UNDERCOVER

UNDERCOVER

How I Went from Company Man to FBI Spy—and Exposed the Worst Healthcare Fraud in U.S. History

JOHN W. SCHILLING

⁄AMACOM

AMERICAN MANAGEMENT ASSOCIATION
New York • Atlanta • Brussels • Chicago • Mexico City
San Francisco • Shanghai • Tokyo • Toronto • Washington, D.C.

This publication is designed to provide accurate and authoritative information in regard to the subject matter covered. It is sold with the understanding that the publisher is not engaged in rendering legal, accounting, or other professional service. If legal advice or other expert assistance is required, the services of a competent professional person should be sought.

Library of Congress Cataloging-in-Publication Data

Schilling, John W.
    Undercover : how I went from company man to FBI spy and exposed the worst healthcare fraud in U.S. history / John W. Schilling.
        p. cm.
    Includes bibliographical references and index.
    ISBN-13: 978-0-8144-7450-1
    ISBN-10: 0-8144-7450-0
    1. Columbia/HCA Healthcare Corporation—Corrupt practices. 2. Fraud investigation—Florida. 3. Medicare fraud—Florida. 4. Schilling, John W. 5. Whistle blowing—Florida. I. Title.

HV6698.F6S35 2008
364.16'3—dc22

                                                                    2007042359

Printing Number

10 9 8 7 6 5 4 3 2

Contents

Foreword

What is it about whistleblowers? What makes them take bold and risky actions most of us would never even consider? When faced with the unethical and even criminal conduct of big healthcare corporations cheating the government, most people would simply say, "It's not my job," without further thought to the financial and human costs of such actions. Perhaps we are too trusting of "the system" and believe in the karmic law that all the bad people will be caught eventually. Perhaps we are reluctant to complicate our lives.

When I was a boy, my grade school teachers enthralled me with tales of the brave and daring individuals whose selfless actions and upstanding principles built our country. I dreamed of a time when I too might face similar challenges and wondered how I would respond to the test. Would I take a stand, make a difference, and contribute to our common good? Or would I back down, shrink from that responsibility, and melt back into the masses?

Then it happened: That crisis of conscience presented itself. I came face-to-face with a huge corporate behemoth operating with reckless disregard for human life and public laws. Through many unexpected twists of fate, I'd uncovered a scheme to defraud the federal government. So now I had to choose. Would I simply accept the situation as something inevitable that I could not change? Or would I try to move some mountains? If I chose the latter course, how could one person turn the tide against a large, powerful, and well-financed adversary?

The answer for me could be found in a once obscure federal law signed by Abraham Lincoln and dating back to the Civil War. It is called the False Claims Act, also known as the *qui tam* law, and it was created to encourage citizens and company insiders to report fraud by unscrupulous contractors during the Civil War.

The False Claims Act remains the greatest legal tool a concerned and motivated citizen can employ to fight and report fraud. I became a whistleblower in 1997 to report the wrongdoing I'd uncovered, and that is exactly what a brave man named John Schilling did when he discovered complex fraudulent schemes at the nation's largest hospital chain. John Schilling is one of my heroes. He was not concerned about complicating his life or looking the other way. That would have been too easy, and for John, failing to act was simply not an option. Because of his actions, John Schilling became one of the top whistleblowers ever. Partly as a result of his efforts, the U.S. Justice Department recouped more than $1.7 billion in criminal and civil settlements from the hospital chain. I am very proud of him.

Here's what happens to whistleblowers. First, we work like mad to assemble evidence without pay and on our own time. Then, we hire an attorney and work to draft a legal complaint, which needs to be flawlessly written, reviewed, fact-checked, spell-checked, rewritten, and finally approved—again on our own time. Once the complaint is filed, it is "under seal," meaning we are forbidden from discussing it with anyone but our attorneys. Our personal freedoms are constricted, and we are unable to turn to the people most likely to help—our friends, neighbors, and political allies. We must behave as though everything is normal, but it is not— and we are not. Friends and relations will notice our changed behavior and will wonder about us.

And once the newspaper headlines trumpet "Feds Raid Offices," we are introduced to a whole new set of enemies: the defense team's corporate henchmen, lawyers, private detectives, and PR staffs, whose goal is to destroy us. Some of us lose our jobs, or are forced to change careers. Our families can plan to move frequently. Our reputations are attacked. The long, arduous *qui tam* process can take years, even a decade. We wonder if we'd have been better off ignoring the problems we confronted.

Luckily for patients, taxpayers, and dreamers like me, John Schilling proved that one person can make a huge difference. He joined the small group of us burdened by the obligation to step up when we see wrongdoing. And that may be what it all comes down to: righting a wrong and standing up for patients and taxpayers alike.

This is a David and Goliath story demonstrating that right can triumph over wrong when an honest man stands against it. And it is also a cautionary tale warning that corporate misconduct and pilfering of government programs will continue unless we care enough to stop it.

How? By sticking our necks out like John Schilling did and fighting fraud and wrongdoing when we find it.

—Kevin McDonough

Kevin McDonough formerly owned and operated Mobile X-Ray Specialists Inc., in central Florida and Mobile X-Ray Specialists of Georgia, Inc. In 1998, Kevin filed a successful whistleblower lawsuit against Integrated Health Services, Inc. (IHS). Kevin resides in Florida with his wife Debbie and daughters Amy and Megan. He enjoys off-shore fishing and volunteer work.

Acknowledgments

Most of all, I want to thank my family for their unwavering support. I am extremely grateful to my lovely wife, Kirsten, for her support and assistance. She was instrumental in all aspects of this book including the development of ideas and review of my work. To my children, Alex, Abby, and Austin, I greatly appreciated your patience while I was writing my story.

I want especially to thank my mother and father. At an early age, you taught me to respect others, be honest, and strive to live with integrity. You instilled the values I possess today.

The efforts of many people went into making this book a reality. I am grateful for their contributions. Stan Wakefield, thank you for believing in this project from its inception and for your encouragement throughout the process. Mark Taylor, your tireless hours of work, thoughtful contributions, and encouragement are greatly appreciated. A special thanks to my friends Jim Alderson and Connie Alderson for all your contributions, support, and comments. Tom Jahnke, thank you for all your creative ideas. Last, I am grateful to my friends and attorneys who worked diligently on my case: John Phillips, Peter Chatfield, Stephen Meagher, Gerry Stern, Chris Hoyer, Judy Hoyer, Chris Casper, Al Scudieri. Without you and your support, this book would have never come to fruition.

Many other people made considerable contributions to this book. Thank you Stuart Rennert, Kevin McDonough, Marcia Taylor, Gillian Klucas, Darlene House, Carolyn Washburne, and Jim Moorman, Jeb White, and Patrick Burns (Taxpayers Against Fraud).

Author's Note

While a great deal of this book is taken from actual court transcripts, notes, and personal interviews, some dialogue has been recreated from actual events. This should not be considered verbatim, but is my reasonable adaptation of the ideas being discussed.

To enhance the reader's experience I have added a Post Script written by health care reporter Mark Taylor. I believe it is important to elicit the opinions of those who lived through and observed the investigation and its impact. My goal was to present a fair, balanced, and objective range of commentary from a variety of perspectives in the words of those who witnessed these events, placing the investigation in a historic context. Some have never spoken publicly about the investigation or its effects on their lives and careers.

UNDERCOVER

Prologue

He drove a dark, nondescript Chevy, its interior strewn with coffee cups and gum wrappers. The four-door sedan badly needed a wash, but I recognized it right away and slid into the front passenger seat. There on the floor lay a 10-millimeter Glock, snug in its brown leather holster. I grimaced and gingerly shifted my feet to avoid touching it. I adjusted the air-conditioning vent to find relief from the stifling tropical heat. The driver flashed me a reassuring grin and stepped on the accelerator as we sped out of the Wal-Mart parking lot. We were in Fort Myers, Florida, and today's mission was to tour each Southwest Florida site that would be targeted. I wondered why this was necessary, but my handler explained that in his experience, guessing only leads to mistakes. He obviously had a lot of experience.

Although the tourist season was over, the traffic was unusually slow for a Tuesday afternoon. The familiar flickering of red emergency lights indicated an accident scene ahead. After we maneuvered past the sheriff's squad cars at the crash site, we arrived at Gulf Coast Hospital, located at a busy intersection. Ford pulled the car into an empty space in the parking lot and produced a yellow legal notepad.

Then he said, "Tell me everything you know about these offices, John. Where are the executive offices and the financial documents?"

As I spoke, he drew small diagrams, mapping the layout of the administrative suites. When he was satisfied that he'd gleaned all the information he needed, he tossed the notepad into the backseat, restarted the car, and headed northeast toward East Pointe Hospital in nearby Lehigh Acres. After briefly discussing the administrative office layout, we returned to Fort Myers.

"Any idea when you'll execute the raid?" I asked on our way back. "Might be another two or three weeks," Ford replied, vowing to warn me beforehand.

Then he cautioned, "After the raids, you might get a few phone calls asking if you know anything." He advised me to say that I was paranoid about talking on the telephone and to arrange a meeting.

"Then, we can fit you with a wire and record the meeting," he said, halting to gauge my reaction. "Are you OK with that?" I nodded. *This is getting interesting*, I thought.

Ahead I could see our next stop: Southwest Florida Regional Medical Center. Southwest is a sprawling, four-story, white and blue stucco building, one of the 350 hospitals then owned and operated by the U.S. healthcare giant Columbia/HCA Healthcare Corp., the world's largest for-profit hospital chain. Ford turned into the hospital's parking lot and stopped near several cars parked at the side of the building. I pointed out a red Buick Regal I recognized, and Ford promptly grabbed the two-way radio wedged into the car's console.

He began relaying the license plate numbers of cars I recognized to a dispatcher. The red car was registered to Jay Jarrell, the chief executive officer for Columbia/HCA's Fort Myers division. Another was owned by the division's office secretary, who was just entering the building. I sat there quietly, observing Ford.

My God, they don't take any chances, do they? I thought to myself. After noting the plate numbers, Ford asked me the locations of the administrative offices in the building. He was particularly interested in the location of the offices of the hospital's chief executive and chief financial officers. Did I know which computer files should be downloaded? Did Columbia/HCA store contracts and other documents in obscure or remote sites around the hospital? I told him what I knew, and he rapidly filled the pages of his notepad. Only a few minutes later, the office secretary reappeared, entered her car, and drove slowly toward us. As she passed our vehicle, I ducked, hoping she hadn't noticed me. I did, however, find myself enjoying my new role as spy.

Heading north a few hundred yards to Swamp Cabbage Court, we veered into the lot at the Central Billing Office at the end of the cul-de-sac. We spent a few minutes there while Ford recorded some additional notes, then proceeded to an offsite record storage facility located not far from Southwest Florida Regional Medical Center. Once he completed his detailed note taking, he swung back into traffic and deposited me back at the Wal-Mart parking lot.

Once there, FBI Special Agent Joe Ford, my handler and the man the U.S. Justice Department assigned to lead the investigation into my case, reached into the backseat, fumbled with a few papers, and finally produced an envelope with my name on it. Inside, he said, was an application. "You're a natural, John. I think the FBI could really use a guy like you. Think about it, OK?" The idea was thrilling and I was tempted to pinch myself: The FBI wanted to recruit an ordinary accountant like me.

CHAPTER ONE

Hornet's Nest

April 1994
Fort Myers, Florida

Sweating in my suit and tie despite the cold air blasting from the vents in Bob Whiteside's new burgundy Toyota Camry, I couldn't shake a feeling of foreboding. Whiteside, normally so jovial and talkative, had fallen silent after grilling me yet again about my conversation with the auditor two days earlier. The trip along I-75, hugging Florida's southwest coastline, took only an hour from Fort Myers to the little town of Port Charlotte. This morning, however, it seemed endless. I hadn't slept much the night before. I was too worried about the upcoming meeting to relax.

My briefcase, heavy with files, leaned against my leg as I watched the tangle of scrubland pass by with each monotonous mile. Most of what I saw out Bob's windows were melaleucas. I'd been in Florida less than a year, but I already knew that the tall, spindly trees were an invasive scourge that threatened native species. The trees, native to Australia, had been imported to Florida in the early 1900s to dry up the swamp with their spongy bark so the land could be sold and developed to accommodate Florida's growing retiree population. The plan worked too well. Like those other transplants, melaleucas had planted roots and proliferated, choking out the original fauna.

Watching the crowded melaleucas' budding green leaves, I saw how difficult it would be to cling to paradise's soil. I reflected on the parallel between those trees and Columbia Healthcare, and I silently replayed the events of the past two days in my head. I'd only been with the company for eight months, but even before the phone call that provoked this worrying trip, I had been feeling uneasy about my new job. At first, I had figured that at Columbia, they just did things much differently than my last employer. Now, though, everything felt wrong—not exactly illegal, but ethically questionable. I had kept my apprehensions to myself, not even telling my wife. I didn't want to worry her with my vague concerns about a questionable interest reserve issue at Fawcett Memorial Hospital, located in Port Charlotte. When I had asked my co-workers about it, however, I had been assured that the practice was standard. "You're young," I had been told. "Don't worry. All the big boys do it this way."

When Thuan Tran called two days before that fateful drive to Port Charlotte, I hadn't thought much of it. Tran was an auditor for Blue Cross & Blue Shield of Florida, the fiscal intermediary (FI) I worked with regularly. Fiscal intermediaries conduct yearly review-like "audits" of hospital Medicare cost reports, the method by which Medicare pays hospitals for treating Medicare beneficiaries. Though FIs have the power to conduct full audits, they rarely do. Tran's call seemed no different from any other call she'd made to me. At the end of the conversation, though, Tran asked offhandedly in her heavy Vietnamese accent, "John, do you know anything about a cost report reopening at Fawcett?" Fawcett Memorial Hospital was one of the facilities I helped oversee from my company's division office in Fort Myers. I hadn't heard about the reopening, a routine occurrence, but promised to look into it. Tran said she would as well and we hung up.

I searched through Columbia's files, but found nothing. My boss, Bob Whiteside, was not in the office that day, so I telephoned Jim Burns, the controller at Fawcett. Hesitating, he said he wasn't sure but thought the reopening might be related to an "interest issue." I had no idea what he meant by that, but nothing in his tone suggested the reactions that later would follow from our colleagues when they heard about Tran's question. I gave up the search and returned to work.

The next morning, Whiteside sauntered into my office. His required suit coat had already been discarded and his tie was askew. I filled him in on the previous day's work, and at the end of my monologue, I mentioned my conversation with Tran.

Whiteside stiffened. "What did she say?" he demanded in a harsh tone. "Do you know why she was asking?" I'd never seen Whiteside react that way before, and it startled me. "She asked if I knew anything about a reopening at Fawcett," I replied. "It's the Fawcett interest issue," Whiteside said quickly without elaboration. Leaning across my desk, he growled, "Let me know if she calls back about it." Then he warned, "Don't tell anybody about this. Jobs could be lost if this gets out." From under his bushy eyebrows, his eyes glared coldly at me. I had no doubt he meant my job.

As the day wore on, I tried to forget about the phone call or the "Fawcett interest issue." Later in the day, though, Whiteside stormed into my office and slammed the door behind him. His face was scarlet, his nostrils flared, and his mouth hardened under his thick moustache. "I thought I told you not to tell anyone about the Fawcett interest issue," he glowered, barely muffling his fury.

"What do you mean?" I croaked, my stomach rising to meet my throat.

"I just got off the phone with Mike Neeb (Chief Financial Officer) at Fawcett, and I don't appreciate being put on the hot seat."

"When you weren't available yesterday, I called Burns to see if he knew about it. I'm sorry," I added regretfully.

Whiteside's scowl deepened. He inhaled a few heavy breaths. "Now I'm going to have to tell Jay Jarrell," he said.

Jarrell, the vice president and chief financial officer of Columbia's Southwest Florida Division, was everything Whiteside was not. Tall, trim, and boyishly handsome, it was easy to picture Jarrell as a popular high school jock. He was also a hard-driving and intimidating force who had advanced quickly in the company. I suspected that Whiteside was afraid of him, which made me wary of him, too.

"You need to gather as much information as you can find about this," Whiteside said. "We're going to be meeting with Jay Jarrell and Mike Neeb at Fawcett tomorrow." He turned and abruptly left my office.

I was worried and confused by Whiteside's behavior. In my eight months at Columbia, I'd never seen him behave like this. What had I stumbled into? What was this "Fawcett interest issue?" (See Appendix A for a detailed description of the Fawcett interest issue.) My mind racing, I turned and left my office and went to the storage room. There, I rummaged through the file cabinets, looking for background information to bring to the meeting—a task that consumed the rest of my day.

At home that night, I tried to act as if nothing was wrong. I didn't want to worry Kirsten, my wife, about something that might blow over after tomorrow's meeting. A few weeks earlier, Kirsten had announced she was pregnant. She'd miscarried twice since our son, Alex, was born, and I didn't want to upset her unnecessarily.

The next morning, I left early for my office, driving slowly through our subdivision, Three Oaks. Newly constructed homes were sprouting around ours, the third house on the block. By next year, it promised to be a quiet, kid-friendly neighborhood perfect for Alex. I also thought about the new baby and prayed everything would be okay this time. I could not afford to lose my job with a new house, a toddler, and a pregnant wife.

I drove to work more slowly than usual—not to marvel at this beautiful, exotic place but to avoid the growing sense of foreboding I felt. Too soon, I'd arrived and parked. The air was already growing thick and warm as I walked under the portico, out of place with the modern building of angles and glass. I stepped into the spacious marble lobby that had so awed me just a few months earlier and drew a deep breath before pushing the elevator button. Riding up to the fifth floor, I remembered Whiteside's anger the day before and closed my eyes while leaning against the wood-paneled elevator. Willing the elevator to stall, I prayed for a reprieve before it reached its stop.

To my surprise, Whiteside seemed normal when we met in his office before he hustled me back to his car for the drive to Port Charlotte. His temperament changed quickly, however, as he drove. I grew increasingly uncomfortable as he barraged me with nonstop questions for which I had few answers. How much did Tran know? How did you respond to her? What prompted her questions? I was slightly relieved when we reached Port Charlotte an hour later, and Whiteside grew silent. Port Charlotte seemed sleepy compared to the bustling city of Fort Myers and the ritzy resort town of Naples farther south. Like those towns, Port Charlotte was populated with retirees. But unlike Naples, the residents in Port Charlotte had migrated primarily from northern blue-collar towns to retire in Port Charlotte's small houses and mobile homes. Instead of beaches, Port Charlotte, tucked inside a bay, is known for its fishing, palm trees, and warm, sunny days.

Whiteside drove straight to Fawcett Memorial, a medium-size hospital of 250 beds, its orange-stucco exterior garishly shimmering against the slightly rundown concrete structures surrounding it.

The butterflies in my stomach fluttered as Whiteside turned into the small employee parking lot. We walked silently to Mike Neeb's spacious corner office in the accounting wing adjoining the main hospital. Neeb was seated at his desk when Whiteside and I entered. Rising from his immaculate desk, he greeted us with professional courtesy. He was about my age—early to mid-thirties—but his intense, deep-set eyes and premature graying hair made him seem older. Like Jay Jarrell, who would participate in this meeting via speakerphone, Neeb was driven and demanding with little tolerance for incompetence. This meeting would be all business.

He steered us to the round table in the corner, where we took our seats. Though he'd already spoken with Whiteside, Neeb was anxious to hear a blow-by-blow account from me of my conversation with Thuan Tran two days earlier. I recounted the conversation I had already repeated several times earlier. Once he was convinced that he understood the conversation, Neeb decided it was time to call Jarrell. Jarrell answered the phone immediately in his booming voice. It was not only his voice but his prominence in Columbia's hierarchy that granted him dominion over the meeting.

At Jarrell's request, I replayed the conversation with Tran. Then the blitzkrieg of questions erupted. What prompted her call? Why did Tran ask about the Fawcett interest issue? Did she ask specifically about anything else? Did I call her back? I had few answers. They queried me repeatedly about the conversation. What were Tran's exact words, her tone of voice? The interrogation continued as if I was withholding some key piece of information that would resolve the problem.

Jarrell's voice, broadcast through the speakerphone, sounded strained. He knew all about the interest issue, he said. He characterized it as a mistake made in the accounting records, stemming from a loan a few years earlier when Fawcett Memorial was owned by Basic American Medical, Inc., an Indianapolis-based for-profit hospital chain Columbia had purchased several years before. The complicated mistake was not discovered by the fiscal intermediary, and as time passed, it had turned into a windfall for the hospital. By this time, that mistake was worth $3.5 million to Fawcett's bottom line. Neeb was worried that if the FI discovered the error and the hospital was ordered to repay the $3.5 million, he would suffer both professionally and financially. Top Columbia hospital executives, such as the CEOs and CFOs, could earn up to half their annual salaries in year-end bonuses.

Although Columbia had not caused the mistake, it seemed apparent to me that the company was concealing it from the federal government. I thought then that I had learned only of a slightly "gray area" in Fawcett's past. Later, I was to learn that Jarrell had not been fully candid in his recounting of the events. There was more going on than a simple mistake.

Throughout the meeting, Whiteside played the peacemaker. "Nothing may come of this," he said. "This is a fiscal intermediary, after all," he noted, reminding everyone of the low opinion private sector executives maintained of the competence of their government overseers. The inquiry was normal. It might all blow away, he reassured us, and remain undiscovered.

Jarrell and Neeb were not easily placated, however. They wanted to know how to ensure that the issue was not identified. "What can we have John do to throw Tran off the Fawcett interest issue trail?" they asked. I gulped in response. Given Whiteside's reaction and my apprehensions, I was concerned by the tenor the meeting had taken on. What began as a fact-finding mission was quickly turning into a cover-up. I had already questioned the reserve cost reports I'd found in Columbia's Medicare reimbursement division. Whiteside had told me that these accounting methods were practiced industry-wide. Perhaps that was true, but I felt even then as if the company was doing something wrong, something unethical. And this meeting—designed to distract the federal government from finding out that it was owed $3.5 million—compounded my misgivings. The attitude seemed to be that if the government was too incompetent to know it was being duped, then that was the government's problem, not the company's.

As the three executives schemed, I took notes, writing down their ideas on a to-do list. Ask Tran questions about starting new hospital programs, they suggested. Ask her how rural healthcare reimbursement works. Question the status of other hospital audits. Could she move up a scheduled audit? The gist was to keep Tran too busy to investigate Fawcett's earlier audit and prevent her from finding the $3.5 million.

As the meeting progressed, I saw I wouldn't lose my job immediately. Jarrell's parting comment before he hung up, however, left me confused and unnerved, and I would replay it in my mind over the next year as I wrestled with my choices. "If all else fails," Jarrell said, his voice filling the room, "let's offer her a job at the company."

After the meeting adjourned, Whiteside and I left Neeb's office for the return trip to Fort Myers. The ominous sense I'd felt on the drive to Port

Charlotte had not dissipated. What they asked me to do seemed unethical. I didn't know it at the time, but it was also criminal. A nagging question persisted: *Why do we need to offer our government overseer a job if we aren't doing anything wrong?* Unknown to me then, I'd stumbled into a hornet's nest that would turn me against the men I worked for and the company that employed me. What began as correcting a simple accounting error mushroomed into the largest healthcare fraud case in history and made me a multimillionaire.

CHAPTER TWO

Morals and Values

It was June 1962, and my parents, Harry and Shirley Schilling, were jubilant. They had been blessed with two beautiful daughters—Sally and Judy—and now, a son, me. When I was baptized, the priest proclaimed that it was their duty to raise me with strong Christian values—a message my parents took to heart.

My father's parents emigrated in the 1920s from Germany, settled in the Milwaukee area, and raised a family. My dad, a machinist, worked for Allen-Bradley for thirty-five years. He was able to provide the necessities—food, clothing, and shelter—but never luxuries such as travel to exotic places or dinners in elegant restaurants. I never felt poor, though. Our modest, beige brick ranch-style home in the middle-class suburb of Menomonee Falls was comfortable, and we lived on a street lined with similar houses. Like most households on our street, we owned one used car—a blue four-door Ford—that my dad drove to work. My mom stayed home caring for my sisters and me.

Every fall, my parents scraped together the tuition to send us to St. Mary's Catholic School, a third-generation family tradition. My mother, grandmother, maternal uncles, and cousins all attended St. Mary's. The school, run by the Franciscan sisters, was known for its rigorous curriculum and strict adherence to Catholic religious teachings. That upbringing at home and at school taught me to respect others, be honest, and strive to live with integrity. I remember one teacher in particular, Sister Berna, as a great person who inculcated in us a strong sense of moral values.

She wasn't stodgy or somber like some of the other nuns, but played football and baseball with us and let me wash her car in exchange for McDonald's lunches—a real treat for me then.

After St. Mary's, I attended Menomonee Falls North High School, one of the two public high schools in town. I excelled in many of my courses—especially math and business—and earned money after school bagging groceries. I also joined the school swim team, a sport in which I lettered. At sixteen, I signed up for the Explorers program at the Menomonee Falls Fire Department. The newly created program promoted firefighting as a career and publicized the fire department's contributions to the community. I was enamored with becoming a firefighter and daydreamed about rescuing people from burning buildings. My parents supported my firefighter career goals.

I graduated from high school in 1980. While most of my classmates went away to college, I stayed behind in Menomonee Falls. Firefighting seemed to offer the exciting, physically demanding, and honorable profession I then sought. So, at eighteen, I graduated from my role as an Explorer firefighting wannabe to a part-time paid on-call firefighter. I reveled in the camaraderie and excitement of the job and advanced to the rank of lieutenant. I learned to be patient and remain calm under very stressful conditions. But a small town like Menomonee Falls had no full-time firefighter positions available, so I spent months crisscrossing the state, taking firefighting aptitude and physical agility tests and interviewing with hiring panels. I knew it could take years before I was offered a full-time firefighting position.

While waiting to be notified of an opening by one of the fire departments, I enrolled in an associate degree program in film and television production at Milwaukee Area Technical College. I fantasized about directing big-budget Hollywood movies. Perhaps my true vocation wasn't firefighting after all. For the next three years, I divided my time between college studies, on-call work at the Menomonee Falls Fire Department, and interning with WMVS/WMVT, the local public television station. I completed additional courses in firefighting and emergency medical services and earned my emergency medical technician (EMT) license. In May 1984, I graduated first in my class with an associate degree in telecasting. Ironically, even though I had interned there, WMVS/WMVT would not hire applicants without bachelor's degrees. My associate degree could land me little more than freelance work in such a competitive field.

But there was one bright spot on the horizon: a quiet, blue-eyed blonde I'd met named Kirsten Genett. Kirsten lived with her parents and sister in a white house on a busy street just across town. She was an eighteen-year-old high school senior I'd met through a mutual friend at a party. I knew after only a few dates that she was the girl for me. We dated for six months and then announced our intent to marry. On a warm July afternoon in 1985, we married in Menomonee Falls in Kirsten's family church, Emmanuel Community United Methodist Church. A Catholic priest from St. Mary's also officiated. Kirsten was nineteen and I was twenty-three.

Now finding a full-time job was imperative. I accepted a position as an EMT with Paratech Ambulance, a private ambulance company providing emergency medical services for the city of Milwaukee. I also continued to work as an on-call firefighter and EMT with the Menomonee Falls Fire Department. By 1986, I was logging more than sixty hours per week, splitting my time between Paratech and the Menomonee Falls Fire Department.

Though I was gaining invaluable experience, I realized that my career advancement would be constricted without a bachelor's degree. I began attending classes at the University of Wisconsin–Milwaukee, while working as an EMT evenings and weekends. I decided to major in business, figuring that with a versatile business degree, I could enter the business world or apply my degree to a firefighting profession. I worked hard in college, taking five or six classes each semester and throughout the summer months. By my second year, I switched my major to accounting because I enjoyed the challenging course work and it seemed to offer great job opportunities.

Just when my future seemed clear, I received a surprise. The Milwaukee Fire Department offered me a full-time firefighting position, providing I passed its rigorous fire academy training. While I pondered which path to take, fate intervened in an odd and unfortunate way. One evening while working as an EMT for Paratech, my partner and I responded to an emergency call in a tough, inner-city Milwaukee neighborhood. With red lights flashing and the siren blaring, we hurried onto a street lined with rundown, neglected flats. Trudging up the steep stairway to the second floor apartment, medical equipment in tow, we found an angry resident who denied requesting an ambulance. Another false alarm! But while quickly retreating down the stairs, I stumbled and fell. Pain shot through my left foot. Later, in the emergency room, I learned that I had broken my foot and because of the severity of the injury, it would not heal in the normal six to eight weeks. (Eventually, doctors had to surgically remove one bone so I could walk comfortably.)

The Milwaukee fire academy kindly offered to postpone my start date, but I felt my dream of becoming a firefighter extinguishing. While firefighting sounded exciting, its dangers were real, as my broken foot attested. Accounting, on the other hand, seemed safe, stable, and not very life-threatening—and it promised a more secure future for my family.

On a blustery, cold day in December 1989, I graduated from the University of Wisconsin–Milwaukee with a bachelor's degree in business administration in accounting. I had achieved something I once believed unimaginable: I'd earned an accounting degree and could select from several job offers in the field. I accepted a position with Blue Cross & Blue Shield United of Wisconsin as an auditor for Medicare, the federal health insurance program for the elderly and disabled. Blue Cross & Blue Shield, the state's largest health insurance plan, was a fiscal intermediary that contracted with the federal government's Health Care Financing Administration (HCFA) to administer and review claims to the Medicare program in Wisconsin.

My job at "the Blues" was to audit and review Medicare cost reports from hospitals. A Medicare cost report is a summary of reimbursable costs submitted to the Medicare fiscal intermediary for services provided to Medicare beneficiaries. Included are costs, revenue, and other data to calculate the actual Medicare reimbursement to that healthcare provider.

For the next three years, Kirsten and I enjoyed our newfound independence. I earned a decent salary and a year-end bonus. In 1990, we purchased our first home, a spacious ranch-style house in suburban Greenfield, Wisconsin, ideal for a young family. Three weeks before Christmas, we became the proud parents of a son, Alex. Our family's first grandchild was the perfect Christmas present.

In 1991, I passed the rigorous Certified Public Accountant (CPA) exam. I took seriously the CPA Code of Ethics. Upholding integrity and objectivity are integral to that oath. The code forbids anyone licensed to practice as a CPA from knowingly misrepresenting facts and subordinating judgment to others.

At work, I supervised several audits at one time. While I enjoyed auditing, the frequent travel the job demanded too often kept me from my family. In the summer of 1992—tempted by recruitment ads for reimbursement managers, controllers, and chief financial officers with salary offers that tripled mine—I began searching for a job on the healthcare provider side of the industry. Perhaps, I thought, it was time for a change. After a short job search, I accepted a reimbursement analyst position with St. Mary's Hospital in Milwaukee. Travel was no longer a problem, so I could spend more time at home with Kirsten and Alex.

My new office was located in the "old" St. Mary's Hospital, located on the east side of North Lake Drive. Beautiful views of Lake Michigan compensated somewhat for the rundown office conditions. Rolling up my sleeves, I began learning the daily reimbursement regimen from a hospital's perspective. At St. Mary's, I first heard about Medicare reserve accounts. Standard in the industry when used properly, a Medicare reserve allows a hospital to set aside money in case Medicare auditors find fault with its annual cost reports and demand additional payments.

Just five months after joining the accounting department at St. Mary's, I received a phone call from an employment recruiter. He told me about a job opening at Columbia Healthcare Corporation's Southwest Florida Division office. The recruiter described the great growth potential this rapidly expanding, publicly traded hospital corporation could offer. In addition, my parents had recently divorced and my father had moved to Florida; moving closer to him in the sunny South sounded tempting. I was already regretting the move to St. Mary's. I might have overlooked its shabby offices, but another factor influenced my decision. My supervisor had recently resigned, leaving the finance and accounting departments in turmoil. The future there looked murky. So, on an impulse, I agreed to a telephone interview with Columbia's reimbursement manager, Robert Whiteside, the following week.

First, I spent several days researching Columbia Healthcare. Its rapid growth and innovative approach to healthcare really impressed me. I wasn't alone. Wall Street revered Columbia cofounder and CEO Richard Scott for leading a healthcare revolution after he cobbled together a patchwork of regional hospitals. Scott—profiled in business magazines as a hot young executive in the growing healthcare industry—seemed on top of the world. His company sales skyrocketed from $499 million in 1991 to nearly $15 billion three years later, mostly through acquisitions. His initial $125,000 investment in 1988 exploded in value to $200 million by 1994, according to federal securities filings. My opportunities seemed boundless at such a dynamic, innovative company.

On the morning of the phone interview, Whiteside called my house promptly at 8 A.M. I was encouraged by our frank discussion and could envision working for him, and he seemed genuinely interested in me. Four weeks later, he invited me to a second interview, this time in sunny Fort Myers. I was ecstatic.

I arrived forty minutes early at the sleek glass and concrete office tower on the corner of Summerlin Boulevard and College Parkway. Not wanting to appear too eager for my 9 A.M. appointment, I sat in the car, mentally preparing for the interview while listening to the radio. At 8:45 A.M., I turned off the car and entered the building. The portico, reminiscent of an ancient Roman structure, led me through glass doors into a spacious marble lobby. A beautiful lake and fountain glistened beyond. While waiting for the elevator, I imagined a wide open career path awaiting me with a bright future and unlimited potential. Already, Columbia and I seemed like a fit. Entering the elevator, I rode up to the division offices on the fifth floor. I was swept away by the sumptuous office decor, rich carpets, and dark mahogany furnishings.

Whiteside, a heavyset man in his early forties with prominent jowls and a bushy mustache, shook my hand heartily and put me at ease. "Call me Bob," he said. We chatted casually, first about our families, then about the office surroundings. "Our philosophy here is, you have to spend money to make money," he chuckled.

The interview lasted three hours, concluding with a tour of the office. Along the way, Whiteside introduced me to several members of the financial staff, including the division CFO, Jay Jarrell—a tall, sleek, impeccably dressed man who exuded success. Before I left, Whiteside asked if I still wanted the job. "Of course, I'm interested," I responded without hesitation.

On my flight back to Milwaukee, I bubbled with enthusiasm. Whiteside and Jarrell sounded impressed that I was not only a CPA but also had Medicare auditing and reimbursement experience. Two weeks later, Columbia made me an offer.

Finally, I thought, *my hard work and education are paying off.* The position of reimbursement supervisor included an annual salary plus stock options and year-end bonuses. The generous offer also included house-hunting costs and relocation expenses. The company was courting me with job security, opportunities for rapid advancement, and unlimited earnings potential. Although only eight employees worked in the Fort

Myers regional division, it was a corporate job and more prestigious than working in one of Columbia's hospitals.

Unlike my dilapidated work environs at St. Mary's, Columbia boasted an elegant office setting and the latest high-tech equipment. I would have new furniture and the latest computer system. The offer sounded almost too good to refuse. The only drawback would be leaving our family and friends in Wisconsin, but my unhappiness at St. Mary's and the allure of palm trees and Gulf breezes tipped the scale in Columbia's favor.

I wondered when in my life I would ever have another opportunity to ride a juggernaut. It was time for a change, and we were moving to Florida. I had no idea then that my choice would lead me to more stress, angst, and excitement than I could ever wish for and ultimately more money than I could ever imagine.

CHAPTER THREE

Chokehold

Headquartered in the Columbia division office as supervisor of reimbursement services, I directed the audits of five hospitals formerly owned by Basic American Medical, Inc. (BAMI). Columbia Healthcare had acquired these hospitals only a year earlier in its huge expansion plan. My responsibilities included overseeing the hospitals' Medicare cost report filings and coordinating audits in conjunction with the fiscal intermediary. Less than two months after I arrived in Florida, the company expanded again when Columbia Healthcare and Galen Heath Care jointly announced shareholder approval for their merger on August 31, 1993. Galen Health Care, a short-lived spin-off of Humana, Inc., owned and operated approximately seventy hospitals. The colossal merger strengthened Columbia's dominance not only in Florida but in other markets as well. Like the proliferating melaleuca plant, Columbia Healthcare—which now owned ninety-four hospitals and complementary healthcare facilities in eighteen states—was now choking out its competition. The two companies' combined estimated annual revenues exceeded $5 billion.

Rick Scott professed to forge a new path in healthcare, building comprehensive physician and hospital networks and improving efficiency while increasing access to quality medical care. The merger had consequences for Bob Whiteside and me. Until a new division office opened in Tampa, we would oversee all the Medicare reimbursement functions for every Columbia Healthcare hospital along the west coast of Florida, which then numbered around twenty. My first few months in paradise would be tested by fire.

Meanwhile, on the home front, the three house-hunting trips Kirsten and I had made had been futile, so we opted to build a house in the quiet, South Fort Myers neighborhood of Pine Glen at Three Oaks. We were impressed with the developer's master plan and beautiful home models and the newly constructed elementary school nearby. We loved the notion that our children would be able to walk to school two blocks away, and it didn't hurt that my dad lived within blocks of us. After renting a cramped, two-bedroom condo for six months, we found our new 2,100-square-foot home palatial. Our home, the third house built on the block, was quickly surrounded by new frames being erected at a frenzied pace. In April, Frank and Eva Pomarico moved in next door. Their children, Sarah and Mark, were only slightly older than Alex. Our families became fast friends.

To those unfamiliar with the healthcare industry, it seemed like Columbia had burst onto the national stage from nowhere. In October 1987, attorney Rick Scott and Fort Worth financier Richard Rainwater each put up $125,000 to form Columbia Healthcare. By 1993, using leveraged cash flow and partnerships, the two quickly amassed a small empire of twenty-four hospitals. The company grew rapidly through aggressive acquisitions and mergers. Columbia planned to build a chain that would provide integrated services, implement strict cost controls, and seek greater purchasing savings through volume buying.

Another healthcare company, the Hospital Corporation of America (HCA), could boast similarly humble beginnings. In 1968, three men—Dr. Thomas Frist, Sr.; one of his sons, Dr. Thomas Frist, Jr.; and Kentucky Fried Chicken founder Jack Massey—pooled their resources to purchase Nashville's Park View Hospital. HCA soon became known as the nation's first for-profit hospital chain. By its twenty-fifth anniversary, HCA owned or managed ninety-six facilities in twenty-one states, and its growth would mushroom from there.

On February 10, 1994, Columbia Healthcare Corporation and the Hospital Corporation of America (HCA) jointly announced their merger, the largest in either company's history. Overnight, the newly formed conglomerate, renamed Columbia/HCA Healthcare Corporation, became the world's largest healthcare services provider, with some 190 acute-care and specialty hospitals in twenty-six states and two foreign countries. Analysts predicted that annual revenues would top $14 billion. The newly formed Columbia/HCA anticipated an annual cost savings of $130 million through national purchasing contracts, the reduction of functions, and the consolidation of administrative programs. My new employer had not only jumped to the peak of the healthcare industry; now it was poised, as Scott had predicted, to drive that industry. Scott himself—famous for his aggressive cost-effective approach to healthcare—was widely admired on Wall Street by analysts, fund managers, and investment bankers.

When Columbia, still a fledgling company in the healthcare arena, had hired me, its reimbursement department was little more than a skeleton crew relying on consultants to perform much of the work. Columbia had neither the resources nor the longevity to fully staff a reimbursement department able to accommodate its growing chain of hospitals. And while the Galen merger had little impact on Columbia's reimbursement department, the HCA merger significantly altered the company's reimbursement hierarchy. Thus, the merged Columbia/HCA adopted HCA's reimbursement structure and retained HCA's top reimbursement management, including the former HCA president of reimbursement, Helen Cummings; the vice president of reimbursement, Jerry Glather; and the Florida reimbursement director, Trish Lindler. Whiteside also capitalized on the opportunities created by the mergers, accepting the position of reimbursement director at Columbia/HCA headquarters in Nashville, Tennessee. He would remain in the Fort Myers office until June 1994 before making the move to Nashville.

I was happy to see Whiteside leave our office. The matter of the Fawcett interest issue was still lingering, and he showed little interest in examining whether it had been properly disclosed. Though he was a CPA, he didn't seem to adhere to the CPA Code of Ethics. Rather than confronting a serious accounting error and creating waves within the organization, Whiteside chose rapid personal advancement.

In one of our last conversations before he left for Nashville, he told me, "With a little more experience, you'll be promoted, John. You're still a little green." And he dispensed what he may have considered fatherly advice: "With time, you will learn when to keep quiet about things." I knew he was speaking of the Fawcett interest issue, and in that instant I lost my respect for him. He was encouraging me to violate our CPA oath and break the law.

With Whiteside relocating to Nashville, I'd now report to Larry Bomar, who'd been hired as the Tampa division's reimbursement manager. Bomar would assume responsibility for all Columbia/HCA hospitals along Florida's Gulf Coast. I would remain in Fort Myers and would oversee reimbursements for the company's six hospitals and numerous ancillary care providers, such as ambulatory surgery centers and home health agencies, from Sarasota south to Naples 120 miles away. Bomar would report to former HCA executive Trish Lindler, the newly merged company's Florida reimbursement director. Before Whiteside had left for Nashville, he had led Lindler on a whirlwind tour of our offices and updated her on all the division's issues—including the troublesome Fawcett interest case.

The Columbia/HCA merger had proceeded smoothly. Bomar initially spent several days each month with me in Fort Myers, familiarizing himself with the division's hospital financial practices. A courtly native Floridian, he proved himself more of a mentor to me than Whiteside had been. I appreciated his candid, straightforward approach, but he raised the hackles of hospital administrators. They grumbled, "It's bad enough to have had three new computer systems in two years, but now corporate sends us 'Bad News Bomar.'" Bomar, an honest, "old school" accountant, commanded hospitals to file their cost reports properly. He was alarmed by some of the reserves the hospitals used and repeatedly warned administrators that some of the prior cost report reserves they maintained were improper and possibly fraudulent.

"These reserves are not normal accounting practices," he told me. "This is fraud." Fraud? I couldn't believe it. Whiteside had lied to me about the entire situation.

Bomar reviewed all of the Fawcett interest documents. He agreed with me that something had to be done to resolve the problem. (Years later, during Whiteside and Jay Jarrell's criminal trial in 1999, I discovered that I wasn't the only executive Whiteside had threatened. Bomar said that Whiteside had also pressured him with the threat of termination if the Fawcett interest issue was uncovered. Bomar also testified that Jarrell telephoned him and asked how the company could hire Thuan Tran, the irksome auditor from the Florida Blues plan. Bomar said he had been shocked.)

Whiteside's warning that I might lose my job haunted me even as Bomar confirmed my misgivings about the Fawcett interest issue. Bomar and I hoped we could resolve the matter internally without being labeled troublemakers or ruining our careers. Bomar assured me that he had contacts high up in the Nashville corporate office, and he could attract the attention of the right official to correct the problem. However, his efforts met resistance or apathy. I believed that was because Columbia/HCA was more concerned with profit than compliance or ethics.

And one way the company created those profits was by courting physicians. From the beginning, Rick Scott's business model included enlisting physician investors to the hospitals he purchased. He knew these physicians were more likely to refer patients to hospitals in which they held financial ownership stakes, and hospitals can't succeed without physician referrals.

Columbia/HCA's philosophy that "to make money, you have to spend money" was exemplified by the gala balls Scott threw to woo some of those physicians. Several of those soirees were rumored to cost more than $100,000 each. The parties were held in Columbia/HCA division offices or posh local hotels and other venues. The company even rented the Thunderdome (since renamed Tropicana Field) in St. Petersburg, the home of the major league baseball team the Tampa Bay Devil Rays, for one division ball. Attendance was mandatory at the parties for company executives.

Kirsten and I, along with hundreds of area physicians and hospital administrators, attended one of those galas in October 1994 at the downtown Fort Myers Harborside Convention Center. I scanned the spacious ballroom, noting the elegantly dressed couples, tables displaying huge carved ice sculptures, and dancers gliding through the crowd of 500, boogieing to seventies music. Tuxedoed waiters offered champagne and hors d'oeuvres.

Kirsten and I took our seats at the beautifully decorated round tables, each topped with white linen and fine dinnerware and crystal. Servers paraded from the kitchen balancing trays of artistically arranged salads, the first of many courses. Across the ballroom, in a scene from a sixties movie, lithe women dressed in mini-skirts and white go-go boots, in giant suspended birdcages, gyrated to "Love Shack" by the B-52's. I tugged at the stiff collar of my rented tuxedo and adjusted my too-tight bow tie.

This was my first black-tie event and I'd never felt so far away from Menomonee Falls.

Throughout the evening, Rick Scott flitted between tables like a pollinating bee, shaking hands and welcoming guests. Scott—a tall, gangly man with a receding hairline—seemed at home in the lavish surroundings. When he approached our table, I stood to introduce Kirsten and myself. Scott firmly gripped my hand and asked how we fit into the new Columbia/HCA organization. Then, with a smile, he left to greet his other guests. It was as intimidating as meeting royalty, I thought then.

I read both amazement and discomfort in Kirsten's eyes. We hadn't wanted to attend the gala, but months earlier Whiteside insisted it was expected. We both felt out of place. The gala, a huge success by all accounts, was designed to achieve one goal: winning physician approval and buy-in for the colossal Columbia/HCA merger.

Two months later, in December 1994, the gala seemed but a faint memory. Bomar reported to me that he had made no progress on the Fawcett matter with his corporate contacts. Our frustrations continued to mount. It seemed clear that the issue would not be resolved by year's end.

That night, not wanting to be late for our subdivision developer's annual holiday party, I left work a little early. The festivities would culminate with a trolley ride through the neighborhood to view the holiday lights and decorations. It was an enjoyable party, but even the trolley ride couldn't shake Kirsten's lingering unease. Strangely lacking an appetite, she felt sure she would go into labor. She woke me at 1:30 A.M., unable to sleep, and asked to go to the hospital. Our darling baby girl, Abby, was born early that morning. We'd been blessed with yet another wonderful Christmas present!

I'd seldom discussed my fears about Columbia/HCA with Kirsten. With the new baby, new house, and growing family, I knew I needed this job and kept hoping I'd convince someone within the company to correct the fraud and repay the government. I also worried about my personal obligations, not only as a law-abiding citizen but also as a CPA who had pledged an oath to uphold integrity and objectivity. I knew I was not supposed to misrepresent facts or subordinate my judgment to others.

By December 1994, Larry Bomar and his boss, Trish Lindler, were established within Columbia/HCA, having weathered the merger storms. (Five years later, while testifying in the criminal trial that my whistleblowing allegations initiated, Bomar portrayed those months as frustrating.

He testified that he believed then that Columbia/HCA's corporate office would disclose the interest issue on Fawcett's 1994 cost report. Any disagreements concerning prior adjustments were customarily revealed in a transmittal letter and the amount disclosed on the protest line of the cost report. However, this was not done. Bomar said at the trial that he strongly felt that he would have been fired if he had objected to the way the 1994 cost report was filed. Since he had already discussed the entire issue with Lindler, including the improperly reported interest issue, he believed he shouldn't disclose it himself.

During Lindler's testimony in the same 1999 trial, she remembered general conversations with some individuals, including me. On the witness stand, she could not recollect what was discussed, except to recall that I didn't like the way "something" was handled. Lindler told jurors at the trial that she grew concerned when she discovered the extraordinary size of those reserves, but not concerned enough to disclose the issue.)

In early 1995, short of quitting—an option I couldn't afford—I could see no way out of my predicament. When Bomar uttered the word "fraud," I understood that what I'd uncovered would not disappear. And what if a new reimbursement supervisor stumbled across the issue as I had? Would Bob Whiteside, Jay Jarrell, and Mike Neeb blame me? Was I to be the scapegoat or the sacrificial lamb?

As my mind swirled with questions, my eyes focused on that morning's edition of the *Wall Street Journal*. On the front page of the January 11, 1995, edition was an article with the headline "Honesty Pays Off: John Phillips Fosters a Growing Industry of Whistle-Blowing." The story was about John Phillips, an attorney and founding partner of Phillips & Cohen LLP, a law firm in Washington, D.C. Phillips, was carving a reputation for successfully representing whistleblowers using the False Claims Act. I reread the article several times, increasingly convinced that this False Claims Act might apply to my dilemma.

As I drove home that evening, I thought about that news story. Like many people, I held a negative impression of whistleblowers and had no desire to become one. I didn't want to be called a "rat" or "snitch," either. Even the term *whistleblower* connotes a pejorative image in American society. Americans don't squeal on others—I'd heard that since grade school.

After washing the dinner dishes and tucking in the kids that night, I told Kirsten that I believed my company was committing fraud and explained how my efforts to resolve the problem within Columbia/HCA's management had repeatedly failed. I told her my bosses threatened to fire me if I revealed the accounting fraud.

I felt trapped in a chokehold.

"What happens if someone else exposes this? Don't you think you'll be blamed?" she asked. "I'm afraid of that. I have to do what's right," I replied.

I had persuaded myself to call Phillips & Cohen.

CHAPTER FOUR

The False Claims Act

It was 6 P.M. on Friday, February 10, 1995, and it surprised me when Mary Louise Cohen answered my call. I had expected to hear a recorded message. Quickly regaining my composure, I said I was calling because of the *Wall Street Journal* article. I launched into a quick version of my story, telling her I was a Medicare reimbursement supervisor at a major U.S. healthcare company.

I told her I believed that the company I worked for was cheating the U.S. government. I said that I had unearthed a long hidden cost reporting error and received no support when I sought to disclose it. I'd also found that my employer routinely prepared two separate cost reports. My company, I explained, ordered me to oversee the preparation of one cost report to file with Medicare that included expenses that I knew were not allowable under federal rules. In addition, I had to oversee the preparation of a second "Confidential" or "Reserve" report that more accurately reflected actual hospital expenses. I asked, "Do I have cause to file a whistleblower lawsuit?"

Cohen explained that she couldn't answer that question definitively yet. She explained that a *qui tam* case is filed under "seal," allowing the government unhampered time to investigate the allegations. Under the False Claims Act, once the seal is lifted, the company would be prohibited from retaliating against the whistleblower. *That's a relief,* I thought.

"How could I possibly afford to retain your firm?" I asked.

She explained that if the law firm decided to take the case, it would be paid on a contingency basis, meaning that in lieu of hourly fees and advances, it agreed to receive a percentage of the award after settlement from the whistleblower. There would be no up-front costs at all. "In fact," she said, "the defendants pay the hourly fees of the plaintiff's attorneys if the case is settled."

Cohen warned me that filing a *qui tam* lawsuit offered no guarantee of any settlement. A complex case like this needed thorough development, she said, requiring a lot of time and money. And in the end, she explained, the U.S. Justice Department might not even intervene in the case, which would lessen the chances of success.

"I am afraid of being held responsible for the fraud, and I've got an ethical responsibility as a CPA to disclose this information," I stammered. I knew I needed to do something.

I weighed the risks of an uncertain outcome with the potential costs of doing nothing. Cohen, who seemed interested in my story, said she really couldn't answer all my questions over the phone. She promised to send me a questionnaire and closely review my story in the office. It was all I could hope for. I hung up the phone, feeling like I had just taken a life-altering first step.

President Abraham Lincoln championed the False Claims Act, which was enacted during the Civil War to combat fraud committed against the federal government. Lincoln was convinced that corrupt practices by war profiteers were not only defrauding the government but also putting at risk Union soldiers and the entire war campaign. For example, Union Army officials discovered that munitions sold to the Union were packed with sawdust rather than gunpowder and that soldiers' boots were manufactured with flimsy cardboard rather than leather. To halt these fraudulent practices and punish the crooked contractors, Congress passed the statute in 1863. The law contained incentives known as *qui tam* provisions. Those novel provisions allowed private citizens, called "relators," to sue on the government's behalf and enabled federal authorities to recover amounts they had overpaid, plus penalties. *Qui tam* is short for a Latin phrase that means "he who proceeds for the king as well as for himself." (The concept traces its roots to English common law.) The 1863 version of the act, then known as "the Lincoln Law," imposed double damages and a $2,000 civil fine for each false claim. The whistleblowing relators were entitled to receive up to half the amount the government collected.

For eight decades, the statue remained virtually unchanged. During World War II, however, Congress took dramatic steps to change the *qui tam* provisions. Until 1943, whistleblowers could still file lawsuits even after the government had commenced criminal prosecutions. To block such "parasitic" lawsuits, the statute was amended to reduce the relator's reward significantly. The amendments went even further to curb private litigation by prohibiting *qui tam* suits based on evidence that the government already had in its possession, whatever the source. This applied even if the whistleblower had told the government about the fraud and authorities had shown no interest in investigating the allegations. Not surprisingly, as a result of the 1943 amendments, the law sat dormant and unused for more than four decades.

But in the 1980s, the public and the press again began to focus aggressively on reports of defense contractor irregularities costing taxpayers millions. Just as newspaper readers today may be shocked by the $6,000 shower curtains and other well-publicized examples of corporate excess, in the 1980s, the U.S. public and Congress were shocked by headlines of $400-plus hammers sold to the military. It had become clear after the 1943 amendments gutted the False Claims Act that the government lacked effective tools to combat such fraud. Budgets and staffing were tight at the Justice Department and other agencies charged with protecting federal programs. And whistleblowers willing to risk retaliation were scarce, particularly in light of the scant rewards and minimal protections. The public clamored for increased accountability, and in response, Congress began to revise the False Claims Act.

Recognizing both the need for reform and the untapped potential of the False Claims Act, Senator Charles Grassley (Republican of Iowa) championed efforts to reinvigorate the law. With Representative Howard Berman (Democrat of California) and a bright, forward-thinking attorney, John Phillips, Grassley sponsored important amendments to the False Claims Act, which President Ronald Reagan signed into law in October 1986. Grassley has continued to support the law. He inserted provisions into the 2005 Deficit Reduction Act, a congressional budget reconciliation bill that encouraged states to pass their own false claims acts and required certain organizations billing state Medicaid programs to educate employees about the False Claims Act.

The amended 1986 False Claims Act substantially increased the potential rewards for whistleblowers willing to bring suit. For example, the law now allows successful whistleblowers to share between 15 percent and 30 percent of the government's recovery. The amendments also raised the stakes for fraud defendants in whistleblower cases, since those found to have defrauded the government are now liable for treble (triple) damages and penalties up to $10,000 for each false claim. The revised law also protects whistleblowers from retaliation and compels defendants to pay the hourly fees of whistleblower attorneys.

The 1986 amendments ensured a strong and powerful role for whistleblowers with the proof, courage, and conviction to step forward. As awareness of the law has grown, the number of *qui tam* lawsuits has skyrocketed. Whistleblowers have filed more than 6,000 *qui tam* lawsuits since the revision. Through the law, government prosecutors have collected more than $20 billion and *qui tam* relators shared in more than $1.8 billion for reporting the fraud.

On September 19, 2007, Grassley co-sponsored the False Claims Act Correction Act of 2007 designed to clarify certain provisions and to override several recent cases interpreting the 1986 amendments to the False Claims Act.

Through the decades, the law has evolved into a balanced and successful approach to a festering problem. Fraud against the government may never fully disappear, but I believe a public-private partnership harnesses perhaps the most effective means of combating it.

I couldn't believe it when I learned that John Phillips had actually assisted Senator Grassley in reinventing this law, the False Claims Act. Now John Phillips might be in my corner. I thought I was finally on the right track and had enlisted a seasoned, well-qualified ally to help me.

CHAPTER FIVE

The Final Straw

The February 21, 1995, shareholder announcement surprised few insiders, but press reports of a proposed merger between Columbia/HCA and HealthTrust, Inc. (a onetime division of HCA later spun off into a separate company), shocked the healthcare world. It was a big, audacious, and gutsy move. The merger would close in a few months, pending Federal Trade Commission approval. Company officials anticipated annual savings of approximately $125 million by controlling costs while maintaining quality patient care.

The previous mergers had created opportunities at Columbia/HCA, but the HealthTrust merger wreaked havoc for many reimbursement executives in the Columbia/HCA corporate hierarchy. The new vice president of reimbursement, Tom Johnson, guaranteed jobs for HealthTrust reimbursement executives, elevating many to top reimbursement slots in the merged company. He also replaced most of the vacancies with his HealthTrust staff. The company's Florida Group regional reimbursement office was relocated from Tallahassee to Winter Park. Trish Lindler, Columbia/HCA's Florida director of reimbursement, resigned. Her Nashville boss, Vice President of Reimbursement Jerry Glather, was demoted in the shuffle.

Shortly before Lindler resigned, she had asked me to clarify the reserve issues in a memo for her and Glather. I express-mailed a memo to both, hoping that they would finally take action. My memo listed six items, including the Fawcett interest issue. I included copies of pertinent documents for their perusal and requested that they inform me of any action. Then I waited. Hearing nothing, I contacted Lindler about the Fawcett interest issue days before she left. "I've pushed it up the ladder as far as I could," Lindler sighed, in effect washing her hands of the matter.

Lindler's replacement, Bonnie Reid, was a trim, well-dressed woman with long, painted fingernails. She had joined Columbia early on and had risen quickly in the organization, recently transferring from Texas to Florida. Reid scheduled a general meeting with ten members of her new Florida reimbursement staff, including Larry Bomar and me, at the recently relocated Florida regional reimbursement office in Winter Park. Before the meeting began, I placed a small pocket-size tape recorder in the center of the conference table. I hoped that might ignite some positive action. In addition, if Reid failed to take action, I wanted audiotaped proof so I would not be implicated later. If she decided to correct the fraud, I wanted evidence that I had worked within the company's internal framework to facilitate the disclosure.

The meeting's goal was to disseminate uniform corporate policies regarding Medicare reserves. Reid listed those issues that company-wide should or shouldn't be reserved for. Certain issues were approved at the corporate level, and many others were left to the discretion of the reimbursement manager. *More of the same*, I thought. The meeting was not geared toward compliance with government rules but rather with how to game the system. I couldn't forget Bob Whiteside's warning that heads would roll if the money were repaid.

After the meeting, Reid asked Bomar and me to stay and discuss the Fawcett interest issue. I thought that maybe then she would listen and decide to finally disclose the interest error and repay the $3.5 million Columbia/HCA owed the government. Since Bomar had struck out with his corporate contacts, I considered Reid our last hope.

Looking solemn, she told us that her boss, Richard Parker, assistant vice president of reimbursement, had inherited the Fawcett interest issue file. She said Parker had instructed her to look into it and report back. Bomar and I restated our belief that Columbia/HCA was legally obligated to disclose the errors made on the prior year's cost reports. Instead of disclosing them, the company had omitted them in subsequent Medicare cost report filings, creating the $3.5 million windfall. I also recounted the meeting in Port Charlotte in which Bob Whiteside, Jay Jarrell, and Mike Neeb brainstormed for ways to distract the Medicare auditor. When I told her that Jarrell had even suggested hiring the fiscal intermediary as a way to buy her silence, Reid laughed. "And I thought we were aggressive in Texas," she joked.

I brought to the meeting a legal opinion prepared for Basic American Medical, Inc. (BAMI) by attorney Norman Tabler of the Indianapolis law firm Baker & Daniels. Using information supplied by William "Steve" Dudley, a former BAMI director of reimbursement, Tabler said that hospital companies and government auditors long had debated how to differentiate operating expenses from capital expenditures and classify them correctly on Medicare cost reports. Operating expenses include items like salaries, utilities, and supplies. Capital expenditures consist of depreciation, leases, and interest expenses for borrowings relating to the purchases of equipment and building. The opinion concluded that this was a gray area open to interpretation. (I later learned that the information Dudley supplied to Tabler as the basis for the opinion was inaccurate and misleading.)

Reid looked at us and bit her lip. She acknowledged that correcting a Medicare auditor's error was the only ethical choice, but she admitted that she had never done it before. In the end, she told us to ignore the earlier errors made in previous cost report filings. She insisted that in the future, Fawcett Memorial Hospital would file its cost reports correctly.

The meeting with Reid left me fuming. This was the last straw. Obviously, nothing would change. I had no choice but to leave Columbia/HCA, and I wasted no time updating my resume. By late August 1995, I'd secured a new job in Naples, twenty-five miles south of Fort Myers. After I gave notice, Columbia/HCA presented a counteroffer, to increase my annual salary by 35 percent, which I immediately rejected.

Ethically and legally, I believed Columbia/HCA had violated its obligations, not only to me but to its stockholders and taxpayers. While many employees chose to look the other way, neither Bomar nor I could continue to condone the company's fraudulent cost-reporting activities. One month after I resigned, Bomar also left the organization.

My new employer was Community Care of America (CCA), a fledgling start-up that owned and operated long-term care nursing homes in rural markets. CCA executives wanted to expand operations by acquiring rural hospitals, and they believed that my hospital financial experience could help them achieve that goal. In dire need of a cash infusion, CCA was preparing to "go public," selling shares in the company on the stock market. CCA saw selling shares as the best way to finance its planned foray into the rural hospital market. As the CCA manager of reimbursement, my initial duties included hiring reimbursement staff and overseeing the filing of Medicare and Medicaid cost reports. As the reimbursement department expanded, my duties shifted to the financial operations of existing hospitals and performing due diligence on potential hospital acquisitions. Due diligence is the process by which an acquiring organization evaluates the true financial condition and operations of a company it intends to purchase. The purchasing company does not want any surprises and seeks to determine the real value of the acquisition.

In the meantime, Phillips & Cohen responded to my completed questionnaire. They believed I had legal grounds to file a *qui tam* lawsuit against Columbia/HCA. The law firm would accept the risk of financing a *qui tam* case, collecting the evidence and working with the federal government in exchange for a contingency fee, based on whatever I would receive from any settlement. If the case was settled successfully, under the False Claims Act the defendants would also pay Phillips & Cohen's legal fees and expenses. I had no qualms about the concept of paying a contingency fee, but I objected to the large percentage the firm demanded: about 40 percent.

Having never hired an attorney, I possessed negligible negotiating skills. However, I really did think that I could bargain for a better deal. I responded, writing a letter to the firm requesting they concede to a lower contingency. In a reply letter dated October 13, 1995, John Phillips wrote "Our willingness to pursue the claim you identified was in fact a close call for our firm. The case is very much on the small side in terms of potential damage to the government . . ." For those reasons, he believed the case might not attract the attention of the U.S. Department of Health & Human Services and the Justice Department. "Pushing this case through the complex web of these federal agencies will be difficult, time-consuming, and therefore, risky," Phillips wrote, so the firm was not willing to alter the retainer agreement. He said that a judge could dismiss my suit if another whistleblower making the same claims filed before me—a strong likelihood given that the whistleblower were filed under seal. My case could also be excluded if news stories publicly disclosed my allegations, airing Columbia/HCA's practices to make them common knowledge. His advice was that I should "seek immediately to retain other counsel if you intend to pursue this claim," if I would not agree to the firm's contingency percentage terms. (Neither of us had any idea then how wrong he was when he characterized my case as "small.")

I knew that if I moved ahead with the case, I'd be blackballed in the industry, ending my career in healthcare. Kirsten and I would need guts and courage to withstand the personal and financial sacrifices to survive the long and arduous legal process that lay ahead. The risks were great, but the potential reward could exceed millions of dollars.

As I struggled with my dilemma in Florida, another man across the country in Whitefish, Montana, had also contacted Phillips & Cohen after reading the same *Wall Street Journal* article I had read in January 1995. Jim Alderson had worked for North Valley Hospital, a small community hospital in Whitefish, before he was fired in 1990 for questioning the fraudulent "reserve," or "dual," cost-reporting system used by Quorum Health Resources. Not surprisingly, Quorum, a for-profit hospital management company, was a spin-off from HCA. After being fired, Alderson had uprooted his family to take a job far from home in dismal Dillon, Montana. Alderson then had filed a wrongful termination lawsuit against Quorum. During that lawsuit process, Quorum staff had unwittingly sent Alderson and his attorney documents detailing the dual cost-reporting scheme that had originated at HCA. Nobody had to tell Alderson the scheme was wrong. Stunned by what he had uncovered, the soft-spoken accountant knew he possessed a smoking gun pointing toward serious misconduct.

On his own, Alderson had researched the law and in January 1993 filed a *qui tam* case against Quorum and HCA. Not long after, in early 1994, HCA merged with Columbia to form Columbia/HCA. Despite Alderson's damning evidence, the Justice Department would not commit to investigating a criminal case. Alderson couldn't afford to take on the healthcare giants alone, so his case had languished in a Justice Department file. When Alderson read the *Wall Street Journal* article, he phoned Phillips & Cohen to see about reviving his dormant suit.

The fraud I had witnessed at Columbia/HCA still disturbed me. I was mired in a moral dilemma. Should I proceed with a *qui tam* lawsuit, risking inevitable career suicide and subjecting my family to the pressures of protracted litigation? And if I did, how would this affect my former colleagues and their families? I had no answers. Back then, Columbia/HCA had no corporate compliance officers—positions that are almost ubiquitous today in every hospital organization—so there was no one within the corporate hierarchy in whom I could confide my concerns. I believed that I'd fulfilled my ethical obligation to Columbia/HCA by reporting the fraud to my superiors within the system. But as a CPA, I had sworn and was obligated to uphold the CPA's Code of Ethics and thus still feared the revocation of my license and potential criminal liability. That oath meant a great deal to me.

Columbia/HCA, on the other hand, had not upheld its ethical commitment to act upon my reports of fraud and disclose the past errors in the Fawcett interest issue. It was time to make a stand.

Three months of research convinced me that Phillips & Cohen, with its breadth of experience in filing and pursuing whistleblower cases, was the top gun in the field. Though I was dismayed that the firm minimized the magnitude of my false claims allegations, I knew that John Phillips had earned a solid reputation for successfully helping the government to expose fraud. After much discussion and soul-searching, Kirsten and I concluded that this firm was the right choice for my case. When I called to accept the firm's terms, I learned that the firm was now representing a new client asserting similar allegations. Phillips & Cohen said they would get back to me. My heart sank. I wondered if someone at Columbia/HCA had come forward to blame me.

A few days later, attorney Stephen Meagher from Phillips & Cohen phoned me. I liked him immediately. Meagher, a former federal prosecutor, had founded and chaired the Healthcare Fraud Task Force for the U.S. Attorney's office in Northern California before Phillips & Cohen named him as a partner. While the firm's response several days earlier had left me feeling uncertain, Meagher quickly calmed my fears. He suggested that the firm's other client and I could combine our lawsuits and work together as a team. Meagher arranged a conference call to introduce me to Jim Alderson. The similarities in our allegations amazed us, despite the huge geographic span separating us. The fraudulent practices in both cases were rampant and widespread—prevalent both in Columbia/HCA and their spin-off companies. Soon, we realized that we could each benefit from a teamwork approach. Jim and I agreed that a written contract between us was unnecessary; our gentlemen's agreement sufficed.

Several days later, Meagher introduced me via teleconference to Phillips & Cohen attorney Peter Chatfield. Chatfield, a Yale Law School graduate, would assume the arduous task of drafting my complaint. My role on our legal team became that of educator, which greatly amused Kirsten because I was schooling an Ivy League scholar.

I spent hours on teleconferences explaining the complicated Medicare reimbursement system. I could tell immediately that both Meagher and Chatfield were extremely intelligent, and I was thrilled that they would represent me. Even though they quickly caught onto the complicated Medicare reimbursement principles, it became obvious that I would need to guide them through the labyrinthine details of reserve cost reporting and the Fawcett interest issue. So I flew to Washington to tutor them on Medicare Cost Reporting 101.

Chatfield greeted me at the airport the night before our scheduled meeting and drove me to my hotel. He was in his mid-thirties, just a couple of years older than me, and looked younger than I'd expected. He was a medium-size man with short, dark hair and a very firm handshake. His blue eyes sparkled behind gold wire-rimmed glasses. Chatting about my flight and Kirsten's third pregnancy, we waited at the airport luggage carousel. My checked luggage was easy to identify: four white banker boxes crammed with more than 11,000 documents. (My clothes fit into a small carry-on bag.) Chatfield was surprised by the volume of documents I brought, substantially more than most clients. We carefully stowed the boxes in the trunk of his silver 1989 Honda Prelude and glided through light traffic onto the Baltimore-Washington Parkway toward downtown Washington. I was so deeply engrossed talking with Chatfield that I completely missed any significant DC landmarks along the way. After completing the forty-five–minute drive, we briefly stopped at Phillips & Cohen's office to unload the evidence boxes for tomorrow's meeting.

Our official meeting was scheduled for 9 A.M. on April Fool's Day 1996. As I exited my hotel—wearing my best gray plaid suit and a red paisley tie—I got my first daytime view of Washington, D.C. The weather was cool and overcast with periodic light rain. I had no time for sightseeing. I flagged down a cab, nervously anticipating the meeting. My driver left me off at 21 DuPont Circle, the unimposing red brick and glass building in which Phillips & Cohen leased office space. Peter met me at the door. I was accustomed to Columbia/HCA's extravagant surroundings and had expected Armani-clad attorneys in opulently decorated offices. I had anticipated feeling out of place and underdressed, even in my best suit. But the offices were modest and I was the one who was overdressed.

Chatfield quickly introduced me to Stephen Meagher, who had flown in from the firm's San Francisco office to meet us. He did not look the way I expected either. Like Chatfield, he was dressed casually, and I felt at ease. About my size, Meagher had reddish brown hair and his ruddy complexion gave him an outdoorsman's appearance. As we shook hands, I sensed that I was being sized up.

At the same time, I was assessing them. My mind was spinning. Could these young attorneys really absorb the complex financial fraud underlying my case? Could we work well together? Or would they respond to my allegations as the Columbia/HCA executives had, with reluctance and denial?

We spent the morning discussing proper Medicare cost reporting requirements and my revelations of the improper dual cost reports Columbia/HCA prepared. That afternoon, we sorted through my fraud claims and the supporting documents. I sensed that I would be intimately involved in my lawsuit and thought we would make a great team. It was a long, productive day, and I was happy to see my attorneys so enthused about my case.

While I was surprised by how young my attorneys were, they also seemed taken aback by my age, compared to other whistleblowers they represented. I was younger than they expected. From the start, they seemed genuinely interested in hearing my story. Chatfield acknowledged my expertise in Medicare reimbursement and pronounced as outstanding the documenting evidence I brought. Meagher quickly concurred.

They sympathized with my moral dilemma and agreed that accountants, like attorneys, swear to uphold the law. Meagher acknowledged that I had attempted repeatedly to address the situation internally, only to be rebuffed and frustrated by the company's failures to respond and disclose the error. Slightly cynical after his years as a prosecutor, Meagher said he had witnessed many whistleblowers motivated to report solely by money, some of whom even encouraged the fraud themselves. Meagher said he saw me as an accountant who understood the highly complex regulations. "Sometimes the accountant knows where the bodies are buried," he observed, "or at least who paid for the burial."

The next two months passed quickly after meeting with my attorneys. I frequently telephoned Chatfield as he labored to draft my complaint, which he eventually would file in federal court. His diligence unearthed many questions that only I could answer.

My first year at CCA also swiftly passed, and now I was traveling often to the small, rural towns of Adel and Hahira in southern Georgia. My colleague Harry Cole, a southern Alabama native, and I raced to complete the due diligence of a potential CCA hospital chain acquisition. We assessed both the operations and the financial conditions of the small group of hospitals owned by a local physician. Even though our backgrounds differed, Cole and I became friends.

Meanwhile, back in Washington, Chatfield continued to pore over my documents and Medicare regulations to understand Medicare reimbursement and draft my complaint. When I reviewed his first version, I marveled at the masterfully worded document he crafted. I sent it back to him after making a few revisions, but I still agonized over my decision. I knew my career would end once the news broke. *Maybe I can still back out*, I reasoned. But I reminded myself that Columbia/HCA had repeatedly broken the law, cheated taxpayers, and deceived its shareholders.

I had exhausted every avenue within the corporate hierarchy and failed to affect a change. Maybe, I reflected, I could still halt the company's fraudulent business practices bleeding the Medicare program. It would be a monumental challenge indeed to confront this behemoth. However, David had beaten Goliath. My law firm and I were up to the challenge.

CHAPTER SIX

An Olympic Event

The phone on my desk rang at precisely 4:43 P.M. on June 25, 1996. "Hello, this is John," I said. "John. It's Peter. Your case was filed at 4:05 P.M., in the United States District Court, Middle District of Florida, Tampa Division" (Civil Action 96–1264-CIV-T-23B).

I sighed with relief. The cumulative stress of discovering the fraud and my struggle to expose it had been immense. But once the decision had been made, there was no turning back. Now, two years later, my life as a whistleblower had just begun. I could not have known that my ordeal would last another seven years or become such an Olympian task.

Just as Mary Louise Cohen had explained to me during our first telephone conversation back in February 1995, all *qui tam* cases, including mine, are filed "under seal" (without public access) in civil court. The "seal" allows the Justice Department ample time to investigate the allegations before they become publicly known. The U.S. attorney general, who heads the Justice Department, certainly does not personally investigate cases, but U.S. Attorneys in ninety-three districts oversee both the civil and criminal divisions of their offices, typically charging Assistant United States Attorneys (AUSAs) to pursue those investigations and subsequent litigation.

Historically, civil AUSAs were not as polished as their counterparts on the criminal side of the bench. While most civil cases that are not dismissed end with a settlement, more criminal cases are actually argued in court. The Federal Bureau of Investigation (FBI) is the investigative arm of the criminal division of the Justice Department. Its investigations can assist the civil division, but the Bureau's primary function is to investigate criminal activity.

When it was filed in the Middle District of Florida, my case came under the jurisdiction of U.S. District Judge Steven Merryday in Tampa. Marie O'Connell, the Justice Department's Civil Division trial attorney, would investigate the case. The initial seal lasts just sixty days, after which the government has three options: to immediately join the case, to decline it, or to request an extension allowing more time to investigate. Civil cases filed by whistleblowers historically fare much better when the Justice Department intervenes. When the government joins or declines, the case is unsealed, becoming public knowledge. If a case is filed in civil court, an additional copy is forwarded to the Justice Department's Criminal Division. Suddenly, Kirsten and I worried that sixty days would pass too quickly, and I was unsure how my current employer would react to the news that I had turned my previous employer in to the feds.

Knowing that the False Claims Act protected me from being fired only by Columbia/HCA, we feared I might be fired by my current employer, CCA. In addition, how would my current and former colleagues react? Kirsten, pregnant with our third child, worried about retaliation from Columbia/HCA. We were also concerned about what our friends and family would think. We didn't like the idea of keeping the case secret and were thankful it would end in just a few months. Already, I had lied to my dad when he took me to the airport for my trip to Washington. He'd asked why my work was taking me there, and I had said I needed to resolve some Medicare issues with the federal government. It wasn't a complete lie, but I couldn't tell him the truth either, and that gnawed at me.

Kirsten wasn't due to deliver for another two weeks, but knowing her other labors had passed quickly I left work early when she complained of feeling ill. The baby was indeed coming. Our neighbors, Frank and Eva Pomarico, watched Alex and Abby that evening. Our son Austin was born that July evening in 1996.

Just after Austin's birth, the world converged on Atlanta for the 1996 Summer Olympic Games. Kirsten and I had purchased tickets a year in advance, but when she became pregnant, she knew she'd be unable to attend. My dad joined me on the trip and Kirsten's mother, Sonia, volunteered to stay with her and the children. I had hoped that the trip would offer a needed diversion from the growing stresses of my real life. Dad and I attended the Olympic events feeling very safe. The increased security measures implemented after the tragic bombing at the Centennial Olympic Park on July 27 eased our concerns. We had a rare opportunity to see the best athletes from 197 nations competing against each other. Watching Michael Johnson, of the United States, race to gold in the 200- and 400-meter events was spectacular. As he stood on the winner's podium, gold medal held high, I thought to myself that if he could take on the toughest competition around the world and win, maybe I could challenge the world's largest healthcare company, too.

Six weeks after my case was filed, the government asked me to travel to Washington, D.C. Peter Chatfield told me that my case had finally piqued the interest of the Justice Department and that the trial attorney, Marie O'Connell, having read the complaint, wanted to interview me in person on Thursday, August 15. *Great*, I thought, *the government is finally interested in talking to me. Someone is willing to listen.* Both Chatfield and Stephen Meagher warned that Jim Alderson had found O'Connell abrasive when he had met her and that his experience with her had not been positive. In fact, his case had stagnated on her desk. Meagher hoped that my complaints would breathe new life into Alderson's case.

On my second visit to Washington, my yellow cab wove through the traffic at Reagan National Airport and headed northeast onto George Washington Memorial Parkway. This time, I marveled at the beauty of our capital. Ahead I viewed the Arland D. Williams, Jr. Memorial Bridge spanning the Potomac. The bridge was named after a heroic passenger on a 1982 Air Florida plane that crashed; he had selflessly offered other passengers the rescue line dropped from a helicopter before eventually drowning.

The afternoon sky looked absurdly blue, as if painted by a child and dabbed with puffy, white clouds for artistic effect. I enjoyed this drive more than I had on my first trip. Once we crossed the Potomac, the driver headed downtown, passing dozens of beautiful landmarks I recognized from school books, postcards, and TV shows. The Jefferson Memorial, the sprawling green lawns of the National Mall, and the shining spear of the Washington Monument rolled past. As we approached Pennsylvania Avenue, I even caught a glimpse of the White House.

Over dinner that evening, Meagher said he had tried to interest Justice's Criminal Division in my case. If the feds charged and prosecuted Columbia/HCA executives with crimes, the Civil Division likely would attempt to recover the losses from that criminal activity. He had invited the FBI to attend the next day's meeting.

"Do you think there really is criminal activity?" I asked Meagher. "Absolutely," he responded, "especially the interest issue at Fawcett Memorial Hospital."

The next morning, the butterflies in my stomach performed nosedives. Hailing a cab outside our hotel, Meagher and I headed to DuPont Circle to pick up Chatfield. We headed to the Justice Department headquarters at 950 Pennsylvania Avenue N.W. As we approached, my stomach erupted in spasms; I had never met a government official or an FBI agent before. My only exposure to an FBI agent was from movies and television.

While the Justice Department dates back to 1870, its current headquarters, an imposing limestone structure, was not completed until 1935. We entered through glass doors and showed our drivers' licenses before passing through security and the metal detectors. It felt like we were being watched, scrutinized before entering the elevator. I pictured some low-level bureaucratic functionary viewing the surveillance tape and analyzing our every move en route to our meeting in Conference Room 3460.

As we walked down the hallway toward the room, I was impressed how well the Works Progress Administration craftsmanship had survived for sixty-one years. But I was astonished by the dichotomy between the grand exterior and the tacky decor of the conference room, which had been shabbily remodeled in the 1970s. We entered through one of several worn doors topped with frosted glass windows. The room included a small chalkboard and lectern and a mirror hung crookedly over an old, discolored porcelain sink. I guessed that the two-tone, brown shag carpet was at least twenty years old. Surrounding a long desk in the center of the room were several vinyl and cloth chairs; nearby stood a metal cart, piled high with copies of my indexed documents, sagging under their weight. In the far right corner, a Panasonic TV and VCR stared blankly. Bookcases filled with legal statutes and disorganized binders covered two walls. The clock above the door announced it was 9:05 A.M., but my watch disagreed. It was actually 10:05 A.M. Apparently, no one had ever adjusted this clock for Daylight Savings Time.

At 10:10 A.M., Marie O'Connell arrived, flustered, and apologized for being late. Based on my attorneys' warning, I had prepared myself for an imposing, high-powered attorney. *Funny,* I thought, *so far no one has looked the way I'd expected.* Marie was thin and slight. She appeared a few years older than me, with graying hair hanging past her shoulders. She was dressed professionally in a blue blouse, a light brown tweed skirt, around her neck hung a long strand of white pearls. Again expressing regret, she said the FBI was unable to attend.

O'Connell said it was important to assess my knowledge of Medicare cost reporting. She also wanted to know about my previous work experience and requested organizational charts of Columbia/HCA and BAMI. She was most interested in what I knew about the Fawcett interest issue and the meeting with Bob Whiteside, Jay Jarrell, and Mike Neeb. She also queried me about the taped meeting with Larry Bomar and Bonnie Reid in which we discussed both the Fawcett interest and reserve cost report issues. O'Connell asked if I had truly attempted to resolve these issues internally, who else knew about these matters, and what actions they took. Finally, we discussed other Medicare cost report reserve issues I considered improper.

The interview lasted nine hours, ending around 7:00 P.M. O'Connell took eighteen pages of notes. She told us that this was one of the longest interviews she had ever conducted. She wasn't as brutal as I had anticipated and appeared pleased by the interview. While she doubted the prevalence of the reserve cost reporting practice within Columbia/HCA, which disappointed me, I understood that it was her job to be skeptical. I also knew that after she had interviewed Jim Alderson several years ago, his case had stalled, growing dusty somewhere in a Justice Department cabinet. Couldn't she see how extensive and egregious the dual Medicare cost report practices were? Didn't she understand that the government's hesitation was unwarranted? If O'Connell did, she hid it well.

My attorneys, who had seen her in action before, were not disturbed. But they were dismayed that the FBI had reneged on their pledge to attend. Still, from what I had heard, my interview had proceeded better than Jim Alderson's. Our lawyers sensed we were making respectable progress, not only in my case but possibly in reviving Jim's. I was happy to have the meeting out of the way and encouraged by how well it had gone.

On the morning of September 23, 1996, I reviewed the transcript Phillips & Cohen had transcribed of the June 1995 reimbursement meeting I had taped with Bonnie Reid. That afternoon, I was meeting with O'Connell, my lawyers, and the FBI in Fort Myers. My brown suit and tie were too heavy for this uncharacteristically warm Florida September. I backed my black Plymouth Acclaim out of the driveway and checked my pocket for the small cassette tape I was to bring to the meeting. The typewritten transcripts were carefully tucked in my briefcase, resting on the seat beside me. I was feeling quite professional but apprehensive of my first meeting with an FBI agent.

The drive south to downtown Fort Myers afforded me plenty of time to think. Traffic was slow. It seemed as though every red light was synchronized to delay me. After I parked, I entered the Sheraton Hotel. In its aging lobby, Chatfield and Meagher introduced me to a new attorney retained by Phillips & Cohen, Karla Spaulding. Spaulding represented my new Florida counsel, the Tampa firm of James, Hoyer & Newcomer. She was a pleasant brunette in her mid-forties who seemed as bright and perceptive as Chatfield and Meagher. Bar rules require that at least one attorney on a case for each party be admitted to the bar of the court where the case is pending (in this case, the middle district of Florida) and that they have an office close enough to the court so that the clerk can deal with them in an emergency.

The afternoon heat and stifling humidity forced us to drive the short distance from the hotel to the Barnett Bank building, where the meeting would take place. Meeting the FBI would be uncomfortable enough, but two years earlier Columbia/HCA's division office had moved into the same building. Now its offices were two floors below the FBI's. On the elevator, I feared someone from my former employer might recognize me, and once again I prayed the elevator wouldn't make any unexpected stops. We exited the elevator without incident and passed through the large wooden doors of Suite 800. I noticed the security camera just above the door as we entered the small lobby. Meagher took charge, announcing our arrival to the receptionist behind the large bulletproof window.

"We have a 1 P.M. appointment to meet with Agent Joe Ford," he said. The receptionist slid a sign-in sheet under the thick glass and requested that we take seats while she contacted Agent Ford.

As we each took a chair, I surveyed the room, noticing a half-hearted attempt to make the waiting area comfortable. The white walls and burgundy carpeting lent the lobby an austere appearance. The sparsely decorated space contained four fabric chairs, a dusty artificial plant, and an end table topped with a glass lamp. The only entry into the office was through an impenetrable-looking security door marked with the unmistakable FBI insignia. Several minutes passed before the security door buzzed open loudly and FBI Special Agent Joe Ford emerged.

Dressed in a short-sleeve dress shirt and tie, Ford appeared to be in his forties. He was of medium build, slightly taller than me, clean shaven with short brown hair. This all clashed with my movie image of FBI agents with starched white shirts, tailored suits, and dark sunglasses. Ford introduced himself, shook hands firmly with each of us, and guided us into the conference room. This conference room was much different from the Washington, D.C., room in which I had first met Marie O'Connell. It featured newer furniture and had a fantastic view overlooking the Caloosahatchee River. My four boxes of documents, logging their own frequent flyer miles, dominated the conference table. Flanking the boxes were O'Connell and Kathleen Haley, the criminal division AUSA who had been assigned to work the case with Ford. Her short, dark hair and fashionable glasses contrasted sharply with O'Connell's more dowdy appearance. We shook hands and chatted briefly.

Ford led the meeting, describing his experience with the FBI and his healthcare background. He modestly proclaimed himself no expert in Medicare reimbursement, despite his accounting credentials. He implied that he actually looked forward to having me guide him through the Medicare cost report process. I was flattered but not surprised. After all, my attorneys had required intensive education in the same arena, and teaching Ford would be no different.

For the next four hours, Ford asked most of the questions and took notes for his "302 Report," the agency's tool for properly documenting a personal interview. The interview was designed to plumb my knowledge of my case. Everyone else in the room took occasional notes as I spoke. Ford focused much of his questions on the Fawcett interest issue. He also queried me on my allegations that Columbia/HCA inappropriately used reserve cost reports. His interrogation explored the improper transactions relating to home health acquisitions. When he wrapped up the meeting around 5 p.m., it seemed likely that there would be a criminal investigation.

As we began leaving, Ford suggested, "Why don't you call me Joe? I think we'll be seeing a lot of each other." In the years to come, Ford and I would forge a strong working relationship.

I cautiously exited the building, careful to pass undetected by Columbia/HCA employees. My attorneys observed that the case was progressing at a decent clip. Even though it had been initially under seal for sixty days and one extension had already been granted, Meagher warned me that the Justice Department would probably request more extensions. This came as news to me. I'd only expected one extension and a speedier process. (It wasn't the last time the Justice Department would surprise me.)

"At this point, there is no reason to object. Give the government some time to investigate," Meagher said. Compared to the excruciating delays of Jim Alderson's case, mine seemed to be progressing well, and being patient made sense.

I removed my suit coat and tie, returned to my car, turned the AC on full blast, and headed home as the setting sun dipped low in the Florida sky.

Three weeks later, I took a different route to the FBI office, stopping first to pick up Peter Chatfield at the airport. He asked about Kirsten and the kids and was eager to hear how Austin's arrival had altered our family dynamic. We argued amiably about the World Series. An Ohio native, Chatfield had been crushed when the wild card Baltimore Orioles had trounced his Cleveland Indians so early in the playoffs.

When we pulled into the Barnett Bank parking lot, my new attorney, Karla Spaulding, was waiting for us. I still felt uncomfortable entering the building that also housed Columbia/HCA, but our quick entry was unnoticed. Inside the FBI office, Agent Ford escorted us to the conference room, where the AUSA, Kathleen Haley, was already seated. Within minutes, Marie O'Connell entered, sporting a straw hat, tennis shoes, and a small backpack. Ford once again led the four-hour interview and took the majority of the notes, and again most of his questions probed the Fawcett interest issue and the meeting I had had in 1994 with Jarrell, Neeb, and Whiteside. Once Ford completed his interview, Haley and O'Connell exhausted their list of questions, but continued to prod me for more details.

In most of the FBI interviews I would have over the next years, the agents and AUSAs repeatedly asked many of the same questions over and over—partly, I sensed, to verify the consistency of my story and partly because they did not share information very well. New AUSAs and agents asked me to repeat my story again and again, tilling the same soil. They seemed to cover every angle and drilled as deeply as they could to understand what had happened. It was awfully frustrating if not boring to answer the same questions repeatedly. I was a little nervous during those first few interviews. Who wouldn't be? We've all seen the movies. We know the power the FBI holds. The FBI can be very intimidating, even if you're innocent and trying to help as I was.

Luckily, the interviews were informal, which put me at ease. I stopped wearing a suit and tie after the first few meetings: I didn't need to dress to impress. Many times I dressed casually in a polo shirt and slacks, looking more like a golfer heading for a quick nine holes than an undercover operative. Ford was always fairly informal, and meeting with him never felt like an interrogation. Most of the time, I felt very comfortable during those interviews, except for the questioning by AUSA Tony Peluso, which felt like oral surgery without an anesthetic and made me squirm.

After this particular meeting, the government officials asked me to sketch a floor plan of the Fort Myers Columbia/HCA division office two floors below. They also asked for a list of the individuals involved in the Fawcett interest issue, when each individual had become aware of the problem, and any correspondence I had relating to it. Finally, they asked me to provide copies of my previous job performance reviews. I completed those tasks in the next few weeks and forwarded them to my attorneys to disseminate to the right federal prosecuting attorney.

CHAPTER SEVEN

Disaster or Opportunity?

Meanwhile, back at CCA, calamity struck. I had been working on CCA's planned acquisition of a small Georgia hospital chain, but stock market analysts publicly doubted whether the company could close the deal. CCA was mired in financial turmoil and could find no lender for much needed additional borrowing. Its stock spiraled downward. CCA's falling stock price had sparked desperation. I saw company officials violate Securities and Exchange Commission laws in ways similar to what Enron would be charged with years later. CCA had manipulated earnings to shore up stock prices.

For example, I had prepared an unfavorable due diligence report for company executives regarding a potential hospital acquisition, revealing that the previous owner's earnings were clearly overstated. I also reported that there was a severe risk of liability due to inappropriately filed Medicare cost reports by this provider. I told the executives that there were too many skeletons in this hospital's closets and that we should reconsider the purchase. They had responded, "It's too late. We have to make it work; we already sold it to the board of directors and they approved the deal. We already announced it to the stockholders." The meaning was clear: Management chose to ignore the harsh reality of the situation, putting the company at future risk.

Investors grew increasingly concerned about how Medicare and state Medicaid reimbursement changes could damage CCA's profits. Cash for operations was tight, vendors were paid late, and employees waited weeks for their expense report reimbursements. The company trimmed positions and demanded that nursing home administrators cut costs. Performance bonuses, including mine, were not paid as promised.

It's just a matter of time, I thought. From the beginning, I had recognized that CCA was poorly managed and overpaid its executives, who did little to improve the overall operations of the company. My boss, CCA's director of reimbursement, had been hired for the position without accounting or cost report experience. His annual salary of $120,000 was quite extravagant, considering he held only a nursing degree and a nursing home administrator's license. I also witnessed corporate fraud and what I believed to be unethical behavior. I saw a pattern of overbilling for skilled nursing time in some skilled nursing units, the failure to disclose related party transactions (deals between company insiders), and the improper billing for non-allowable Medicare costs.

Returning from lunch on December 6, 1996, I mulled over Alex's birthday party, which we were having at our home that evening. *Maybe,* I thought, *I can sneak away a little early today.* Sorting through the work on my desk, I answered the phone when it rang, expecting it to be Kirsten. It wasn't. It was CCA's chief operating officer, Deborah Lau, briskly summoning me to her office. I knew something wasn't right. When I arrived, I saw Lau at her desk and Vice President William Krystopowicz sitting across from her. Nervously, I sat in the only empty chair. Krystopowicz didn't mince words, telling me immediately that the company demanded my resignation.

"We heard you were snooping into the company regarding fraud. You apparently are too concerned with compliance and fraud, and we're not committing any," he said curtly. "Therefore, we're asking you to pack your belongings and leave."

I remained silent, surprised but not shocked.

Lau piped in, "You're the reason Harry Cole left the organization."

I said nothing but thought, *Boy, is she off base.* Cole had left the company several weeks before because he could see it was floundering and agreed with me that the company was participating in unethical behavior. Breaking the silence, Lau repeated, "There is no fraud in our organization, but if you know of any, you should tell us."

I couldn't believe what I was hearing. *She has the nerve to fire me because I am too interested in fraud, tells me there is no fraud in the organization, and then asks me to reveal what I know,* I thought.

I kept quiet. These two people did not really want to hear what I had to say. Besides, their strange reasoning and odd behavior confused me. I left the office without comment, packed my personal belongings, and was escorted out by Krystopowicz. When I arrived at my car, I chuckled to myself, *If they knew I was spending time with federal investigators, they might think twice about their actions.*

Though I had expected that my days at CCA were numbered, I didn't think the end would come so soon. I felt humiliated by being fired. I pondered the situation as I drove home.

It was true that as I preformed my job, I had been looking into the company's dubious accounting practices. I was stunned to find that CCA's director of reimbursement had exaggerated Medicare revenue in financial meetings and I had seen the company claim non-allowable expenses on cost reports. Recently, I had been floored to learn that even though the financial position of the company was tenuous, the executive management had held a corporate board meeting at a Bahamian resort. In addition, I had uncovered company loans paid to upper management that were not repaid. In fact, one $600,000 loan to a corporate officer had let her purchase a house in the posh Florida community of Bonita Bay. That loan had been reported, but no payments were made, I was told by a staff accountant.

I had sensed that I was under the microscope when I discussed legal compliance issues or pointed out proper accounting principles and Medicare regulations. CCA management had begun to ignore me or to exclude me from financial discussions altogether. I'd created more trouble than intended.

By the time I neared home, I was almost relieved to have escaped drowning on the sinking CCA ship. Maybe, I thought, the feds would be interested in CCA's unethical business practices. First, though, I needed to cement their interest in Columbia/HCA.

Then reality struck me: How would I support my family? I wasn't sure how to tell Kirsten, our family, and friends.

As I walked in the door around 2 P.M., I found Kirsten decorating our lanai (a screened-in patio or pool area) in a barnyard theme for Alex's birthday party. "What are you doing home so early?" she asked, looking concerned. "I was asked to resign," I replied, the words suspended in the air.

"What?" she asked.

I shook my head, unsure what to say. I told her not to worry. I reassured her that I would find something, maybe healthcare financial consulting. We agreed not to discuss it at the party. I immediately phoned Chatfield and Meagher about my firing, and they agreed that we should share what I knew about CCA's dubious accounting practices with the government. My journey as a whistleblower had just hit a pothole.

CHAPTER EIGHT

Undercover

Though it multiplied the stress in my life, my abrupt departure from CCA proved a blessing in disguise. Not only was I now available to help with the investigation, my lack of employment allowed me to infiltrate Columbia/HCA with the FBI's blessing, further assisting the government's investigation.

I quickly told former colleagues that I was now a self-employed health-care consultant and sent out resumes to numerous healthcare companies. Within days, several former Columbia/HCA colleagues contacted me with news of job openings with the reimbursement office in Winter Park. Stephen Meagher quickly saw how my employment there could boost my case. Agent Joe Ford agreed that my becoming an insider would help his investigation immensely. Soon, I had a phone interview scheduled for a reimbursement coordinator position with Robin Gaffney, Columbia/HCA's reimbursement reporting manager in Winter Park. Ford wanted me to surreptitiously record the interview from his office.

On December 17, I drove to the FBI office to begin my stint of undercover work for Ford. To protect my anonymity, he asked me to use the alias "John Smith" when I signed in at the reception desk. *More cloak and dagger precautions,* I thought. He escorted me through the security door to the conference room. There on the table was a common cassette tape recorder with a small black wire leading from the recorder to a suction cup. *So much for high-tech surveillance equipment! Where's MI6's Q when I need him?* I thought. The recorder didn't look very complex or difficult to operate. Ford showed me how it worked, then he reviewed several questions he wanted me to ask designed to extract information regarding reserve cost reports. "Be sure not to use questions that elicit yes and no answers," he reminded me.

Nervously, I pushed the record button and stated my name, the date, and the name of my interview subject. Then I dialed the phone number. Robin Gaffney answered the phone and placed the call on speakerphone. Bob Riley, another reimbursement reporting manager, was with Gaffney in her office for the conversation.

Ford left the conference room, allowing me to conduct the interview in private. Gaffney and Riley knew my background and experience, so they skipped the typical introductory interview questions. Instead, they explained the job position they thought I'd be best suited for. The position, they said, would require me to prepare and file Medicare cost reports for approximately five Florida hospitals and assist each hospital with its Medicare audit. This presented an opportunity for me to ask Ford's questions.

"Who is responsible for preparing the reserve cost reports?" I asked casually. Without missing a beat, they stated that the reserve cost reports were prepared by the reimbursement coordinator, with input from the reporting manager and the division reimbursement staff. They also confirmed reserve cost reports were not limited to Florida, but were commonplace company-wide. Concluding the interview, Gaffney expressed interest in hiring me for the open position.

Afterward, Ford and I listened to the tape. "Nice job," he concluded.

The FBI interviews of other witnesses were proceeding well, and he was excited. He hoped I would be hired again by Columbia/HCA. As an insider, I could assist his investigation of the company and its operations. He even considered the possibility of bugging my home phone. Ultimately, he decided against it; either he didn't obtain permission from the U.S. Attorneys office or he thought I could accomplish what he needed using just the tape recorder. Ford did instruct me that if anyone unexpectedly phoned me from Columbia/HCA, I should say I was busy and would return the call in a few minutes. This would give me time to set up the recorder and tape the call.

I told Ford that if I was offered a job with Columbia/HCA, Kirsten would not want to move to Winter Park, particularly if it was just a temporary move. Alex had begun kindergarten and we were happy in Fort Myers.

"No problem," Ford said. The government would provide me with a furnished apartment in Winter Park and a car allowance. *This spy thing might not be half bad*, I mused, especially after Ford assured my protection, saying he would pull me out before my name was released to the public or if my safety was jeopardized.

I conducted a number of interviews for the FBI, recording my conversations. My undercover role was increasingly exciting. I conducted one interview in person with Trevor Sylvester, a middle manager with Olsten Kimberly, a for-profit home healthcare firm in Orlando, Florida. Columbia/HCA had purchased hundreds of Olsten's home health agencies. In return, Columbia/HCA retained the company to manage the agencies. In the interview, Sylvester confirmed my suspicion that the management fees Columbia/HCA paid to Olsten were inflated and that Columbia was improperly shifting costs to obtain higher Medicare reimbursements. Those practices cheated Medicare of millions of dollars.

Sylvester also confirmed that Olsten knew that Columbia/HCA was improperly and illegally filing its cost reports. He pointed out that Olsten could only advise Columbia/HCA on proper procedure and that Olsten was not responsible for how the cost reports were eventually filed. "We can only warn them of the consequences," he said. When I asked why Olsten didn't report the wrongdoing, he said the company did not think it was appropriate business practice to turn in a client. This new information fascinated me.

I was not the only person fascinated by the information. During the course of the Phillips & Cohen's interviews and the FBI's investigation, this new information corroborated new allegations that had been unearthed. Ford urged me to have my attorneys amend my complaint to assert additional false claims, including home health issues against Columbia/HCA. Without divulging any details, he hinted that there was another whistleblower filing a false claims case, and he suspected our cases might overlap. (Later I learned that Don McLendon, the former vice president for client development and marketing at Olsten Kimberly, had filed a *qui tam* suit, and Ford was conducting an investigation similar to mine with his help.)

Some time after my phone interview with Robin Gaffney of Columbia/ HCA, I had a phone interview with Bonnie Reid, Columbia's director of reimbursement. (Of course, I recorded the conversation.) Reid wondered if I'd be happy in the job for which I'd interviewed with Gaffney. She said my old division reimbursement position might be open soon. Until then, she said, the Winter Park office could use me as a consultant to help out until that job became available. I accepted the offer and officially became a consultant.

Before I reported for duty at Columbia/HCA in Winter Park, I had to meet with Ford once more so he could further prepare me for my undercover role. We met at the Hampton Inn on Daniels Parkway near I-75. We exchanged recorded cassette tapes for new blank tapes, and he instructed me on the legal boundaries of my spy role. It was a little underwhelming. Nothing earth-shattering had happened to me. No one had threatened me, but if they had, I was instructed to page Ford immediately and leave my return number followed by 911, signifying an emergency. He promised that no matter where I was, he would send an agent to respond. He reminded me that I was not an employee of the FBI, nor did I represent them, but I was voluntarily helping the agency.

Ford looked at me gravely. "Do not participate in any acts of violence or use any unconstitutional means to obtain information," he explained. "Don't take any documents out of the office. If you see something of importance, take notes on what it is and where it is kept. Just don't take it."

"If they ask me to do something illegal, what should I do?" I asked. "Go along with it at first, then call me as soon as possible and I'll get you wired," he answered. "But do not, I repeat, do not initiate any criminal activity."

In exchange for my "good behavior," Ford said the FBI would not disclose my identity. *That's odd,* I thought, because my name was supposedly protected already under the law through the seal.

"If you do something wrong, you're on your own," he warned.

Finally, Ford assigned me a mission to help other agents performing later searches under search warrants. He requested a detailed layout of the Winter Park office, a list of employees and their titles working in the office, and details of the type of records located there, along with any offsite record storage sites. He also asked me to elicit specific information about the company's reserve cost reporting process, computer system, and e-mail system.

Early one morning in January 1997, I began working undercover at

Columbia/HCA. Up at 5 A.M., I got ready, headed out the door, and stashed my briefcase and luggage in the car. Then I set out on the three-hour drive to Winter Park. The drive provided plenty of time to prepare myself for my new James Bond role. I knew that I would need to hone my acting skills to pull this off.

Arriving in Winter Park at 9 A.M., I located the company's office at 1375 Semoran Boulevard within a sprawling office complex. This mundane office facility seemed a step down from my grander former office. I found the suite and told the receptionist, "I'm here to see Bonnie Reid."

The receptionist escorted me to Reid's office and knocked on the door. Reid stood, hand outstretched, and said, "Glad to see you again, John." We discussed the open reimbursement job and others she knew would become available soon. Then she showed me an empty office that I would use while doing my consulting work. "Make yourself at home," she said. I knew she didn't realize my real purpose there.

The first week of undercover work passed without incident. I spoke with numerous reimbursement staff members who confirmed my lawsuit's allegations and acknowledged the widespread company use of reserve cost reports. Not only did I obtain the information Ford requested but I was able to garner additional statements and information that proved useful to the FBI's investigation. The government later incorporated that information into the affidavit, which helped secure search warrants for later raids.

Each night, back at the hotel, I reported the day's events over the phone to Ford and my attorneys. Ford sounded encouraged by how events had shifted in our favor. However, while he called me one of the best informants he had worked with, Ford cautioned me not to overstep my bounds. Everything must be handled in the most professional manner without any hint of misconduct, he reiterated. He did not want to be criticized for mishandling the case, nor did he want me attacked or allow anything else to jeopardize our case. Our motives and actions needed to remain clean and beyond reproach.

On Friday, the long drive back to Fort Myers offered time for me to mull over the information I had gleaned that week. That evening, Ford asked some questions about two interviews he had conducted that week with Steve Dudley, who'd worked for BAMI and Trish Lindler, former reimbursement executive at Columbia/HCA. He wondered how loyal they were to the companies. He was frustrated that Lindler conveniently seemed to forget everything.

After my consulting assignment at Columbia/HCA ended, I taped several more telephone interviews, flew to Las Vegas and Atlanta for consulting jobs, and continued my daily phone calls with Ford and my attorneys. I also met with other FBI personnel and auditors from the U.S. Department of Health and Human Services in Fort Myers to discuss the documents I passed on to the investigators. Once again, the investigators asked me to repeat my allegations of wrongdoing and instruct them on the complexities of Medicare cost reporting. I chuckled at the irony that I had to educate the government about its own program.

Several weeks later, Bonnie Reid called, offering a second consulting assignment at the Winter Park office. This would be a longer assignment than the first. She wanted me to return to Winter Park to help prepare cost reports for Gulf Coast Hospital in Fort Myers and Ed White Hospital in St. Petersburg. Each job would take at least two weeks to complete.

"It's just a matter of time," she replied, when I inquired about the reimbursement position for which I had interviewed. (A few weeks earlier, the company had offered me a full-time budget position at Southwest Florida Regional Medical Center in Fort Myers, but I had rejected the offer, still waiting to hear about the Winter Park reimbursement position.)

I was becoming concerned that the civil side of my case, the *qui tam* portion, was slowing down, but Meagher and Chatfield assured me that the criminal investigation was flourishing and would only strengthen our civil case. (Criminal cases involve the prosecution of persons or entities accused of violating a specific law. If convicted of the crime, that person or entity will receive a monetary penalty, imprisonment, supervision in the community, or any combination of the three. A civil case usually involves private disputes between persons or entities. In general, a civil suit seeks to uphold a contract or seeks compensation for harm done, or both.) Meagher's government sources told him that the Justice Department investigation was progressing smoothly. Joe Ford and Kathleen Haley diligently interviewed former Columbia/HCA employees, who corroborated my accusations.

Back home, Kirsten and I began to worry about our safety. Even though we did not expect the seal on the case to be lifted soon, my name could surface, which would probably wreak havoc in our personal lives and damage my career aspirations. We debated whether to move back to Wisconsin. But Meagher calmed our fears, explaining that during his years as a prosecuting criminal attorney, he had known only one incident involving witness safety, and that was in a drug case. "People don't generally threaten witnesses in white-collar cases," he reminded us. He also noted that while doubtful, the best-case scenario would be for the case to settle by the end of summer. His crystal ball envisaged Columbia/HCA fighting the charges for awhile and then agreeing to settle.

"This case could be the largest *qui tam* settlement in history," he predicted. I was astounded. After all the denial I had received from Columbia/HCA and all the time I had spent educating my attorneys, the FBI, and the Justice Department, I couldn't believe what I was now hearing. Suddenly my quest to tell the truth had turned into a potentially colossal event.

In the meantime, I continued my amateur sleuthing role. I met Reid at the Winter Park office to discuss my new consulting arrangement. I felt like an actor portraying a spy. I had to be convincing to avoid detection in my covert mission. My consulting role this time was to prepare the 1996 Medicare cost reports for Columbia/HCA's Gulf Coast and Ed White hospitals. I would not be responsible for filing these reports, nor would I prepare reserve cost reports, but I would compile the cost reports and submit them to the respective reimbursement managers, Bob Riley and Robin Gaffney.

I began preparing the 1996 fiscal year-end Medicare cost reports for Gulf Coast Hospital using documentation received from the hospital. Since Gulf Coast was one of my hospitals when I worked in the Columbia/HCA division office, I was already familiar with many of the inappropriate reserve items there. But I had no similar oversight experience with Ed White Hospital, so I was tilling fresh ground. Reviewing the documents there, I again found more examples of inappropriate reserves. My theory that this was a common and widespread company practice was confirmed.

I also found time to talk with other cost report preparers. At one lunch with a cost report coordinator, Tommy Stoves, we discussed the Olsten home health management agreement with Columbia/HCA. Stoves confirmed that the financial terms of the five-year management agreement between the two companies were inflated. He explained that this was how Columbia/HCA disguised "goodwill expenses" and attributed them to the purchase price. Normally, "goodwill"—which is the premium a purchasing company pays above the book value for the acquired company—is a non-allowable expense under Medicare, meaning it cannot be submitted for reimbursement. However, by masking and reporting it as a management expense, the company transformed it into an allowable and reimbursable Medicare expense. Stoves knew about other irregularities and openly disclosed them. Unknown to him, everything he said was relayed to the FBI.

At one point, Stoves joked, "I hope you're not going to go work for the fiscal intermediary." "Of course not," I replied. We both laughed. I played the clandestine role well, never revealing my true purpose.

By Friday afternoon, I had a good handle on the cost reports. Reid agreed that I should complete the reports back in the accounting offices in Fort Myers. I started home early, not wanting to miss Alex's Little League game that evening.

Three hours is a long time to spend alone in the car. I began speculating why no one else besides Jim Alderson and me had challenged Columbia/HCA's reserve cost reports and illegal accounting practices. While cost report preparers in general are well educated, many have also achieved certification as public accountants. The CPA Code of Ethics mandates that accountants must maintain integrity and objectivity while correctly representing facts and applying their own best judgment. I soon learned that many cost report preparers were strictly "following orders" without realizing that what they'd been told to do was wrong. It seemed that those who knew better justified their actions by characterizing the practices as common and industry-wide. The culture of the healthcare industry was driven by the mantra that the bottom line was king. I blamed greed as the primary motivator. I hoped that once this case became public, providers would change and correct their cost reporting practices. Was I being naive?

The U.S. government shares responsibility for creating such a mess. The Medicare program has mushroomed into an unwieldy administrative system, burdened for years by excessive complexity, arcane rules, and lack of flexibility. As the bureaucracy grew, oversight funding shrank and enforcement of the endlessly complicated Medicare rules suffered. Many healthcare providers operating on a self-reporting "honor system" have exploited legal and illegal loopholes within the poorly enforced program to benefit themselves. Too often, providers have viewed unreported errors as multiyear, interest-free loans with no penalties imposed for repayment.

In the years since I filed my suit, I began to view the investigation differently. What began as an effort to correct a simple error that should have been reported grew into a deeper personal crusade to expose loopholes, unethical accounting practices, and fraud costing taxpayers millions of dollars annually.

CHAPTER NINE

Covert Missions

Three months into my undercover role, I was summoned to appear before the federal grand jury looking into practices at Columbia/HCA. I dreaded the thought that on March 19, 1997, I would have to testify in front of a group of strangers in what seemed like a very intimidating setting.

Before that took place, though, I worked on a consulting assignment preparing Gulf Coast Hospital's cost report in the accounting offices of Southwest Florida Regional Medical Center. While I was there, Jim McGonnell, Southwest Florida's assistant controller, told me he was uncomfortable with the recent practices of Richard Pearson, the reimbursement manager at Columbia/HCA's Fort Myers division. McGonnell was worried that his hospital might not be in compliance, but he said that it did not seem to concern upper management. McGonnell also said he was concerned about the legality of some ideas Pearson had implemented to increase Medicare reimbursement.

"Accounting for some of his ideas has been a nightmare for us," he complained. "Specifically, what ideas are you concerned about?" I asked.

"Intercompany transactions relating to marketing expenses," McGonnell said, describing an accounting term that captured the cost of division marketing expenses and allocated them to the various hospitals. McGonnell wasn't sure how the company was reporting the expenses on hospital cost reports, but he said it didn't feel right to him. I was suspicious that Pearson was disguising non-reimbursable marketing expenses (promotions, public relations) as an allowable patient care–related expense so the hospitals in the division could claim Medicare reimbursement.

"But we no longer have our own marketing department. All the marketing expenses are run through the division office and then allocated back to us," McGonnell said.

"That's interesting," I observed. "Marketing is a non-reimbursable expense under Medicare. How are they going to report it on the Medicare cost report?"

"I don't know," he sighed.

"Jim, the Orlando reimbursement office already told me to offset this intercompany marketing expense on the cost report. I'll look into it further," I told him.

Reviewing the questionable issues, I began investigating how they were reported on previously filed Medicare cost reports. I contacted Richard Pearson—whom I'd never met—to discuss the issues of the Gulf Coast Hospital's 1996 cost report. Pearson, a thin man in his fifties with a deep, raspy voice and weathered face, introduced himself as he strolled into the conference room. Soon after, I launched into my questions about his new cost reporting practices. I asked him to explain the intercompany accounting of marketing expenses.

In his gruff baritone, he responded, "Yeah. That was my idea. It should be picked up as an adjustment on the cost report on Schedule A-8–1." When I asked why he was doing it this way, he said, "By doing it this way, we avoid the Medicare auditors from setting it up as a non-reimbursable cost center, which would allocate additional overhead expense. That overhead expense would also become non-reimbursable."

If each hospital maintained its own marketing and public relations department, the direct expenses of that department, such as salaries and supplies, and the indirect overhead expenses, like utilities and housekeeping, would be considered non-reimbursable under Medicare rules. What Pearson's accounting maneuver accomplished was to remove only the direct marketing costs. The indirect costs would remain, so Medicare would overpay the hospitals.

"Okay, I understand what you're doing," I said, sounding like I grasped his concept. I caught on all right. I well understood what he was doing and vehemently disagreed with it. It was a clever maneuver designed to confuse the Medicare auditors, and it would have increased Medicare reimbursement to the hospital for non-reimbursable marketing expenses had cost report auditors not uncovered the scheme.

Pearson and I spent the next thirty minutes discussing the other reimbursement issues at question. All were based on increasing reimbursement but flouting company compliance with existing laws. Pearson told me he would be transferring soon to the Miami division office and that his post in the Fort Myers office would be vacant. Now it was just a matter of time before I could return to my old position at Columbia/HCA.

The evening after my conversation with Pearson, I relayed my new information to Joe Ford, describing the blatantly fraudulent cost reporting procedures Pearson had initiated. Taking notes, Ford asked if I was able to glean any new information for the search warrant. He asked me to sketch a floor plan of Southwest Florida Regional Medical Center's accounting office and list the occupants of each office. He also requested a list of the current CEOs and CFOs of each hospital in the Southwest Florida division and the locations of every hospital's accounting and central billing offices and the offsite storage facilities.

I told Ford that I was a little nervous about a rumor I had heard at work. I expressed my concern that Joseph "Mickey" Parslow, the CFO of Southwest Florida Regional Medical Center, and his family were moving into our neighborhood only a few houses down the street. "What should I do?" I asked.

"Don't get too neighborly with him," Ford answered. "Just say hi and wave. Don't invite them over." "That's easy," I relaxed.

"Mickey will probably wish he disclosed the information that you have. He is not going to be indicted but he will get interviewed," Ford said.

The day before my appointed testimony in front of the grand jury, Stephen Meagher and I prepared for my session. "The grand jury is fairly laid back. Don't be surprised if some are reading newspapers, knitting, etc.," he told me. "Really?" I asked, surprised. I thought the grand jury was an extremely official proceeding that required the jurors' complete attention.

"The grand jury is very casual," he answered. "They'll be listening, though. Don't be surprised that behind those newspapers, all cylinders are firing. There will be intelligent questions. Remember, any time you need a break, just ask."

The federal grand jury is made up of between twelve and twenty-three citizens, usually selected from the same pool of local residents providing trial jurors. Unlike trial juries, grand juries do not decide guilt or innocence; instead, they determine whether a prosecutor has developed enough probable cause to issue a criminal indictment. Since the grand jury decides only whether a defendant will be charged with a crime, jurors may never hear all the evidence. The proceedings are conducted in private, and jurors are sworn to secrecy and forbidden to discuss what they hear. The prosecutor determines which witnesses to call and if and when to offer immunity to guarantee testimony. Witness attorneys are barred from the grand jury room, but witnesses can halt the questioning at any time to consult with their attorneys. During the proceedings, jury members can question any witness to assist in their decision making.

The next day I drove to downtown Fort Myers to meet with Agent Ford, AUSA Kathleen Haley, and my local lawyer, Karla Spaulding, to prepare for that afternoon's testimony. At 10 A.M., we met in the U.S. Attorney's modular conference room. Haley talked me through the grand jury process. "Relax and don't be nervous," she said. "It will be a casual atmosphere. There won't be any surprises."

Haley had conducted many grand jury proceedings and said that most were not as somber and intimidating as those portrayed in films. She then drilled me on the kinds of questions she would ask me before the grand jury. She started with my background, probed my employment with Columbia/HCA, and then delved into the meat-and-potato issues of the Fawcett interest payments and reserve cost reports. She asked about my *qui tam* lawsuit and my role as a cooperating witness working with FBI Special Agent Ford. My responses were concise because I'd answered these questions many times before. *And this won't be the last time either*, I thought.

Jotting down notes to my responses, Haley instructed, "Just be brief. Don't get too technical. The jury might get confused." By noon, she was satisfied that I was prepared.

Over lunch, Karla Spaulding and I discussed my recent consulting assignments. I was eager to share the information I had learned from McGonnell and Pearson. After lunch, we walked the short way to the U.S. District Court. The two-story stone building, built in 1933, sat on the corner of First and Lee. I was beginning to detect a theme in government buildings: They had grand, imposing exteriors, but the interior offices had not been modernized or well maintained and presented a worn and shoddy image to those visiting or unlucky enough to work within them. In the small waiting area just outside the grand jury room, we met Agent Ford and sat down. Around 2 P.M., Haley entered and asked me to follow her into the grand jury room.

"John, if you need anything, I will wait here until you're done," Spaulding told me. "Okay," I smiled faintly. Excited as I was to see what a grand jury proceeding was really like, I couldn't shake a nagging feeling: *What if someone in the jury recognized me? What would I do?*

Scanning the room as I entered, I noticed mostly older men and women making up the jury, sprawled out among several rows of chairs. I was pleased not to recognize anyone. The room had none of the expected trappings of most courtrooms: no judge's podium, jurors' section, or tables assigned to prosecutors and defendants. Haley directed me to sit at a small folding table on the opposite side of the room from the jury beside a court reporter, who swore me in. Haley then told the jury that I was currently a cooperating witness working with FBI Special Agent Joe Ford and that I also had filed a *qui tam*, or whistleblower, lawsuit. I knew I was well prepared and should feel comfortable with Haley, but my stomach had other ideas. I prayed the questioning would end quickly.

Haley first asked about my background, my employment, and the issues identified in my complaint: the Fawcett interest problem, reserve cost reports, and multiple home health fraud allegations. Keeping the butterflies in check, I responded with no trouble, articulating slowly and carefully. My goal was to make very technical issues simple and easily understood for this layman's jury.

True to Haley's word, there were no surprises. I had answered these same questions countless times over the last several years. Occasionally, I snuck a glance at the jury, noting that most members were listening intently and taking notes. A few, however, were nodding off, seemingly bored. After an hour of testimony Haley turned the questioning over to the jury. They had only a few questions. Haley interjected a few times, explaining that I would be unable to answer because, while the grand jury was told about my *qui tam* case, there were other parts of the investigation about which I knew little or nothing. When the jurors had no more questions, Haley excused me and I left. My time in the witness chair had been brief. Outside, Spaulding and Ford were waiting for me.

"How'd it go, John?" Spaulding asked. "I think it went well. There were no surprises," I answered.

Ford, eager to leave the courthouse, told me that something was happening at Columbia/HCA today, but he would not elaborate. "Keep your ears open. Let me know if anyone says anything to you," he said.

Spaulding and I left the courthouse, puzzled and curious. As we walked to our cars, we discussed my testimony. I felt confident I'd done my best answering the questions, but I still wondered whom the Justice Department would indict based on my testimony. That night on March 19, I was watching the TV news and learned that the FBI had executed a limited search warrant on two Columbia/HCA hospitals, physician offices, and other company facilities in El Paso, Texas. News reports said the raids were related to alleged physician kickback arrangements.

Years later, a former Columbia/HCA attorney I became friends with told me that corporate executives were almost shell-shocked by the El Paso raids. As I knew only too well, the corporation lacked a compliance plan that might have caught, reported, and dealt with its many legal problems. But CEO Rick Scott shrugged off the raids as "just part of doing business." He claimed it was no big deal and vowed that the company would return to business as usual.

The next week, I prepared for another early morning drive to Winter Park for my next consulting assignment at Columbia/HCA. Even though I was not looking forward to the drive, it gave me time to reflect on the criminal investigation and my case against Columbia/HCA.

It still amazed me that only the week before, I had testified before a grand jury, and soon someone I knew would likely be indicted for a crime. Days after my testimony, Ford had called to congratulate me on Haley's behalf. She was delighted by how well my testimony had gone. We also discussed media coverage of the FBI raid in El Paso. While I tried to pry information from him about that case, he revealed nothing, explaining that it was a different case. The main purpose of his phone call, he said, was to complete his 302 Reports. Once again, Ford reminded me to persuade my attorneys to finish and file my amended complaint quickly. Hearing the urgency in his voice, I realized that my suspicion of another relator had been correct. Someone had come forward and might be filing a *qui tam* case with similar issues. I wondered whom it could be as I pulled into the Winter Park office.

By now, the office had grown familiar, very welcoming and extremely accommodating. Unlike the working climate in the Fort Myers division office, the attitude at the Winter Park office was low-key and business casual. Lunch groups readily included me.

That day, I had lunch with three reimbursement coordinators, Ray Shaw, Tommy Stoves, and Mark Poppell. I knew they were dying to talk about the El Paso raids.

Shaw, the most vocal of the group, asked, "Does anyone know what's going on in El Paso?" Without waiting for a response, he continued, "I saw in the papers that the records seized seemed to be related to physician practice purchases."

Poppell interjected, "I talked to someone in the Dallas reimbursement office and I was told they have a pretty squeaky clean operation. There isn't anything wrong. The feds won't find anything."

Then, out of the blue, Shaw revealed, "The Tampa division office occasionally hires a temp to shred documents. John, does the Fort Myers division office do the same?"

Document shredding, I marveled. "I've never seen them do that," I said.

Shaw concluded, "Well, they'd never find anything in the Tampa office."

Of course, those Winter Park employees could not have known that each night I was passing information on to Ford and my attorneys. Each seemingly innocent conversation included snippets of potentially valuable information for my team. My insider role was working quite effectively. My attorneys added new allegations to my amended complaint, promising that the revisions would be ready by week's end. Ford, working on the search warrant affidavit, requested additional information on the locations of division and group offices. I learned that the search warrant would include multiple Columbia/HCA hospital and division office locations and encompass all cost reports and computer files. Ford was convinced that as an insider, I could help when the search warrants were executed. Given what I'd learned in Winter Park, he suspected the company might attempt to obstruct justice by shredding documents.

Days later, when I asked Ford how other indictments were progressing, he said, "We're working on it. Jay Jarrell is in deep shit right now. You know, John, there is more than one bad egg at Columbia."

I received a surprise on April 3, 1997. My former boss Larry Bomar called to offer me a three-week consulting assignment in St. Petersburg. Bomar was then the manager of reimbursement of BayCare Health System, a Tampa Bay consortium of nonprofit hospitals.

"Absolutely," I told him.

It was good to hear from Bomar and I was excited to work with him again. He and I shared some common beliefs, and I was interested to hear his current opinion of Columbia/HCA.

That afternoon, I received a letter from the administrative assistant in Columbia/HCA's Fort Myers division office, who confirmed that Richard Pearson, the division reimbursement manager, was leaving. She wrote that I should contact Jay Jarrell, then the division president, if I wanted to return to my former job. I contacted Ford right away to ask if he wanted me to make contact with Jarrell.

"Yes, try to get some statements from Jay. A face-to-face meeting would be best," Ford suggested. If I was successful in obtaining an interview, he would wire me beforehand.

The next day, Ford told me that he'd seen a copy of my amended complaint, which Karla Spaulding had filed the day before in Tampa. I was happy I had heeded his warnings. He said, "I told you to get it filed for a reason. If something good eventually comes out of this investigation, you need to have protected your interests." "Thanks, Joe," I replied. "I understand."

I understood, but I didn't fully realize then that amending my complaint by including the home health allegations would result in millions of additional dollars in recoveries for the government and an unknown percentage for me.

My attempts to arrange a meeting with Jarrell were unsuccessful. Instead, I set up a meeting in the division office with Pearson to discuss additional Medicare reimbursement issues while preparing the cost report for Gulf Coast Hospital. First, I met Ford at the Hampton Inn near the airport on April 18. More practical than covert, this motel had become our regular rendezvous location over the last few months. I wondered if anyone there ever noticed us passing envelopes and folders. If they had, what would they think we were up to—something illegal? If my life were a movie, I imagined what would happen if Lee County sheriff deputies swooped down without warning, guns drawn, shouting, "Freeze!" But Ford would probably slide his hand into his jacket and retrieve his badge in an official, FBI style, making the deputies cringe and apologize. *All in a day's work*, I mused.

Pulling into the hotel parking lot unnoticed, as usual, I saw Ford waiting. He held a rather old-fashioned recording device. The reel-to-reel recorder, about the size of a notebook, looked like a seventies antique. I chided Ford about the FBI using such unsophisticated recording equipment. Even Fisher-Price produced better spying tools—and those were for kids. He laughed and eyeballed my suit, opting instead to hide the recorder in my black computer bag. Unceremoniously, he affixed it to the inside of the bag with gray duct tape. Near the opening of the bag, he taped two microphones. "It's easy to operate," he said, pointing to the controls. "Just turn it on and off in the elevator."

He advised that the bag should be placed on a table or desk so the microphone would be able to pick up the best possible sound. Ford instructed me to treat this meeting just like my phone recordings and ask questions designed to generate discussion. Enjoying the cloak-and-dagger part of being an informant, I asked, "What does it take to be an FBI agent, Joe?" "We do need CPAs that understand healthcare," he replied.

"Because of my involvement in this case, would they even consider me if I applied?" I asked.

"That shouldn't matter. You didn't do anything wrong. Your starting pay would be around $42,000. I would wait to see what happens with your case. You may not be interested in the end."

I was only a consultant at the time, so any steady job would be an improvement for my family. That $42,000 with benefits sounded good at the moment, though it was far less than the $60,000 to $90,000 I should have been earning with my experience and background in healthcare accounting. Did Ford know something I didn't? Would my case be worth more? At that point, I sure hoped so.

We spent the next thirty minutes talking. I told him that yesterday I'd heard that Columbia/HCA would fill both Fort Myers division positions with other applicants. Bonnie Reid had apologized for not offering me either job. Apparently, a qualified internal candidate applied for one job and the company hired someone with more than twenty years of experience for the other position. She did tell me that when Pearson moved to the Miami division office, he would require an assistant. She felt I should discuss the reimbursement coordinator's position in Miami with him. Ford suggested that if I was hired in Miami, he would set me up the same way he would have in Winter Park. I told him I'd find out more when I spoke to Pearson.

Ford then informed me that he was keeping his 302 Reports confidential and had not shared them with Marie O'Connell, the Civil Division trial attorney. Curious, I asked, "Why not?" He told he was keeping them confidential to protect my anonymity after learning that O'Connell had already revealed my identity to the Health Care Financing Administration, the government agency responsible for the Medicare program. *So much for all the secrecy,* I thought.

"I don't want your name to be leaked. I just want to be careful," he explained. "If Marie will just let me make the criminal case, her job will be very easy. It will come down to how much Columbia/HCA is willing to pay the government to get out of the trouble they're in."

At 9:30 A.M., I left the Hampton Inn and headed northwest to the Barnett Bank building. The twenty-minute ride gave me time to prepare myself. *I should have taken up acting,* I told myself. This mission, however, made me more nervous than most. When I arrived at the parking lot, I noticed that I was ten minutes early. Before climbing out of the car, I checked my computer bag to make sure the recorder was still in place. Inside the lobby, the elevator was waiting. Alone in the elevator, I opened my bag and turned on the recorder just before the door opened. At the reception desk, I stopped and chatted with a former colleague while the receptionist located Pearson, who greeted me as I crossed the lobby toward the conference room. With its sweeping view of the Caloosahatchee River (just like the FBI office two floors above), I thought that it was a great location for our meeting. The long conference table provided an opportunity to position my computer bag on top of the table where the microphones could pick up our conversation. Not wanting to jar the tape recorder, I carefully removed my pen and white notepad from the side pocket of the bag.

I began the meeting by asking Pearson about the open items from my preparation of the 1996 Medicare cost report for Gulf Coast Hospital. We spent the next forty minutes discussing it item by item, each at length. I told him I needed further clarification to finalize the cost report before sending it to the Winter Park office. Pearson, of course, didn't know that I had other motives for calling this meeting.

I truly hoped he would display the same corporate arrogance he'd shown in our earlier meeting when discussing the company's questionable cost reporting practices. Ford had provided me with a few questions he wanted answered. Casually, I inserted these queries into our conversation. Pearson, happy to talk, never seemed skeptical. His responses supported my allegations. At one point, I became irritated about how he denigrated another fiscal intermediary, Mutual of Omaha. He explained that the FI had erred in allocating home health payments for several hospitals in his division. Some of the hospitals were overpaid and some underpaid. The combined result, however, constituted an overpayment to Columbia/HCA of more than $1 million.

"Richard, have you disclosed the error?" I asked. Nodding, he indicated that he had and that Mutual of Omaha to this point had not made the correction. "Did you contact them again?" I inquired. Pearson said he hadn't and explained that he was now waiting for Mutual of Omaha to find the overpayment itself.

"Sometimes you have to tell them more than once," I said. He chuckled, "If I handed them a road map to the hospital, they still wouldn't be able to find it. Fiscal intermediaries are so ignorant." *This is just like the Fawcett interest issue*, I thought. *The company's attitude hasn't changed at all. It's still too arrogant to be compliant.*

As we wrapped up our meeting, I told Pearson I was interested in the coordinator position in Miami. He said one internal candidate was being considered but he would keep me in mind. Departing, I thanked him for his time and the opportunity to work with him. I told him I would send the completed Gulf Coast cost report to Winter Park and the division office would make final adjustments before it was filed. They also would prepare the reserve cost report.

As I left the conference room, I stopped at the reception desk. Under her breath, the receptionist told me that Pearson was not well liked in the office. I asked her if Jay Jarrell was in the office. I told her I hoped that Jarrell could sway the hiring decision in my favor. Secretly, I was hoping that Jarrell would make some incriminating statements on tape.

"Unfortunately, he's not in today," she responded. I left disappointed, but was happy with the recorded statements from Pearson. *An Academy Award performance*, I thought.

Boarding an empty elevator, I turned off the recorder, pleased that almost the entire tape had been used. I loosened my tie and removed my jacket, relieved this covert mission was complete. *That was a breeze*, I thought. I had remained extremely calm and didn't even break a sweat. As I exited the elevator, I paged Ford from my cell phone. Then I slowly drove to our prearranged meeting spot in the post office parking lot. Ford was already waiting for me.

"Did it go well?" he asked as I approached his car.

"No problems. I think you will be happy with some of the statements I got." I proceeded to recount details of the conversation. He said he couldn't wait to see the transcript.

Then he said, "John, don't expect the search warrant before June. I'm still working on it." The indictment process was under way, he said, but the timing would be a surprise.

Stephen Meagher called me one week before the May 15 seal expiration. We were willing to agree should the Justice Department request an extension of my case's seal for another six months. According to Meagher, the Civil Division had labeled Ford a "loose cannon" and worried that he wasn't sharing information with them. He believed that the Civil Division was jealous of Ford's success. It seems that the two divisions, even though under the same umbrella, do not always work well or efficiently together. Joe Ford had told me that he was not sharing all information with Marie O'Connell—that he felt she was not altogether trustworthy. Obviously Marie could tell that Ford wasn't being altogether candid and felt he was a loose cannon. The Criminal Division focuses on the crimes, while the Civil Division focuses on "breach of contract" sort of issues. Like any bureaucracy, they don't always play nicely together in the sand box. In any case, I couldn't see the whole picture at that time; I only understood what I was told, which was very little.

Ford called me in the afternoon to ask how my consulting assignment had gone with Larry Bomar in St. Petersburg. I told him Bomar was happy to escape the Columbia/HCA tentacles. We had recalled the egotism of our former colleagues and the self-indulgent corporate culture at Columbia/HCA. We expressed mutual relief that we'd not become entangled in it.

Bomar told me about another quarrel between Michael Neeb and Trish Lindler at Columbia/HCA. According to Bomar, Lindler had disclosed an error on a previously filed cost report at Southwest Florida Regional Medical Center to a Medicare auditor during a period in which Neeb had been the CFO. In preparing the report, a consultant had inadvertently double-counted a property tax expense, so Medicare overpaid the hospital. Lindler notified the Medicare auditor without consulting Neeb, which made him furious. He apparently blasted Lindler for making the disclosure, telling her, "It's not fraud unless you're caught."

Larry and I both played our cards close to our chests then, not revealing too much information. Although we didn't talk about it, I knew Bomar had been interviewed by the FBI. I was glad to see him happy and doing well. Just like me, he'd stepped in a hornet's nest when he joined Columbia/HCA.

Ford's ultimate purpose in calling me was to ascertain my availability for the next mission. I told him I was ready any time he was. "So what do you have in mind?" I asked. "I would like to see the hospitals and the central billing office," he answered.

"Why do you want to see the hospitals? Aren't the records you want in the division offices?" I asked. "Yes, but the hospitals may have tidbits of information we may not find anywhere else," he explained. I agreed to meet him the next morning in the Wal-Mart parking lot. It was May 8, 1997, and my role as an FBI spy intensified.

Ford had other motives for looking at these locations, which he kept secret. I had no idea then, but Ford was organizing the execution of a massive, multi-state search warrant, one of the largest ever conducted by the FBI. That seventy-four–page search warrant affidavit would be submitted to obtain search warrants for twenty Florida locations and additional hospitals and offices in six states for a total of thirty-five locations. Five confidential witnesses provided the information for the affidavit.

While I was pleased that the Justice Department had shown such intense interest in my case, the stress it caused in our lives was unfathomable. I shared the anxiety Kirsten and I felt with Stephen. While he was steeped in the law, he also played an unofficial role of therapist. He understood the fears and the stress we were experiencing and was always ready to allay our fears. We discussed the progress of the case and my feeling that I needed to work full time to support my family. We both understood that having committed "career suicide," my future job choices would be limited. Meagher and I agreed that once the search warrants were executed, my identity as a government witness would likely be publicly disclosed and my anonymity would vanish. Although Meagher assured us that our family would be in no danger, we agreed that a move out of state away from the media attention might be beneficial. With that in mind, I had begun reconnecting with my Wisconsin healthcare contacts.

Two weeks after my scouting mission with Ford, I received a phone call from Jim McGonnell, the assistant controller at Southwest Florida Regional Medical Center. McGonnell wanted to know if I was interested in the reimbursement manager's position at his hospital. "Certainly," I responded. We arranged to meet for an interview. Since we had worked closely in the past, the interview would be merely a formality. A full-time job with benefits would not only be helpful at home, but might afford me even more flexibility in my spy role.

At home each morning, our household routine revolved around preparing our son Alex for kindergarten. After the short walk to school, Kirsten and I would stroll through the neighborhood. I used our walks as a form of therapy. Kirsten didn't mind listening or playing devil's advocate. After our walk, I would spend most of the day in a corner of our master bedroom at my small workstation, which I jokingly called my office. A desk, phone, computer, and fax machine were all I required. The hours passed quickly as I worked on consulting assignments, prepared data for my *qui tam* case, and compiled information for the FBI.

But now I was preparing to return to the 9 to 5 world, dressing in typical accountant attire—white dress shirt, red tie, dark blue suit, and black wing tips—for my interview with McGonnell. As I drove north to the hospital, I reflected upon the progress made since I filed my *qui tam* case twelve months earlier.

I arrived at the hospital's accounting offices for my job interview with McGonnell. Leather briefcase in hand, I headed into the office. Inside, McGonnell was waiting to introduce me to his boss, Controller Tim Williams. In McGonnell's office, we discussed the responsibilities of the reimbursement position. Since they knew my background, the hospital already was prepared to make me an offer, he said. To make it official, however, the hospital requested a copy of my resume and asked me to complete an application. The offer was respectable, but I needed some time to get approval from the government and my attorneys. Stalling, I responded, "Thanks Jim, give me some time to think it over. I'll let you know by the end of the week." "Okay, let me know soon. We need you as soon as possible," McGonnell replied.

As I drove home, I pondered this new development. Full-time work without relocation was perfect. Kirsten would be happy to hear the news. Even though it would be temporary (temporary because the main purpose was to be a spy and I'd likely be fired or dismissed when my case became public knowledge). The full-time position promised a steady paycheck and health insurance. The last five months we had paid for our own insurance, a costly venture for a family of five. Luckily, the position wasn't located in the division office; however, if I took it, I would again become entangled in the company's unethical practices. *I'd better polish up on my acting skills again*, I thought.

"In this job," I told Kirsten, "I might be able to help when the search warrants are executed." When I told Ford about the offer, he quickly approved. He welcomed having me on the inside of the company because the FBI would soon execute the search warrants.

I could hear the urgency in his voice when he asked me to help prepare a list of the former CEOs and CFOs of Fawcett Memorial Hospital and of the Fort Myers division office. He stressed, "This could be one of the most important things I am asking you to do."

"Sure, but why?" I asked. "I can't tell you at this time," he replied.

Glancing at the time, I asked, "When do you need it?" "Tomorrow, he said. I'll meet you in the morning at 9 at the usual place."

Next, I called my attorneys to apprise them of McGonnell's job offer. They agreed that a job at the hospital would definitely help my case. Even though I was fearful of Columbia/HCA at the moment, the offer was too good to refuse.

I met Ford promptly at 9 A.M. the next day and provided the list he had requested. He scanned it, questioning Bob Whiteside's background and seeking the locations of several offsite record storage facilities.

"So Joe, any idea when you're going to conduct the search warrants?" I fished. "Maybe a couple months," he countered. "I'll tell you in advance. But don't tell anyone, including your legal counsel, when it's happening!"

On June 2, 1997, I met Ford for lunch in Fort Myers. He surprised me with news that he had been promoted and introduced two new agents, Deanna Clark and Steven Miller, who were now assigned to the investigation.

"Don't worry, I'm still the lead agent on the case even though I'll be moving to Tampa," he assured me. Clark, Miller, and other agents from the Tampa office would be taking more significant roles, however. Clark, a young, petite woman, told me she had seven years of FBI experience. Miller, on the other hand—a towering, beefy fellow—was only two weeks out of the FBI Academy. I was skeptical. Were these agents as good as Ford, my longtime handler? Would they protect my interests as well as he had? Later, Ford refused my offer to pay for my share of lunch. "It's on the FBI," he said. "You deserve it."

The next day, I officially accepted the hospital job offer. Our family needed the stability of a routine paycheck. The anxiety of the last five months had been overwhelming, and Kirsten seemed most affected by the financial insecurity and the double life I'd been leading. Our children—Alex (age 6), Abby (age 2½), and Austin (age 1)—demanded all of her attention. Kirsten couldn't remember the last time she'd enjoyed a full night's sleep. In addition, and especially troubling, she had been experiencing numbness in her leg, which wasn't going away. At first, doctors feared a brain tumor. Further testing at the end of June revealed the slightly less ominous diagnosis of relapsing remitting multiple sclerosis (MS). MS, an autoimmune disease, affects the central nervous system and can cause a variety of symptoms, including pain, impaired mobility and balance, slurred speech, depression, and fatigue.

Unconvinced of the diagnosis, Kirsten blamed her ailments on the stress of the case. Having little faith in the Fort Myers doctor who had diagnosed her, in July we consulted with an MS specialist in Milwaukee, who, sadly, confirmed the diagnosis. We learned that the condition primarily affects adults and is more prevalent among women than men. (In 2000 Kirsten began taking daily injections of Copaxone, an MS therapy drug. While Copaxone does not cure MS, it has been proven to slow the disease's progress. She continues to take it to this day with few noticeable symptoms.)

The diagnosis of Kirsten's MS validated my decision to return to Columbia/HCA. I told Meagher about the diagnosis, and he felt confident that the hospital job would reduce some of our financial pressures, at least for a while.

Then, back in his attorney's role, Meagher updated me on the case. He had organized a meeting for June 18 in Tampa with both the Criminal and Civil Divisions of the Justice Department. His goal was to bring the Civil Division attorneys, Marie O'Connell and Dan Anderson, from Washington to join the Criminal Division attorney, Kathleen Haley, and FBI Agent Ford. Meagher had prepared a list of issues he wanted to discuss with both groups. One item was allegations against my former employer, Community Care of America (CCA). Another was the preliminary damages analysis prepared by experts in Jim Alderson's Quorum Health Group case. Meagher hoped the same methodology could be applied to the Columbia/HCA case. Ultimately, his goal was to persuade both sides to share information and work as a team.

I left the house on June 18 for the drive to Tampa. Taking the same route as I had with Whiteside the day of our fateful meeting in Port Charlotte in 1994, I drove north on I-75, surprised by the changing vista. The melaleucas, so prominent three years before, had dwindled. The state now required developers to clear each parcel of the weed, allowing native species to reestablish themselves. I mused that Florida's eradication initiative was much like mine against Columbia/HCA: Each small step constituted an increasingly debilitating blow against a much larger foe.

I found myself sailing over Tampa Bay on the Sunshine Skyway Bridge. My first stop was the Tampa office of James, Hoyer & Newcomer, my Florida counsel. The offices of James, Hoyer & Newcomer were much more imposing than the plain headquarters of Phillips & Cohen in Washington, D.C. The glass multistory complex looked impressive. This was more like what I expected from a law firm.

Meagher, who had flown in from California, and Spaulding were waiting for me when I arrived. We spent a few minutes discussing Meagher's agenda, and once we felt sufficiently prepared, Spaulding drove us to the FBI offices. They were located in the Robert Timberlake Federal Building at 500 Zack Street in downtown Tampa. Little did I know then that the route along Kennedy Boulevard from Spaulding's office to the federal building would become as familiar to me over the next few years as washing my hands.

The seven-story concrete monstrosity, built in the early 1960s, was visible from where we parked two blocks away. Behind it towered its polished granite and glass annex, built in the 1980s. We passed through security and a metal detector as we entered the federal building. Entering the FBI office lobby, Meagher approached the receptionist behind the thick bulletproof glass and told her Agent Ford was expecting us. After paging him, the receptionist required us to sign in. Ford soon appeared and led us to the conference room. Unlike the Fort Myers office, this conference room offered no aesthetically pleasing views. O'Connell, Haley, Miller, and Clark were already seated at the large conference table. Meagher had hoped that the other Justice Department attorney, Dan Anderson, would attend, but O'Connell explained that he was unavailable.

Kirsten topped Meagher's agenda. With our approval, he disclosed her recent diagnosis of MS and said he sought to minimize any added stress this case could deliver my family. O'Connell appeared to be the most sympathetic. (In future meetings, she asked me how Kirsten was doing.) Next up, Meagher introduced the damage analysis examples from Alderson's Quorum case and proposed that the same methodology could work well in the Columbia/HCA case. Meagher responded to the government officials' questions with pointed answers, sometimes pausing to let me address any technical issues. Once satisfied, he allowed the government to ask questions. I provided answers without any trouble.

Finally, Meagher introduced the fraud I had witnessed at CCA. Everyone present knew I'd been fired, but they seemed stunned when I told them the extent of the fraud I'd seen there. It took me thirty minutes to enumerate the Medicare fraud I'd seen and describe the multiple SEC violations I had witnessed. Ford and Haley showed the most interest, promising to have an FBI agent from the Naples office contact me for further investigation. In the meantime, they requested that I organize the documents I had and list the alleged violations.

(In hindsight, I wonder whether the FBI was honestly interested or if the agents were simply pacifying or playing me. I believe the government had too much on its plate and lacked the will, resources, and depth of prosecutorial talent to begin another complex investigation. Everyone was aware that I would be testifying in the criminal case against Columbia/HCA as one of their key witnesses. Perhaps they didn't want to muddy the waters with another case. No doubt they considered the CCA case inconsequential and had to minimize the matter.

In one ill-fated attempt at contact with me regarding CCA, an FBI agent from Naples did leave a phone message for me. Subsequently, I was unable to reach him and my messages went unanswered. One year later, in August 1998—when it seemed apparent that the FBI would not investigate CCA—I suggested to Ford that I send a fraud referral package to CCA's fiscal intermediary, Wellmark. Ford agreed that it was a good idea, but I came to believe that Ford either foiled Wellmark's investigation or discouraged the FBI's inquiry. Having worked with fiscal intermediaries for many years, I knew their policies. If contacted by a current or former employee, the FI fraud unit was instructed to contact federal law enforcement. In addition, policy required that the FI inform the complainant of its findings.

While Wellmark admitted receiving the complaint, I was never contacted nor did I receive its disposition. After many frustrating months, I gave up. The company that purchased the sinking CCA, Integrated Health Services (IHS), suffered its own financial and legal difficulties. I wondered if Ford had stymied the investigation or whether the Naples FBI office or the fiscal intermediary, Wellmark, were simply incompetent.)

As my attorneys and I left the FBI office in the afternoon, Meagher jokingly predicted that only three locations would be raided when the warrants were executed: the reimbursement office in Winter Park, the division offices in Fort Myers, and Fawcett Memorial Hospital. We had no idea how mistaken that prediction would be.

I settled into my full-time job at Southwest Florida Regional Medical Center, and the first two weeks went smoothly. In fact, the job was rather easy. My covert missions continued for Ford, and I sensed that he would soon execute the search warrants. Ford grew increasingly interested in the company's billing and information systems and how to access them. Specifically, he wanted to know who maintained our computer systems and how these different systems were password-protected.

Ford admitted that he was working on the final version of the search warrant affidavit and thought he might have to call me at work while working out the details. He was familiar with deception and practiced it when needed. "John," he said, "if you're not at your desk when I call, I'll leave a message for you to contact Jack Fordham. That will be my code name."

CHAPTER TEN

FBI Raid and Aftermath

Driving to the office the morning of July 16, 1997, I tried to control my excitement. I arrived as usual at 7:30 A.M., dressed conservatively in dark trousers, a red tie, and a crisp white shirt. Sitting in my parked Plymouth Acclaim, I gathered my thoughts. *Avoid arousing suspicion,* I told myself. As my glasses slid part way down my nose, I realized I was sweating profusely. Shoving them back into place, I quickly glanced in the rearview mirror, nervously running my fingers through my hair. I couldn't shake the feeling I was being watched. *Stop being paranoid; it's just another acting job,* I told myself as I walked into the office.

The night before, Joe Ford had phoned to tip me off to the FBI's planned raid of Columbia/HCA offices at 9 A.M. Ford swore me to secrecy and said I was the only civilian to know what the FBI planned. While my wife knew the raids were imminent, even Kirsten was in the dark. Needless to say, I didn't sleep much that night.

I had to admit that the accounting job at Southwest Florida Regional Medical Center had proven useful, both to our family and to the government. Consulting work wasn't terribly lucrative, and without a regular paycheck, Kirsten and I often worried about our bills. Besides the financial security this new job offered, I knew it would allow me to aid Ford's investigation. In addition, although I had misgivings about working again for Columbia/HCA, even temporarily, I knew the job was a perfect fit. Unfortunately, the position did not offer much prestige. The office was not located in the hospital but across the street in a rundown office complex featuring tinted windows, low ceilings, and the faint odor of mildew. That morning, sitting behind my desk, I tried to look busy. Opening one of the files on my desk, I found it impossible to concentrate. How was I supposed to look unconcerned when I knew what was about to happen? I glanced furtively at my watch and decided a stroll through the building might help calm my nerves. Stopping in the break room, I encountered several co-workers sipping coffee, discussing the brutal murder of fashion designer Gianni Versace the night before. Not feeling sociable, I filled a paper cup with water, gulped it down, and headed back to my office.

Back at my desk, I checked e-mail and resisted the temptation to look out my office window for signs of the FBI's arrival. I wondered if Columbia/HCA's big event for its financial staff, a two-day Orlando reimbursement seminar scheduled to begin the following day, would be canceled. Now I began to worry. How would my fellow employees react when the FBI raided the offices? Would anyone resist? Would there be gunfire? And would anyone point the finger at me?

Exactly at 9 A.M., a swarm of FBI agents descended upon the office. The siege on this hospital's office was just one small piece of a coordinated raid that Agent Ford conducted. In a precise, sweeping move, thirty-six Columbia/HCA offices were raided simultaneously in six states. It was the largest concurrent execution of search warrants on a publicly traded corporation. The FBI was seeking more than just reserve cost reports. The agency had compiled evidence of physician kickbacks, false Medicare claims involving home health agencies, and overbilling. The scandal was exploding in size and scope far beyond what I'd imagined.

"Everyone, step away from your computers!" the federal law enforcement agents commanded, holding their badges high. Just like in the movies, the agents were dressed in suits and ties and sported firearms at their waists. No one panicked, but there were sounds of bewilderment and cries of surprise as the FBI team moved swiftly through the building. Employees were asked to gather in the conference room. I did my best to look as surprised as everyone else as we filed down the hallway. No one could believe what was happening. Throughout the building, phones rang unanswered.

The agents informed employees that they had a search warrant and would completely sweep their offices. They said that once an office had been thoroughly searched, employees would be allowed to return to their desks. One co-worker asked if she could go home, and an agent told her she could leave only with her employer's permission. Agents warned that anyone who left would not be permitted to reenter the building. The FBI allowed no one to leave without first supplying personal identification information, such as their home address, telephone number, Social Security number, and the passwords used to access their computer files.

As some agents began the interview process, other agents began the arduous task of boxing up thousands of pages of documents. In private, one agent asked each employee identifying questions, such as name, address, and Social Security number. I don't remember any Columbia/HCA attorneys coming to our office, but our controller received a phone call from the CFO instructing everyone to cooperate. Confiscated items were carefully recorded on an inventory sheet. I watched as agents downloaded computer files to an external hard drive and carted away entire filing cabinets containing documents of particular importance. Later, I learned that this was also the largest search warrant ever executed on a health-care organization. The FBI seized nearly 14,000 boxes of records from Columbia/HCA offices in the six states they raided. Obviously, the information I'd passed to Ford had been studied thoroughly. A small, satisfied smile crossed my lips. *I can't wait to tell Kirsten how well this went,* I thought to myself.

At noon, I looked out the reception area window to discover that the local WINK-TV crew had gathered outside the building. I couldn't imagine how the news media had learned about the FBI raids so quickly. I reached for the reception telephone and called Kirsten right away to ask if she was watching the news.

"Yes, I turned on the TV and there it was on all the local stations and CNN. I've started recording some of it so you can see for yourself," she said. "And guess what? They are reporting the company's stock price has already fallen about $2 a share and will likely go lower."

The press demanded a response from Columbia/HCA. A flustered spokeswoman, Beth Tuttle of the Fort Myers division, assured reporters that the public had no reason to fear. She said the FBI search did not include patient medical records and pointed out that Columbia/HCA was cooperating fully with the government. It seemed to me that Columbia/

HCA viewed this full-scale invasion of their offices as nothing to worry about, simply "normal operating procedure."

By 2 P.M., Tim Williams had told all but three of the accounting staff who were still in the office that they could go home. I was among those asked to stay behind because my office had not yet been searched. As the afternoon wore on, one of the FBI agents, Jim Trotter, recognized me as the whistleblower. Ford had previously provided Agent Trotter with my description and told me Trotter would be looking for me. When no one was looking, he approached me with a few questions.

"Are we getting all the documents you think we need?" he asked, as he loaded files into a large brown box. "Are we missing anything important?" I pointed out many other documents I thought should have been included in the search, while trying not to be caught talking with Trotter.

Two other FBI agents, one from El Paso and the other from Cleveland, searched my office. Some items were considered so important that they were immediately placed in a cardboard box called the FBI "hot box," a term I'd never heard before. Documents relating to reserves, reserve cost reports, or home health cost report issues were collected in the hot box.

Finally, around 7 P.M.—ten hours after they'd stormed our offices—the agents completed their search and allowed those of us who were still there to leave. As I climbed into my car, I heaved a sigh of relief. When I got home, I described the scene to Kirsten and then to my attorneys. It had been a long day.

The FBI raids rattled many top executives at Columbia/HCA, but not all. The next day, Bonnie Reid, the director of reimbursement for the Florida Group, met with nearly 200 Florida hospital financial managers at the Hyatt Regency Orlando International Airport hotel for the planned two-day seminar. Reid began her remarks by apologizing. She joked that the FBI had carted away all the overhead materials she'd prepared for the meeting. A small ripple of laughter could be heard in the room. As usual, however, Reid was well prepared. She outlined the new structure of the corporate reimbursement department and what services it would provide the hospitals. Then she discussed what the reimbursement department expected in return and urged everyone to seek "creative" ways to add more dollars to their hospital's bottom line. Seated at one of the tables near the front of the room, I couldn't believe what I was hearing.

I had assumed that the company and management would have been more shaken by the FBI raids. The search warrants offered some insight into what was being investigated, but to management, the raids seemed more of a minor inconvenience than a major embarrassment.

"I have taken on a $50 million challenge from our Florida Group's CFO for this fiscal year," Reid told the delegates. "My department will be looking at any possible opportunities at your hospitals that will help us reach this goal." Reid seemed to be conducting a Medicare reimbursement pledge drive, passing the hat to hospital executives to boost reimbursements. *She has to be kidding,* I thought.

Reid said her department had already uncovered a way to generate an additional $15 million in Medicare reimbursement and had identified another $18 million the department could potentially secure through Medicare cost report re-openings and aggressive cost report filings. At the mention of the words "aggressive cost report filings," my spine stiffened. I knew it meant that the company once again was asking financial managers to stretch Medicare accounting rules to the limit. As far as I was concerned, Columbia/HCA was already too aggressive in its cost report filings. Now Reid was urging managers to expand the practice! I found her comments especially startling in light of yesterday's FBI raids. Didn't she realize that these questionable accounting practices were already under investigation? Obviously not! Her comments revealed that the company had no idea the reserve cost reports composed a key component of the FBI's probe. *So far, I'm safe,* I slowly exhaled.

During the day, a lawyer from the company's legal department addressed the group. His message was designed to calm the fears of the company managers. The scope and nature of the FBI raids was unknown, he said, but Columbia/HCA was fully cooperating with the government investigation. The attorney took a few questions from the floor, and it became apparent that many managers were worried they might be contacted by federal agents. He explained that no one was obligated to talk to the government investigators without legal representation and offered the services of the company's legal department. Then he discussed the False Claims Act, telling everyone that it allowed ordinary citizens to sue, on the government's behalf, people or companies allegedly defrauding the government.

"I mention this because the entire FBI investigation could be related to a whistleblower within the organization," the attorney said offhandedly. "And by the way, as managers, I must point out to you that whistleblowers are protected from retaliation under this legislation." I stared straight ahead and tried to avoid making eye contact with anyone. The room suddenly felt too warm.

On the second day of the two-day seminar, I was invited to join a group of colleagues for lunch. There was no way to decline the invitation. Seated with me at the table were Mike Neeb, CFO of the North Florida Division; Jim Burns, CFO of Fawcett Memorial Hospital; Mickey Parslow, CFO of Southwest Florida Regional Medical Center; and Jim McGonnell, assistant controller of Southwest Florida Regional Medical Center. The conversation quickly turned to the FBI investigations. Had anyone heard anything new? What was the FBI looking for? Was someone in trouble?

Parslow, who had been served with a subpoena on the day of the raid, requiring him to appear before the same grand jury that I testified before, initially panicked. Today he seemed a little more relaxed. He said that was because he'd learned that several other top-level managers also had been summoned to appear. Everyone wanted to know what Parslow would say to the grand jury.

"Well, I know what some of my answers will be," Parslow told the group, feigning an innocent expression. "I'm sorry, sir, I can't answer that because it might incriminate me." Neeb joked, "Sounds good. Keep practicing." I chuckled with the group, playing along.

Right after the seminar, I took my family to visit relatives in Wisconsin. I had to lie when asked what I knew about the raids. I shrugged it off as a cost of doing business, just like Columbia/HCA's management had. I couldn't tell them I was behind those raids and knew exactly what they involved.

A week after we returned from Wisconsin, the accounting office at my hospital was buzzing again. A rumor was circulating that Jay Jarrell, the CEO of the Fort Myers Division office, was in jail. He wasn't in jail, but Jarrell—along with my former boss, Bob Whiteside, then the director of reimbursement for the Single Market Division, and Mike Neeb, CFO of the North Florida Division—had been indicted on five counts of Medicare fraud, conspiracy, and making false statements to the federal government.

I felt guilty, even remorseful, that if convicted, my former colleagues could face up to twenty-five years in prison and maximum fines of $1.25 million each. That evening Ford and I discussed the fact that I had not set out to ruin the lives of these men and their families. I simply wanted to correct the fraudulent Medicare cost reporting practices and see those overpayments returned to the government. He reassured me that coming forward had been the right thing to do. Ford held no pity for the men who had been indicted and told me that he hoped the FBI investigation might eventually lead to an indictment against Rick Scott. I too could have been snared in the same web of fraud, but I had been able to foresee the consequences and avoid entanglement. Ford said, "You should be proud of yourself. What you did, John, took courage. I know the last few weeks have been hard on you. You made the right choice and the others did not."

Meanwhile, at Columbia/HCA, corporate changes were being introduced at an alarming rate, contributing to an uncertain atmosphere in the office. In late July, Chairman and CEO Rick Scott had been ousted by the board of directors. Dr. Thomas Frist, Jr., one of HCA's founders and the largest shareholder, was named the new CEO. Frist promised a changed company when he took the reigns of Columbia/HCA in early August 1997.

Frist's first step in reshaping the company's corporate culture simply was to allow each facility the option to drop "Columbia" from its name. Issuing a number of directives, he proceeded to position himself as a corporate "white knight." At the administrative level, he banned the long-standing Columbia practice of tying performance to bonuses. He halted the legally suspect practice of offering lucrative cash incentives to physicians, which some claimed violated the federal anti-kickback law. He announced that the company would implement cost-cutting measures, including the sale of Columbia/HCA's home healthcare division. And Frist issued another edict: Destroying documents would no longer be tolerated.

On the operations side, Frist ended the policy of improperly coding patient diagnoses to increase Medicare payments and said the company would correct its laboratory billing problems. He also expressed his intent to build Columbia/HCA into a leader in corporate ethics and compliance and named prominent corporate attorney Alan Yuspeh as senior vice president for ethics and compliance. In a company-wide video teleconference, Frist said that Columbia/HCA's new corporate compliance program would ensure that Medicare cost reports were filed fairly and honestly. I recognized that many of these changes resulted from Columbia/HCA attorneys carefully scrutinizing the FBI search warrant to focus on the areas targeted by government investigators.

Of course, the public didn't know that Jim Alderson and I had compiled evidence that the reserve cost report scheme dated back to Frist's early days as CEO of the original HCA. Frist was certainly no white knight and should have borne some responsibility for illegal practices under his watch.

If I thought the worst was over, I was sadly mistaken. In the past few weeks, Kirsten and I had been receiving strange phone calls, mostly hang-ups. Kirsten had changed our home phone number twice and was starting to worry. We wondered if someone had learned that I was the secret FBI informant.

Complicating that stress was our new neighbors. Mickey Parslow, the CFO of Southwest Florida Regional Medical Center, and his family had indeed moved in just down the block. Parslow's presence in our neighborhood embodied our worst fears. Kirsten grew increasingly worried that agents of our powerful adversary, Columbia/HCA, were living down the street and watching our children play. Allowing our kids to play in the front yard or driveway now seemed risky. The law may protect the whistle-blower from retaliation by the company, but Kirsten wondered if that same protection extends to the whistleblower's family. The sooner I found another job in another state, the better, she thought. Perhaps we overreacted. (Later, in fact, we learned that Parslow also had filed a *qui tam* lawsuit against the company.)

I, too, was worried. Leaving Columbia/HCA was all I could think about. What if the seal was lifted from my lawsuit and my identity became publicly known while I was still employed at Columbia/HCA? I had seen many movies in which witnesses were conveniently silenced. It was a scary thought. My instincts told me to leave Florida.

My insider status within Columbia/HCA had served the FBI well, and with the search warrants already executed, Ford said the FBI didn't need me to continue working undercover. I was free to work elsewhere. Trusting my instincts, I found a job in Wisconsin with my first employer, United Government Services, a division of Blue Cross & Blue Shield United of Wisconsin, as a senior fraud investigator. Although the job—set to begin in September—paid nearly $20,000 less than I was currently earning, I accepted it anyway, reasoning that it would only be temporary. I was wrong. For the next four years, I would work diligently there as a Medicare fraud investigator while my lawsuit languished in the judicial system.

It was, indeed, a tumultuous time. That same month, in August, Jarrell, Whiteside, and Neeb appeared in federal court in Fort Myers, entering pleas of "not guilty." Their appearance in court created a media frenzy, attracting all the major news organizations, including the *New York Times*, the *Wall Street Journal*, *USA Today*, the Associated Press, and the Dow Jones wire services. Soon, I feared, my name would be leaked to the press and reporters would camp at my doorstep.

The Columbia/HCA criminal investigation and scandal drew a number of attention seekers looking for money or fame. Peter Young, a healthcare consultant living in Cape Coral, Florida, briefly grabbed headlines claiming he was the mysterious whistleblower who had uncovered Medicare fraud at Columbia/HCA. I called Ford, livid over Young's obviously outrageous claims. He reassured me that Young was not an informant. And, while he understood my anger, he cautioned me to remain silent.

Until I left Florida, the tension at work was high, and rumors abounded regarding the raids, company malfeasance, and government snitches. I was becoming increasingly nervous that company lawyers soon would demand to interview me. On September 9, 1997—just three days before I'd be off to Wisconsin—I was jarred by the ringing phone on my desk. It was an attorney hired by Columbia/HCA to defend Jarrell in his criminal trial. I reluctantly answered some of his preliminary questions. Then, questioning whether the caller was really Jarrell's attorney or a Columbia/HCA investigator, I hesitated before evoking my right to refuse to answer. Then I referred him to the division CFO. Agreeing to obtain corporate clearance, the caller hung up. I frantically called Peter Chatfield at Phillips & Cohen in Washington.

"Jarrell's attorney, or someone claiming to be him, just contacted me," I stammered. "I would suggest that you delay him," Chatfield said. "Just stall him."

Ultimately, my attorneys decided it would be best to refer the caller to Karla Spaulding at James, Hoyer & Newcomer. James, Hoyer & Newcomer was known to specialize in fraud litigation, and I worried that this might identify me as the FBI informant within the organization. With a sinking feeling, I realized the company was probably on to me when Spaulding informed them that I would not be available for their interviews since I was leaving their organization. Their message to her was clear: "Make sure to tell your client, Mr. Schilling, that he is not to take any documents when he leaves."

Because of our financial position, Kirsten and I agreed that she would remain in Florida with the children until our home had been rented. We anxiously awaited the day when she could move with the children to Wisconsin. I counted down the days until they could join me in Wisconsin, scouting homes for us in the Milwaukee area and starting my new job.

One morning in October, shortly after I joined United Government Services, the telephone rang. It was Kirsten, and I could tell from her voice that something was wrong. In an agitated voice, she told me that the FBI affidavit—the seventy-four–page document used to secure the search warrants for the July raids—had been unsealed by the U.S. District Court in Fort Myers and was becoming a big story. She said the local TV news programs reported most but not all of the details. Parts of the document had been heavily blacked out, but Kirsten remained very concerned. I was, too. The last thing I wanted was my name leaked to the media! I promptly called Meagher in San Francisco.

Hearing the panic in my voice, he tried to allay my fears. By blacking out the names—or "redacting" the document, he said—the government is trying to conceal the identities of the informants. People extremely close to the case, reading between the lines, may be able to identify you as one of the confidential witnesses. The government refers to you only as Confidential Witness 2 (CW2) in the affidavit, Meagher said. Relieved, I hung up, satisfied that I was still protected. Later, upon reading the affidavit, I realized that while my name was redacted, I could still be easily identified. The biggest hint: The affidavit indicated that two witnesses had left the company, claiming "integrity" issues. I was one of those people.

Later that evening, Meagher faxed a copy of the *New York Times* article on the case, which was titled "U.S. Contends Billing Fraud at Columbia Healthcare was 'Systemic.'" The article confirmed that the affidavit implicated managers at many levels of the Columbia/HCA system, including the company's headquarters in Nashville, as participants in a complex scheme to defraud the government. No names were mentioned in the article. It simply reported that the government had secured the cooperation of several witnesses who had worked for Columbia/HCA. The article went on to say that twenty-eight pages of information remained under seal and because of that, it was impossible to identify the witnesses whose testimony the affidavit cited.

However, the unsealed portion of the affidavit listed at least five cooperating witnesses, including a former reimbursement manager with

Columbia/HCA, a former company employee responsible for supervising the preparation of cost reports for Columbia's Tampa and Fort Myers hospitals, and a current consultant who helped the company prepare cost reports.

I knew that kind of detail could help identify me. Later that evening, I called Kirsten again and told her to be very careful. "Check under the car before you leave the driveway and keep the doors locked," I warned her gravely. Perhaps it was paranoia, but I knew I would be on edge until my family moved to Wisconsin.

The next week, a former colleague from Fort Myers contacted me. "There is a new controller in place at Southwest Florida Regional Medical Center," she told me. "She is spreading the rumor that you are the FBI snitch and had all the locks and security codes on the doors changed. She's paranoid and thinks you'll sneak back in and bug the place."

Paranoia can be contagious, I thought.

I was even more worried about retaliation now. I was certainly relieved to have left Columbia, but I knew I would breathe more easily once Kirsten and the kids joined me in Wisconsin.

CHAPTER ELEVEN

Escape to Wisconsin

Perhaps we overreacted when we decided to uproot our family and move back to Wisconsin. But when the case would finally be unsealed, we wanted to have as much distance as possible between us and the Columbia/HCA officials who knew me. Our families still weren't aware of the monster that had consumed our lives since we had moved to Florida four years earlier.

At the time, returning home to Wisconsin seemed like an obvious solution to our dilemma. From the distance and safety of our hometown and surrounded by family, we could brave any storms created by the unsealing of my whistleblower lawsuit, secure in the knowledge that few in Wisconsin knew or cared about Columbia/HCA. The company operated no facilities in Wisconsin. The nearest Columbia/HCA hospitals were located ninety miles south of Milwaukee, in Chicago. News about the ongoing FBI investigation and the looming Tampa criminal trial barely registered on the local media radar.

The offices of my new employer, United Government Services (UGS), were headquartered in the former bottling plant of the Joseph Schlitz Beverage Company, built in the 1850s along the west side of the Milwaukee River. Most of the original brewery had been demolished, but the expansive, three-story bottling plant remained and had been converted into office space and later remodeled in the mid-1980s.

Arriving slightly before 7:00 A.M. on my second day at work, I took the elevator to the third floor and inserted my magnetic employee ID card into the electronic lock of the solid double doors. I entered a cavernous room stuffed with fabric-lined modular office cubicles. I found mine in the fraud unit near the back and settled down to work.

At 10 A.M., I joined my managers in a sparsely decorated modular conference room to discuss the FBI's interest in me and how it could impact my job. On my first day at work, I'd told them I was a cooperating government witness in the Columbia/HCA investigation. Today, we were to have a teleconference with Joe Ford, which I hoped would dispel any of their misgivings and answer any lingering questions. The management team gathered around the large boardroom table. I introduced them to Ford via the speakerphone. Their nervous voices matched the apprehension expressed on their faces.

Ford took the lead. "John is a great asset to your organization," he began. He said that not only had I gained valuable experience working on this case with the FBI but that I had instructed him as well. He assured them I was not personally involved in the alleged criminal activity at Columbia/HCA and was only acting as a cooperating witness for the government. "You should be proud of John because he came forward, volunteering his time to help us with this investigation. He's done a great job," Ford said. I could feel my face begin to flush.

Then Ford asked if there were any concerns. One manager wondered if the company needed to beef up security to protect me or other UGS employees. Ford assured her there was no immediate threat to safety.

The department's director asked a more pointed question: "Is John a whistleblower?" No one expected the question, but I answered quickly and honestly. "I'm unable to answer that," I said. It was true. Answering that question would jeopardize my *qui tam* lawsuit. Under the law, I was not allowed to discuss my complaint in any way until it was unsealed.

By the end of the half-hour teleconference, my managers understood the gravity of my situation and agreed to keep our discussion confidential. They also allowed me time away from work to fulfill my obligations to the FBI.

Meanwhile, our plan to move to Wisconsin proceeded unhampered. With a rental contract in place for our Fort Myers house, Kirsten was ready to move the kids to Menomonee Falls. I bought a one-way ticket to Fort Myers and planned to drive with the family back to Wisconsin. As I got off the plane, I was still surprised to notice the contrasting climates. The November air in Florida was considerably warmer than in Wisconsin.

The trees and grass remained green. It didn't seem possible that only two months had passed since I'd left Florida. By the time I reached our neighborhood, the movers had already packed the moving vans and left, so I entered a very empty home.

I thought back to the day we had moved into our new home and how elated we had felt. For only a little while, I succumbed to nostalgia, reliving the birth of our daughter and second son here, the birthdays and holidays and good times we had spent together as a family. Our early days here had seemed enchanted. Moving a world away from our families in Wisconsin had been both frightening and exhilarating, but it brought Kirsten and me closer together. Our family had formed roots in the neighborhood and community and cherished the wonderful friends we'd made. And I recalled the genuine optimism I felt in joining the healthcare juggernaut Columbia/HCA and the friends I had made there.

But the magic had faded, and the stress of clinging so tenuously to paradise's soil overwhelmed us. We knew we had to leave.

Saying good-bye to our friends, the Pomaricos, was heartbreaking. Despite their age differences, Alex and his best friend, Mark, were extraordinarily close, and Sarah doted on our Abby like a big sister. It was even harder to leave their parents, Eva and Frank. Like us, they had uprooted from the north and followed the Florida sun to Three Oaks. We had forged a tight bond living next to each other for three years and would miss each other sorely. We had walked the kids to school, attended masses, and spent many holidays together. Eva and Frank, who were Abby's godparents, were our mentors and confidants. Other than family, we trusted no one but them to look after our children. Our kids were inseparable and at times we seemed like one extended family.

Waving as we pulled away from their house, we all cried for miles as we began our journey north. Despite promising to return to our home next door, vowing to call and visit often, no one could imagine the geography between us as anything but a huge barrier. Alex and Abby were devastated, consoled only by their floppy stuffed hound dogs, matching the ones they'd given Mark and Sarah.

Kirsten and I had found a fine house for the five of us in Menomonee Falls. The three-bedroom, two-bath, gray saltbox was located in a family-friendly neighborhood. After borrowing money from my mom for the down payment, we obtained the financing and moved in.

Our families couldn't fathom why we had not sold our house in Florida. We massaged the truth a little, explaining that the Fort Myers real estate market was stagnant then and we had chosen to wait it out, rather than suffering a big loss by selling now. Our families knew nothing of the secret lives we'd led for the last four years in Florida. But that was about to change.

CHAPTER TWELVE

Big Money or Bust

When the weather cooperated, I ate lunch at my desk and then headed outdoors for a brisk walk south along Water Street toward downtown Milwaukee. That one-hour break in the fresh air, so different from the oppressive Florida heat so prevalent while I worked at Columbia/HCA, helped clear my mind. Perhaps that's why the unexpected telephone call from the FBI jolted me so.

I had just returned to the office one blustery day in November 1997, when FBI Agent Deanna Clark called from Tampa. *What now?* I thought.

Clark said that although no date had been set for the criminal trial, she had been asked to perform routine background checks on all cooperating government witnesses. *It's a little late for that,* I thought to myself. Still, I took it as a good sign when Clark said she was asking these questions now so that the prosecutors at the trial would not stumble upon any "surprises."

"What sort of surprises?" I asked. Clark explained that the defense attorneys would be looking for ways to discredit the government's witnesses and would attempt to portray me as untrustworthy to the jury. She asked if there was anything about me that would concern prosecutors.

"Is there anything unusual in your past?" she asked. "Do you mean anything besides a parking ticket or a speeding ticket?" I responded. "Well, do you use any drugs?" Clark asked. "No," I said. "What about alcohol?" she asked. "I have a glass of wine on occasion," I replied.

"Are you a cross-dresser?" "What?" I asked incredulously. Clark laughed. "Just had to be sure," she said, and we both chuckled. I assured her that I was neither a cross-dresser nor did I have a checkered past. *I'm an accountant*, I imagined telling her. *Everybody knows what dull, boring lives we lead.*

It was routine for the AUSA and the federal judge to meet at status hearings to discuss new developments in the case. Slated as the target date for new indictments, we were disappointed when the March 20, 1998, hearing passed without any being issued. Federal officials were being cautious. They told my attorneys that any new indictments issued now would only relate to the Fawcett interest issue. Additional indictments unrelated to the Fawcett interest issue would come much later. The criminal trial, Stephen Meagher suspected, would most likely be delayed until the autumn of 1998. He was concerned by the setback and the Justice Department's hesitation. Meagher had hoped the criminal trial would begin earlier and that the government would have gotten additional indictments by now. Though the government would never admit it, criminal cases take precedence over civil lawsuits. The criminal trial posed a very real roadblock to any discussion of a civil settlement with the company. It was disappointing but obvious to me that we would have to wait it out.

A fourth indictment was finally issued on July 22, 1998. Federal prosecutors charged Carl Lynn Dick, director of finance for HCA's Central Florida Division, with conspiracy to defraud Medicare and making false statements. Furthermore, Bob Whiteside, Jay Jarrell, and Michael Neeb were charged with two additional charges—impeding a federal auditor and making false statements to obtain benefits under Medicaid. A year had passed since the first indictments. In that time, the media hype and market analyst speculation had predicted many more indictments against Columbia/HCA, with some expecting top current and former executives like Rick Scott to face charges. Thus, the solitary new indictment of a relatively small fish felt like a letdown.

Industry leaders howled that the government was blowing a lot of smoke without any fire. Those of us on the inside disagreed. I knew the government had assembled incriminating evidence against several top executives at Olsten Kimberly (the home healthcare firm that Columbia/HCA was involved with) and Columbia/HCA. Where were those home health indictments? Meagher urged me to be patient. "John," he said, "this case will not go to trial for at least another six months."

Experts hired by Phillips & Cohen for my civil *qui tam* case completed a damages analysis that Meagher planned to introduce to government attorneys. Phillips & Cohen hoped the analysis would be used by the government as a starting point for settlement negotiations when it came time to negotiate a civil settlement with Columbia/HCA. Meanwhile, Marie O'Connell, the Justice Department attorney, had also contracted with professionals in the field to calculate the cost of Medicare losses attributable to the fraud. While agreeing on the fraud loss model used to assess damages, the experts ultimately differed on the estimated amounts. Phillips & Cohen's cosultants predicted that the potential cost report damages stemming from our lawsuits could reach $1.5 billion. That figure represented only the single damages estimate—the average amount allegedly stolen from government programs through false claims submitted over several years.

Under the False Claims Act, however, prosecutors can seek triple that amount, plus up to $10,000 per alleged false claim. Using that formula, the total damages could exceed a staggering $4.5 billion. Convincing Columbia/HCA to pay that figure was impossible. Seldom does the government ever collect treble damages, except if the charged party loses in a court trial.

Whether Columbia/HCA would be willing to pay or not, the amounts were compounding by the hour. I now realized how big the case had grown and was offered a glimpse of the unimaginable fortune I could claim if we succeeded. It was big money! The damage analysis Meagher presented to the government produced the desired effect, and Meagher was thrilled that the government's attorneys did not flinch at his firm's estimates, a good sign we could be on the same page.

Having crafted such a strong *qui tam* lawsuit against Columbia/HCA, Meagher's colleague at Phillips & Cohen, Peter Chatfield, was charged with drafting a second and separate *qui tam* lawsuit on my behalf. This lawsuit targeted the business practices of international accounting giant KPMG Peat Marwick, which operated in more than 100 countries and employed thousands of professionals. KPMG also had a sizable presence in the healthcare industry, providing audit, tax, and consulting services to clients around the world.

Years earlier, BAMI—one of Columbia's acquisitions—had retained KPMG to prepare both filed and reserve Medicare cost reports. Those dual cost reporting documents KPMG created clearly showed that the

accounting firm was complicit in perpetuating the fraud and had conspired with BAMI to file false cost reports. The government did not object
to my filing a separate *qui tam* case naming KPMG as a defendant. In fact,
the government welcomed it and reported that KPMG was uncooperative,
almost obstructive. The second lawsuit was filed under seal on April 27,
1998, in U.S. District Court in Tampa (Case 98–901 CIV T 17F).

In the suit, I alleged that KPMG, its agents, and its employees knew
that its clients and co-conspirators, BAMI and Columbia/HCA, had filed
false, exaggerated, and ineligible claims for reimbursement on their annual Medicare and Medicaid cost reports for fiscal years 1990 through
1992. The complaint alleged that KPMG violated its fiduciary duty to report known errors that resulted in unwarranted government overpayments to BAMI and Columbia/HCA. I also accused the company of
unlawfully concealing those errors from fiscal intermediaries and allowing the hospital companies to keep money to which they were not entitled.
In short, I alleged that KPMG aided and abetted other parties in perpetuating this fraud.

The documentation I had collected regarding KPMG's involvement
was pretty hard to refute. Those same documents had been passed on to
the Justice Department. The government told us that even when faced
with ironclad documentation of its complicity, KPMG was unwilling to
cooperate in the Columbia/HCA investigation. Phillips & Cohen needed
little persuasion to battle the accounting giant.

While the excitement of completing and filing the KPMG *qui tam* lawsuit occupied my thoughts, another potentially damaging drama was unfolding in the halls of Congress. The normally cool-headed Meagher
called me, his voice genuinely agitated.

"Sit down John, I have bad news," he said. His tone conveyed his sim-
mering anger. He explained that a Florida representative had crafted a bill
that would gut the federal False Claims Act, the law that allowed my
whistleblower suit. Bill McCollum, a Florida Republican, had conjured up
a cleverly disguised plan to eviscerate the law. If successful, McCollum's
changes would have significantly impacted my lawsuits. Under his proposed legislation, many pending whistleblower cases would have been
dismissed, leaving the government with few remedies to recover money
stolen from it.

"How can this happen?" I asked, stupefied. Meagher said that while
the proposed amendments to the False Claims Act didn't seem to make

sense, following the proverbial paper trail showed that McCollum's plan was supported and heavily financed by the American Hospital Association (AHA). The AHA represents most U.S. hospitals, including many that Jim Alderson and I had sued.

"In actuality, it does make sense," said Meagher. "This is largely Columbia/HCA's cunningly conceived plan to take direct aim at the legislation that our lawsuits are built around."

I was incredulous. The implications were scary. At the time, the federal government had not yet ramped up its enforcement of federal healthcare laws, including the Fraud and Abuse Anti-Kickback Law and the Stark Ethics-in-Patient Referral Law (also known as the physician self-referral law, which prohibits doctors from referring patients to medical facilities in which they hold financial interests). Hundreds of U.S. hospitals, including some of the country's most prestigious academic medical centers, faced scrutiny from national investigations into hospital billing practices, many stemming from whistleblower lawsuits. An army of healthcare consultants were pitching new, aggressive, and sometimes illegal means of increasing Medicare reimbursements by overbilling, exploiting legal loopholes, and paying doctors through a variety of sham measures, essentially for physician referrals. The hospital industry viewed the False Claims Act as an attack upon itself.

However, healthcare costs and Medicare spending had risen astronomically by the late 1990s, and the government had finally begun to seriously fight back. Several laws passed in 1996 and 1997 had increased the budgets of healthcare fraud enforcement agencies within the Department of Health and Human Services and the Justice Department. Healthcare fraud task forces were assembled in many U.S. Attorney's offices, and the FBI and Justice Departments went on hiring sprees to bring in seasoned investigators and prosecutors and train new ones. Attorney General Janet Reno declared healthcare fraud one of her top priorities.

But government investigators couldn't be everywhere. Insiders with intimate knowledge of fraud schemes and the evidence to prove it remained vital to government enforcement agencies, and one of their top tools was the False Claims Act. Lacking that, prosecutors needed to rely on tips from jealous rivals, antiquated federal computer systems, and other less effective measures to ferret out healthcare fraud.

I had a personal stake in the matter. By this point, Jim Alderson and I had already committed career suicide to help the federal government, and for us there was no turning back. We would never work within the private healthcare sector again, and our chances of sharing in any recovery from Columbia/HCA seemed to be rapidly vanishing.

Meagher and Chatfield were just as apprehensive. Not only had John Phillips, cofounder of Phillips & Cohen, helped to revise and strengthen the law, but the firm's entire practice hinged on the False Claims Act. Meagher theorized that because Columbia/HCA frequently said in its defense that the company's business practices were commonly accepted within the industry, now the entire healthcare industry had reason—self-preservation—to attack the False Claims Act. The healthcare industry, especially its hospital trade associations, worried that the prosecution and the huge civil liability facing Columbia/HCA could metastasize and spread to other providers if the Justice Department succeeded.

Chatfield had seen other attacks on the law over the years, and he felt confident that the powerful official who had cosponsored its modern version and continued to champion it—Senator Charles Grassley (Republican of Iowa)—would fight Representative McCollum to protect Lincoln's law. In addition, Chatfield pointed out that the Washington, D.C.-based Taxpayers Against Fraud (TAF), a nonprofit, public interest organization dedicated to combating fraud and supporting whistleblowers, would also fight to preserve the law.

On March 19, 1998, McCollum introduced H.R. 3523, a bill designed to limit the False Claims Act and protect the healthcare industry from it. A companion bill was introduced in the Senate in April. However, the bills stumbled and faltered shortly after their introduction. And on June 3, the Justice Department issued written guidance on the appropriate use of the False Claims Act in healthcare matters. Shortly after this, the bills in Congress lost their support and were denounced as ill advised.

In an impassioned Senate speech in July 1998, Grassley railed against McCollum's assault on the law. "The AHA used its notable clout to systematically and cleverly orchestrate a major grassroots campaign to 'gut' the False Claims Act . . ." he said. "The False Claims Act is, and will remain, a target of those industries that accept billions and billions of taxpayer dollars annually and balk at strict accountability. I ask only that we, as legislators, remember the history of the assault made upon the False Claims Act by the AHA in the present. I ask further that we agree to be strong despite the strength of an industry, simply because it is the 'right' thing to do."

Ironically, McCollum—who had accepted large campaign contributions from pharmaceutical companies and other healthcare organizations, first as a member of Congress and later as a lobbyist and consultant—became a big supporter of Florida's state False Claims Act when he ran for Florida attorney general in 2006. Then he claimed that as attorney general, he would vigorously prosecute fraud and use every tool at his disposal to protect state programs.

My journey was far from over. It was good to savor a small victory. The False Claims Act challenge was a bumpy detour, but I would need more than just endurance to complete this whistleblower marathon.

CHAPTER THIRTEEN

Case Unsealed

The Justice Department, that monolith that moved at a glacial pace, had actually shifted. The once "marginal" civil case with little likelihood of success, as John Phillips first described my *qui tam* case, had grown very large and important to the government. It was Stephen Meagher's hope to simultaneously unseal my lawsuit along with Jim Alderson's, creating a media frenzy that would increase pressure on Columbia/HCA to negotiate a settlement.

But on October 5, 1998—five years after it had been filed—a federal judge unsealed Alderson's *qui tam* lawsuit first. The press devoured it, unable to resist Alderson's long, tangled journey from Montana to Washington, D.C., and back. Though weeks earlier the Justice Department had verbally committed to intervene in both of our cases, mine would remain sealed for months longer as Justice attorneys requested another extension. Even though we objected in principle, we knew that the Justice Department's Criminal Division continued to investigate. U.S. District Judge Steven Merryday in Tampa granted the government extension until December 29, 1998. Scaling back the planned media blitz, Meagher now focused exclusively on Alderson's case.

On the afternoon of October 5, the Justice Department issued a press release, "U.S. joins lawsuit against Columbia and Quorum Hospital Chains." Phillips & Cohen issued its own press release, "Government's probe of Columbia/HCA prompted by whistleblower lawsuit." Phillips & Cohen's release reported that, despite Dr. Thomas Frist's persistent denial of misconduct at Columbia/HCA, the lawsuit alleged that there was substantial evidence of longstanding, systemic wrongdoing at Columbia/HCA.

Elated for Alderson, I called and congratulated him on the government's intervention. We agreed that we'd cleared our first major hurdle to a successful resolution.

The next day, every major U.S. newspaper carried the story of the government's joining Alderson's lawsuit accusing Columbia/HCA of scheming to defraud the Medicare program. The stories consistently reported that the fraud, contrary to Frist's claims, was widespread and systematic and revealed that many of the claims predated HCA's merger with Columbia Healthcare. Indeed, Frist was leading HCA when many of the fraudulent activities began there. His carefully engineered image as the white knight who rescued his company from the clutches of Rick Scott was beginning to tarnish. Several journalists reported that the fraud might ultimately cost Columbia/HCA more than $1 billion. (Interestingly enough, Alderson's *qui tam* lawsuit was the first of more than a dozen such false claims cases filed against Columbia/HCA that the government eventually joined.)

Less than two weeks later, the *New York Times* Sunday edition featured a profile of Alderson. It's embarrassing to admit it but I was slightly envious of the media attention focused on his case and disappointed that I wasn't sharing the spotlight with him, especially considering all we'd gone through together. The *Times* story, a heartwarming account of the rocky road he and his family had traversed over the past six years, provided an insightful look at the hardships endured by whistleblowers. It was clear to me that the reporter was unaware of my case since he incorrectly attributed the 1997 FBI raids to Alderson's lawsuit, when my case had ignited the entire criminal investigation, including the raids and the upcoming Tampa trial. When it was unsealed, I knew that my lawsuit would substantiate Alderson's claims. After reading the *Times* article, the producers of the television show *60 Minutes* contacted Phillips & Cohen and told them veteran newsman Mike Wallace would introduce the Columbia/HCA case to a national television audience in December.

It would be nice to have been able to tell our family, friends, and coworkers the truth. But since my case was still under seal, I was forbidden to speak of it. Would December 29—the date my case had been extended to—be the magic day to finally free me, or would the Justice Department request yet another extension?

At my fraud investigator's job at United Government Services, it was becoming increasingly difficult for me to pretend to know nothing about the Columbia/HCA investigation. When asked about it by co-workers, I couldn't respond and would usually skirt the issue or tell them I didn't know anything. Playing dumb was growing old. I felt guilty that once again I had to lie by omission and hoped my colleagues would later forgive my deceit.

Agent Joe Ford had kept his promise to me, though, and so far my name had been protected, even within the government. As a fraud investigator, I was introduced to numerous Assistant U.S. Attorneys and federal agents in the Milwaukee area. With only one exception, none of those government employees ever connected me to the Columbia/HCA investigation. When one federal prosecutor heard about my earlier employment at Columbia/HCA, though, he chided me good-naturedly.

"John," he joked, "who knows, maybe you're the CI [confidential informant]." "Sure," I responded with surprise. "I have two words for you that can make you some money. *Qui tam*," he said. "Really," I murmured.

I was flabbergasted. Did he really know who I was? I don't think he did; I'm sure he was just joking. *Won't he be surprised when it becomes public?* I thought.

After dinner on November 3, 1998, I headed upstairs to the desk in our bedroom/office and typed the stock symbol of Columbia/HCA into the Bloomberg website on our computer. I was shocked to see what popped up on the screen. I reread it several times, astonished by what I was reading.

"Kirsten!" I yelled. Out of breath, she entered the room. "You've got to see this," I exclaimed. "What?" she asked.

"Read this article. My name is public."

"Oh my god! It can't be. Your case isn't unsealed yet."

Supposedly still under seal for another forty-five days, I was surprised to see my name in black and white. Bloomberg broke the news with a story titled "Columbia/HCA Indicted Execs' Motion Suggests 2nd Whistle-Blower." The story described a motion filed by Bob Whiteside's defense attorney linking me with Phillips & Cohen. In the article, Whiteside's attorney, Charles Lembcke, said, "I expect there is another lawsuit out there and that's the one with John Schilling."

"Wow! Does that mean we can talk about it?" Kirsten asked. "I don't think so. My lawsuit isn't officially unsealed. Somehow my name was leaked."

In panic mode, I phoned Meagher. "Stephen, did you see Bloomberg News?" I asked. "I did. I was just contacted by Bloomberg and was quite surprised. Apparently, the government provided a document to the defense that you drafted."

"Can I discuss my case now?" I pleaded. "No. Not yet. We can't comment on anything that remains under seal." "Why keep it under seal?" I persisted.

"I'll try to convince the government to lift the seal sooner than December 29," he replied. "But don't count on it. Even though it was entirely the Department of Justice's mistake, Marie O'Connell will probably find a way to keep it under seal. If I'm successful getting it unsealed, maybe we can get your story on *60 Minutes* with Jim Alderson."

Great, I thought excitedly. *That would be pretty cool.*

The next day, the attorneys for Bob Whiteside, Jay Jarrell, Mike Neeb, and Carl Lynn Dick served Phillips & Cohen with a subpoena requesting many other documents that we had presented to the government. Phillips & Cohen, bound by the seal, decided that the judge would have to rule on whether the firm could comply with the subpoena. Waiting for the court's response, Kirsten and I remained silent. Our family and friends, who weren't big Bloomberg newswire watchers, had not seen the article. And no local news organizations carried the story that I was possibly the second whistleblower.

While diligent in his efforts to unseal my case, Meagher conveyed the disappointing news that my case would remain under seal until at least December 29. The window of opportunity had closed on joining the *60 Minutes* episode. It would feature only Alderson's story.

But my name would be leaked again. Every Monday afternoon, at work, I would check the website of *Modern Healthcare*, a weekly national health-care trade publication, for news. I scanned the magazine's website on November 23, 1998, for news of any Columbia/HCA stories. When I saw the headline "Sued Again: Second Whistleblower Nails Columbia, Its Accountant," I was floored. *Modern Healthcare* had obtained court documents revealing that I had filed two *qui tam* lawsuits, one against Columbia/HCA and another against KPMG. Interestingly, *Modern Healthcare* knew the exact dates of my lawsuits' seals but offered no other details of either case. The article quoted Meagher saying he could not confirm or deny the existence of my lawsuits.

Rereading the article, I called Kirsten. "My name has been leaked again." "What do you mean?" she said. "It's in *Modern Healthcare*. They know about both lawsuits." "How did they find out?" she asked.

"What's baffling is that I still officially can't talk about it."

I wondered what Joe Ford was going to think when he saw this article. When we had spoken the previous week, he had sounded pleased with the progress of the criminal case but had added, "I wish your attorneys would stop talking to the press." "Why?" I had asked.

"They can accomplish the same pressure by other means. It's done all the time. I just don't want to read about it in the *Wall Street Journal* or *New York Times* prior to the trial."

"I'll let them know," I had responded.

"John," he had continued, "I know about the *60 Minutes* piece on Alderson. When is that coming out?"

"It should be out in a couple of weeks," I had told him. "I hope there is nothing about you in it," he had warned. Ford's tone had portended the seriousness of his warning that the defense would attack me for anything I publicly said.

"The defense will try to make you look bad. They will make you the 'Linda Tripp' of healthcare. Just remember, I never made you any promises," Ford had said ominously. "There is no doubt that you have put your life and career on the line. You have done the right thing, and you should be proud of it. The defense, however, is going to come at us hard. That's why it's important to remember that neither I nor anyone from the government made you any promises."

I printed two copies of the *Modern Healthcare* article just before I left the office. I placed one copy on my manager's desk with a sticky note saying, "Let's discuss." I took the other copy home to Kirsten. She was flabbergasted to read my name in print. Fortunately, no other media outlet had picked up the story. There were no phone calls from probing reporters or market analysts, and we felt relieved that our family and friends did not read healthcare trade publications. Our secret was still safe.

The next day, my manager summoned me to her office. The discussion was brief, since I was prohibited from commenting on my lawsuit and the criminal investigation. She was not shocked because she already knew

I was a confidential informant and had suspected that I might have filed a *qui tam* lawsuit. Later that day, she called a staff meeting to air employee concerns.

"There have been some media sources that have named John Schilling as a witness for the investigation into Columbia/HCA," she explained, asking those attending to keep what was discussed confidential. She offered me a chance to speak, and I reminded them I was a confidential informant in the criminal case. I told them I could not comment on the case, since any statements could be used to impeach my testimony. My co-workers sat in disbelief. A few said they were concerned about my safety and well-being. The meeting ended with everyone agreeing to keep the discussion and my identity our secret. They walked out looking shell-shocked.

In the early morning darkness of December 30, 1998, I drove to work in the frigid cold. My eight-year-old Plymouth Acclaim could produce only lukewarm gusts of air on this Midwest winter day.

Today could be the day, I reflected. Excited and anxious, we were unsure how the holidays would affect the media coverage Meagher had planned for the unsealing of my lawsuit. The *60 Minutes* piece on Jim and Connie Alderson that aired a few days ago was enthralling. We had sat spellbound as Alderson, in his deep, Montana accent, chronicled the years leading up to the government's intervention in his case. I wished I had been with him to fill in the missing pieces of the story for Mike Wallace. Soon, I hoped, I too would be free to express my true feelings and not have to lie about my case.

While Kirsten and I had been raised in Wisconsin, it no longer felt like home to us. We were unsure of what to say to our families, who believed we'd returned north out of homesickness. In the five years since our Columbia/HCA ordeal began, we had no one outside of our attorneys to confide in. Kirsten and I had learned to keep things to ourselves. It would be a challenge to explain the situation to our families and friends when the news broke and became public. The night before, we had sat down with our older son, Alex, and explained why we'd separated him from his best friend, Mark, and left Florida the year before. We tried to simplify the lawsuit and the secrecy rules surrounding it, but at eight, the complexities proved too daunting for him. Besides, he was far more interested in his new Christmas toys.

When we reminded him not to answer the phone, he quipped, "It's always Stephen. Why would I talk to him?"

That morning, the office was extremely quiet, and I was relieved to find it nearly empty. I nervously wondered when the government would "officially" intervene and was so excited that I couldn't concentrate on my work. *And it's only 7 A.M.*, I thought, flicking my watch to make sure it hadn't stopped. No news would come for at least two or three hours. I couldn't wait for the fax machine to spit out the Justice Department's "Election to Intervene" document.

Finally, at 10 A.M., my phone rang. It was Stephen Meagher. "Congratulations, John, the Department of Justice intervention was filed this morning on the Columbia/HCA case. Your KPMG lawsuit will remain under seal. I'm going to fax you a copy right now."

"Thanks, Stephen," I said. "It's been a long time. I am relieved it's finally out in the open."

He said Phillips & Cohen would issue a press release soon and he would spend the rest of the day contacting reporters and speaking on my behalf. "I think it was a good thing your lawsuit did not come out with Jim's. Now we're hitting Columbia/HCA a second time with negative publicity," he commented. "I can't wait to see what happens," I said.

By the time I walked to the fax machine down the hall, the document was already sitting in the tray. The surprisingly brief government document spanned only two pages. The first page was only two sentences long, and the second page consisted of the signatures of Justice Department officials. The title, "**United States Notice of Election to Intervene**," was in boldface print and underlined.

Alone in my office, I savored a glorious but odd celebratory moment. Uncharacteristically, I pumped my fist in the air and quietly shouted, "Yes!" *Pretty emotional response for an accountant*, I thought.

I called Kirsten with the good news. She excitedly told me she would continue to monitor the Internet for stories.

Phillips & Cohen and the Justice Department quickly issued press releases. The Phillips & Cohen release identified me, stating that the *qui tam* lawsuit "was brought by John W. Schilling, a former reimbursement manager for Columbia in Florida. He filed the case in federal district court in Tampa in 1996 under seal. . . . The case is related to the whistleblower lawsuit the federal government joined in October filed by James F. Alderson. Both lawsuits allege a systematic scheme to defraud the

Medicare program through the 'cost reports' Columbia submitted annually for Medicare reimbursement."

The phone rang around 11:00 A.M. "Hello, John. Welcome to the club!" Alderson's deep voice resonated from far away in Montana. I congratulated him on the *60 Minutes* segment, and we chatted about the encouraging media coverage and the pace of the government's investigation. "Do you see settlement soon?" I asked. "Let's hope," he replied.

Unspoken was the knowledge that while Columbia/HCA's spin doctors were weaving their own slant on the lawsuits to the public, the company was resisting settlement. In reality, Columbia/HCA was stalling. In hindsight, I viewed the delay tactics as politically motivated. The Republican Frist family not only enjoyed strong ties to George W. Bush (then a presidential hopeful), but Dr. Bill Frist (Republican of Tennessee), the brother of Columbia/HCA CEO Thomas Frist, was running for his second Senate term and vying for majority leader. While Senator Bill Frist publicly espoused healthcare values, his brother's company was far from a paradigm of virtue.

Kirsten called around 1 P.M. She told me that Bloomberg had issued its first story about my lawsuit and the government's intervention. I went online myself to follow the Bloomberg updates, hoping that Columbia/HCA stock would take another significant hit that would lure them to the bargaining table. (The company's stock had taken a large tumble after the FBI raids in March 1997, losing 40 percent of its value.) But since it was a holiday week, trading was light. Nothing significant would happen to the stock until the opening bell the following Monday.

In spite of the slow holiday news cycle, that morning I found six online stories about my unsealed lawsuit. Within minutes of Kirsten's call, the phone rang again. This time it was my brother-in-law, Tom Jahnke.

"John, what's going on?" he asked. "What do you mean?" I said, surprised to hear from anyone in my family. "I was just online and checked Bloomberg. They are reporting that John Schilling filed a whistleblower lawsuit against Columbia/HCA. Is that really you?"

"As of 10 A.M. today I can finally talk about it, Tom. You're the first person who wasn't aware of it being filed to call me."

"Does Judy know about it?" he asked (referring to his wife, my sister). "No, but you can tell her when she gets home," I told him.

"Wow, I'm just blown away by this," Tom said. "Read the papers tomorrow. There will be more coverage," I replied.

"Can you tell me more?"

"I'll tell you all about it tomorrow."

What began as a quiet day in the office turned into an exciting one. I was elated that the silence and deceit imposed by the lawsuit for the past five years had been lifted from my shoulders.

That evening Kirsten and I called our families to tell them the news. I tried to explain the situation to my father in Florida. He was quite surprised and didn't fully understand it. He knew I had had employment issues in Florida but said Kirsten and I had done a fine job concealing the truth. We called my mother next and finally my sisters, Sally and Judy. They too were surprised, but now understood our secrecy. Kirsten called her parents, Sonia and Gerold Genett, and finally her sister and brother-in-law, Laurel and Bob Parbs.

"Watch the newspapers," we told them. "Tomorrow the lawsuit might get some more attention."

The next day, New Year's Eve, major newspapers from coast to coast covered the story that the federal government had joined a second suit against Columbia/HCA. Settlement estimates ranged up to a billion dollars. Florida news outlets pursued the Justice Department's decision extensively, and the story made the front page in the *Fort Myers News-Press*. In less than twenty-four hours, we found twenty-three articles in print and online, including the *Wall Street Journal*.

Columbia/HCA spokesman Jeff Prescott responded in news stories by saying, "There is nothing really new." The company, he went on to say, hoped to reach an agreement with the government in the first quarter of 1999.

The New Year approached, and Kirsten and I planned to welcome it with a bang. Conversation would flow like the bubbly at our family dinner that night. Over dinner, I wove the intricate tale of the preceding five years. My family brimmed with questions: How did you know you were right? Why didn't your colleagues do the right thing? Were you ever threatened? Why did you move back to Wisconsin? We distributed copies of the many newspaper articles answering their questions. They read and reread them with great interest. My family was supportive, and my mom was proud that her son's moral compass had not faltered.

Kirsten's family had questions that mirrored my family's. They were generous in their praise and grateful that I had done the right thing.

Knowing what our family had sacrificed, they offered to help. "We're proud of you" was the New Year's mantra.

The press continued to explore the unsealing of my *qui tam* lawsuit against Columbia/HCA and the issues I raised. A flood of articles appeared for weeks after from news organizations around the nation.

My colleagues at work congratulated me, expecting my immediate resignation. The uninformed thought I'd won the lottery and had become an instant millionaire. I realized I needed to dispel an enormous misconception. I explained the long legal process and the current status of my lawsuit, but not everyone grasped the enormity or complexity. I told them the case was far from over and no money had yet changed hands. In fact, despite the government's intervention in my case, there was no guarantee of any money. After the news stories broke, some people in my office who didn't know me stared or whispered when I walked past, which felt strange, but I did receive congratulatory calls from former colleagues applauding my actions. It was good to finally be out of the closet and candid with friends and family. Kirsten and I would continue to lean on them for moral support in the years ahead.

CHAPTER FOURTEEN

The Health Care Financing Administration

Many healthcare trade publications published stories focusing on alleged cost reporting fraud in January 1999, partly because of the lawsuits filed by Jim Alderson and me and the growing government scrutiny into Medicare cost reports. Some articles offered advice ranging from the importance of compliance to the dos and don'ts of cost reporting. The issue, while not quite yet mainstream, was front-page news in the healthcare world.

At work, I tried to incorporate my inside knowledge of reserve cost reports to fiscal intermediary policies. Columbia/HCA had declared that reserve cost reports were commonly accepted practices throughout the hospital industry, so it made sense for FIs such as UGS to request and review the appropriateness of reserves maintained by all providers. After all, the entire government investigation into allegedly fraudulent business practices at Columbia/HCA began with reserve cost reports.

Initially, my fraud department manager and I attempted to enlist the cooperation of United Government Services' provider audit department. The department quickly rejected our request, though, claiming that since all providers prepared reserves, requests to review them would prove too labor intensive. Baffled by this curiously inadequate response, I asked the department to address the issue at an upcoming technical conference that included other fiscal intermediaries. At that conference, representatives of other FIs also expressed their trepidation about requesting reserve cost reports.

In what I found a laughable attempt to disguise their true reasons, they told me that because of the Columbia/HCA investigation and the recent *60 Minutes* story, active investigations could be adversely affected. *What a bunch of trumped-up baloney*, I thought. I couldn't believe their apathy. Instead of taking steps to stop the bleeding, these so-called professionals were retreating and allowing the Medicare system to spin out of control. Undeterred, my manager and I surveyed FIs to see if they'd agree to review reserve cost reports. Most would not even consider the request, explaining that their policies prohibited requesting reserve cost reports.

There was one exception, however. Jeff McVicker, a bright young fraud investigator with a California fiscal intermediary, told me that his unit had occasionally requested reserves. Furthermore, he said his unit was investigating a local case involving cost reporting fraud that he believed would become nationally significant. Armed with this tidbit of information, we continued to press our provider audit department to implement some form of reserve review. They reluctantly agreed, but only on a very limited basis. It was a partial win. I helped develop an audit program for the department that included requesting and reviewing reserves. In exchange, I sought the department's continued cooperation in sharing the results. Several audit supervisors were cooperative, forwarding cases to me when they reached an impasse with a provider.

On one occasion, a large Milwaukee hospital refused to confirm whether it prepared reserve cost reports, nor would it provide a schedule of its reserves. I notified the provider that without cooperation, UGS was fully prepared to suspend its Medicare payments. A flurry of activity followed, concluding with the hospital's denial that it prepared reserve cost reports. I doubted it then and still doubt today that the hospital told the truth.

My earlier request for cooperation from UGS's provider audit department was largely ignored. Despite this increasingly uncooperative attitude, I continued to stress the importance of compliance with Medicare regulations. Although the national implications were clear to me, I was bewildered by the department's continued resistance to seeking reserves and reserve cost reports from providers. After reviewing their audit work, I came to believe that many auditors couldn't distinguish proper from improper reserves.

But then I saw a ray of hope. It looked like the Department of Health and Human Services might be looking for innovative ways to fight fraud through its "Operation Restore Trust" program. The DHHS agency that oversaw the Medicare program was then known as the Health Care Financing Administration (HCFA)—now called the Centers for Medicare and Medicaid Services (CMS)—which was Medicare's policy-making arm, was offering contract bonuses to its fiscal intermediaries' benefit integrity units, sometimes called fraud units, to create fraud-fighting initiatives that could be adopted nationwide.

With my assistance, my manager submitted a proposal to fully review provider reserve cost reports. The HCFA responded, calling our proposal a worthy project, but only accepting part of the request. Because its funding was limited, the HCFA asked us to trim the costs of our project initiative. Based on that request, we reduced the scope of our proposal and slashed its projected cost by 40 percent. But when we resubmitted, the HCFA rejected the refined proposal.

While I knew it made perfect sense to require all providers to submit reserve cost reports and reserve work papers for review, I wondered whether the government was already turning its back on healthcare fraud and abuse. This project held the potential to recover millions, if not billions, of Medicare dollars improperly paid to providers. Was the HCFA afraid to pursue fraudulent providers? Or were healthcare industry lobbyists simply too powerful and entrenched?

My persistence finally seemed to pay off. Several years later, either by coincidence, my perseverance, or some other motivation, the HCFA finally agreed. The administration implemented a policy requiring fiscal intermediaries to request and review reserve cost reports. It further required them to obtain letters from providers verifying that they kept no reserve cost reports (unless they already provided those). Because reserves and reserve cost reports are not defined in any HCFA manual, the agency issued correspondence to the FIs clarifying its definition of a reserve cost report.

"A reserve cost report is prepared in conjunction with the as-filed cost report, but is not filed with the fiscal intermediary," the HCFA explained in its guidance. "Instead the reserve cost report is used by a provider to record the allowance adjustment, which is the difference between the submitted cost report and the reserve cost report, and, often, to claim costs that are not appropriately protested on the cost report and which the provider has reason to believe are unallowable."

At last it looked like the HCFA would finally correct this flagrant flaw within Medicare. The Medicare cost reporting system was built on the cornerstone that providers are honest and truthful. But it's an easy system to cheat, and some dishonest providers had exploited the cost report system. Some providers saw nothing wrong with bilking Medicare. What Alderson and I witnessed was a greedy healthcare industry, where many providers cheated the U.S. taxpayer while robbing the Medicare program designed to help the elderly.

Unfortunately, months later, the HCFA weakened its policy on reserve cost reports. In June 2001, without explanation, the agency issued correspondence to FIs substantially altering its earlier stance. The HCFA still asked FIs to review provider financial statements for reserves and determine whether those reserves involved Medicare issues. But the HCFA abandoned its earlier policy requiring signed statements attesting to knowledge of those reserves.

"We are eliminating the policy in 'budget and performance requirements (BPRs),' which requires you to get a signed statement from a provider's representative stating that this individual had no knowledge of a reserve cost report. Effective immediately, you are no longer required to have the provider's representative sign this statement during an audit. Where a provider's representative has refused to sign such a statement, take no further action to secure the signed statement," the agency told its FI contractors.

While I've never been able to substantiate it, I suspected that powerful hospital industry lobbyists pressured the agency. I was disappointed that the HCFA had defanged its policy, but I was content to make a change in the industry, however small.

CHAPTER FIFTEEN

Co-Conspirator

The subpoena issued by U.S. District Judge Susan Bucklew arrived February 9, 1999, commanding me to appear in the Tampa federal court three months later. The government had my assurances that I would cooperate and testify in the criminal Columbia/HCA trial.

As the dust settled, Joe Ford introduced me to a new FBI agent, Michele Yaroma. She was the first and only agent on the case with any prior Medicare cost report experience. As I had innumerable times before with other government investigators, I briefed Yaroma on every aspect of my case, including the Fawcett interest issue and the reserve cost report practices. This time, though, it took less than an hour for me to realize that for the first time, a federal agent actually understood the concepts I presented. I knew she would prove valuable to the team.

"The criminal trial is set to begin the first week of May," Ford said. He predicted that I would testify on the witness stand for an entire day. The Justice Department and FBI planned to fly me to Tampa several times to review documents and to prepare for the trial. Ford again warned that the defense attorneys would attack me brutally on the stand. "They will try to trick you. The defense will do anything to make you look bad. Remember to stay calm," he advised.

It was not unusual for me to speak with Stephen Meagher or Peter Chatfield frequently throughout the duration of my lawsuit, often several times in a day. Sometimes the calls would be short; other times we spent hours on the phone. Since Meagher lived in San Francisco, the two-hour time difference meant that most of his calls arrived during dinner. On hearing the phone ring at dinnertime, the children would groan in unison, "Not Stephen!" Inevitably, our lengthy conversations would lead to other calls and extend well into the night.

In one conversation in the spring of 1999, Meagher's tone belied his disgust as he divulged an earlier phone call he had had with Kathleen Haley, the AUSA. "She mentioned naming you an un-indicted co-conspirator," he sputtered, barely able to contain his anger. Stephen explained that an un-indicted co-conspirator is a term that refers to a person who allegedly agreed with others to violate the law. The prosecution, he continued, does not charge the co-conspirator with an offense, but the negative stigma remains: un-indicted co-conspirator.

Startled, I blurted, "Why would she do that to a key witness?"

"John," Meagher replied, "I'm not willing to have you forced into a false admission. The Department of Justice, you, and I all know that you were not a co-conspirator. You didn't do anything wrong. I will not have you forced into admitting to a crime you didn't commit."

I was perplexed. The week before, when I had spoken with Ford, he hadn't mentioned this possibility. In fact, Ford had told me the opposite, that as a key witness I was very important to the prosecution. In that conversation, he had also told me that defense attorneys would fight hard and dirty to discredit me with anything potentially damaging. That much I understood. But this was my team! I was working with the Justice Department! I delivered the evidence that launched the entire criminal investigation! I wondered who was behind this sneak attack and why they were targeting me.

"Don't worry," Meagher advised. "The prosecution is getting anxious. It will pass." Trusting his seasoned legal instincts, I hoped the issue would not resurface.

The night before my first witness preparation session in Tampa, Meagher and I met for dinner to discuss the next day's meeting. He figured that the government would want me to explain the Fawcett interest issue to a new member of the prosecution's legal team in the criminal case, AUSA Ernest "Tony" Peluso. The U.S. Attorney in Tampa, recognizing how large the case had grown, had assigned Peluso to assist Haley. In addition, Meagher anticipated that the prosecutors would want to discuss the defense team's likely claim that I was motivated solely by personal gain.

The next morning, Meagher and I met for breakfast before walking to the firm of James, Hoyer & Newcomer. At the office, Stephen introduced me to Chris Hoyer, and Al Scudieri, a former FBI agent now working as an investigator with Hoyer's firm. After our brief meeting, the four of us drove to the FBI office where we were ushered into the FBI conference room. There we were greeted by Agent Ford, Agent Clark, and Assistant U.S. Attorneys Haley and Peluso. Peluso handed me the grand jury transcripts and asked me to familiarize myself with my grand jury testimony.

Once I'd finished, Peluso rapidly fired a series of classic background questions. Then he questioned me about my knowledge of the Fawcett interest issue. Suddenly and without warning, Peluso transformed into a pseudo–defense attorney, grilling me with loaded questions designed to provoke me. In an interrogation style, his nonstop barrage of questions were designed to confuse me. Peluso had every intention of confusing me to the point of admitting guilt. But I didn't budge.

"I disagree!" Meagher cried out in anger, arguing that Peluso's interrogation style was unnecessary.

Peluso tried another tactic. He hoped to trick me into admitting something criminal. For example, he tried to goad me into confessing that the 1994 Fawcett interest meeting constituted a criminal conspiracy and that documents I had prepared under orders made me a co-conspirator.

Meagher wouldn't stand for this. His skin burning red above the collar of his starched white shirt, he interrupted, "I know what you are trying to do. But this questioning is out of line."

For a few minutes, the two men heatedly debated Peluso's tactics. Haley and Ford took notes throughout the process, awaiting my response. Haley, having heard enough, suspended the "bad cop" interrogation to return to normal lines of inquiry.

At 3 P.M., the meeting adjourned. As we walked to the car, Meagher, Scudieri, and I discussed the prosecution's interrogation style strategy. Meagher was furious and found Peluso's provocations unnecessary. Star witnesses are not usually treated so callously, he observed. However, he reasoned that the prosecutors wanted me accustomed to all forms of questioning. (Later, I found out that Peluso employed the same strong-arm tactics with my former Columbia/HCA boss, Larry Bomar. Bomar, another key witness for the government, was asked to admit to being a co-conspirator.)

One month after this contentious meeting, Meagher and I met in

Tampa again with Hoyer and Scudieri for a second witness preparation session and to discuss the government's trial strategies. Meagher fretted that Haley could "over-try" the case. "I'm worried that the Department of Justice is sensationalizing this trial," he said. "This case is simple. Let's hope they don't blow it by making it too complex."

We went to the downtown Mercantile Bank Plaza, the temporary FBI storage facility, to meet with Haley and FBI Agents Yaroma, Ford, and Bill Estevez. Document-filled boxes were stacked floor to ceiling, creating narrow passages like a rat's maze. Before we began the meeting, the agents warned us that defendants Bob Whiteside, Jay Jarrell, and Mike Neeb and their legal teams were also in the building, but on different floors preparing for their trial defense. They advised us to avoid contact.

During the four-hour session, I answered the prosecutor's questions and identified documents stamped "confidential" or "Do not show to Medicare Auditors," that were now being called "exhibits," evidence that was expected to be introduced in the criminal trial.

Several weeks later, on April 9, 1999, Kirsten and I were enjoying a beautiful, warm Wisconsin day in the park with our kids when my cell phone rang. As usual, it was Meagher. I flipped open the phone and without even a hello, Meagher rushed ahead.

"John, the Justice Department intervened in another Columbia/HCA whistleblower case today in Tampa," he explained, a case filed by Joseph "Mickey" Parslow that alleged that Columbia/HCA inflated management fees in a wound care clinic. I gasped, "Stephen, do you know who that is?" "The name sounds familiar. Do you know him?" he asked.

"Sure I know him. His family moved in down the street from us in Fort Myers. He was the CFO at Southwest Florida Regional Medical Center and he also had worked at Fawcett Memorial," I said, stunned.

Meagher told me that the government had been quick to join Parslow's case, which had been filed less than ten months ago. We speculated that the Justice Department's speedy intervention was a legal chess move designed to preempt the defense team. The defense would probably have subpoenaed Parslow to testify on behalf of the defendants. But by intervening in his sealed case, the Justice Department had nullified his friendly witness status. Meagher and I agreed that it was brilliant strategic coup by the prosecution.

I told Kirsten the news. She was quick to point out that it wasn't just coincidence that two people living just four doors apart had filed lawsuits against the same company. There was enough fraud to go around.

The next week, I was off to Tampa again for another witness preparation session. I wanted to know what the prosecutors thought the defense would ask me. On the morning of April 17, 1999, Meagher and I drove to the meeting with Scudieri and Judy Hoyer (Chris Hoyer's wife, who was also a lawyer at James, Hoyer & Newcomer and a well-respected former AUSA). I grew nervous as we approached the Mercantile Bank Plaza. Waiting for us in a makeshift office among the narrow corridors of boxes were AUSAs Haley and Bob Mosakowski, along with FBI Agents Ford, Yaroma, and Tim McCants. (I was relieved to see that AUSA Peluso was not there.) The prosecutors again handed me a copy of my grand jury testimony and asked me to familiarize myself. As I read through the transcript, my legal team and the federal agents quietly discussed the case. Once I finished reading the transcript, Mosakowski began describing the upcoming courtroom proceedings and explained that he would conduct my direct trial examination. He asked me to identify which documents would relate to each question. This process continued throughout the day until we ended at 6 P.M. We'd meet again the next day.

I saw it as a good sign the next morning when we met and AUSA Peluso was still absent. We reconvened where we'd left off the day before: Mosakowski asked the questions and I described each document that would be introduced into evidence. After lunch, we resumed our earlier positions. But without warning, Mosakowski announced that the Justice Department had decided it would label me an un-indicted co-conspirator. "We're treating Steve Dudley and Larry Bomar the same way," Mosakowski stated. I was astounded.

Meagher's face turned crimson as he growled, "You don't need to do this. There are other ways to get to the same result." Then Haley interjected, "Stephen, it's unanimous and final."

The discussion grew even more heated, with Meagher and Judy Hoyer battling to protect me and the government unwilling to budge. Meagher, a great debater, was outraged by the government's decision. "This is so absurd," he barked. "It's embarrassing. He hasn't done anything wrong and I would never advise him to say that he did!"

After several minutes of arguing, Meagher exploded. He angrily blurted, "Well, charge him with something then!" Shocked, I almost fell off my chair. What did my attorney just say?

"We're offering immunity," Haley retorted. "Excuse me," Hoyer interrupted cautiously. "I think we should take a few minutes to regroup and gather our thoughts."

My legal team and I left to discuss our options. My attorneys theorized that the government prosecutors were hedging their bets against a possible loss. After several minutes of discussion, Meagher and Hoyer agreed that our team would not continue to argue with the Justice Department and vowed to prevent the government from mistreating its key witness.

Reentering the tense room, Hoyer announced, "Co-counsel and I have advised our client that we are withdrawing from any further cooperation." Her words caromed off the walls, and the ensuing silence was almost deafening. "This comes as a shock to us," she continued. "We'll need to discuss this unfortunate turn of events."

Haley and Mosakowski seemed as shocked by our reaction as we were by their ultimatum. The tension in the room crackled. I caught Ford staring intently at me. I was insulted that the man I'd thought was my ally now sat silent, failing to come to my aid. After all I'd done for his investigation I'd expected at least some support from him. The criminal investigation had been a thorn in our sides and had hindered and delayed any civil settlement. But I'd believed all along that cooperating with the criminal investigation was the right thing to do. Now I wasn't so sure.

Meeting Ford's gaze, I shook my head in disgust as he quickly looked away. At that moment, I lost respect for both Haley and Ford. *How could I have misread them so badly?* I wondered.

With nothing left to say, my attorneys and I abruptly stood up and marched from the room. We spent the next three hours discussing the development. I was offended. Never had I envisioned such an unfair, intimidating, and wrongheaded government ploy. During our lengthy discussion, Meagher accepted a call on his cell phone from Chris Hoyer. After Meagher recounted the afternoon's events, Hoyer agreed to appeal the Justice Department's position.

The next morning, Meagher and I met with Chris Hoyer in his office. They told me that they had never encountered a dilemma like this in their decades of legal practice. They felt that it was extremely ill-advised for the government to attack a cooperating witness. Meagher's frustration mounted as we once again rehashed the previous day's events. "The case," he told me, "did not exist before you stepped forward."

Why did the Justice Department resort to intimidation when the case had been laid out on a silver platter? Meagher theorized that the prosecution was probably trying to "crime it up." He said the prosecutors didn't know how seriously the jury would treat the evidence, because so much of it was based on abstract Medicare rules and arcane regulations. But jurors might find much more compelling a scenario in which participants and co-conspirators confessed to the serious nature of a crime. We believed their gambit was unnecessary and thought the evidence spoke for itself.

We theorized that the government team must feel insecure in its own abilities and a little gun-shy considering the high profile of the case and all the time and resources invested in it. Perhaps that's why they made such an imprudent choice. There was absolutely no need to cast aspersions on me or Larry Bomar. In the meantime, we agreed to let the Justice Department sweat for awhile.

"Will they charge me with a crime?" I asked. "John, it's plain and simple," Meagher answered. "You did not commit any crime. They have absolutely no evidence that you did. Anyway, if they do charge you, I'd have fun defending you." Meagher's aura of complete confidence reassured me that at least *this* team was on my side. "I am also sure that the Justice Department attorneys are simply insecure. They are afraid of losing the trial," he rationalized.

I agreed, but I wasn't about to accept their offer of immunity. "If they want to charge me with a crime," I said, "then tell them to go ahead."

My flight back to Milwaukee afforded me plenty of time to mull over the weekend's events. With Meagher and Chris and Judy Hoyer in my corner, I knew I was in good hands. But the Justice Department's actions reflected badly on our government. *It's no surprise that some people distrust the federal government*, I thought. *How could I have been so naive?*

After ten days, the government was still unwilling to budge. Amazingly, the FBI even had the gall to ask me to review new documents recently obtained from another witness. The Bureau even Federal Expressed them to my home, hoping I'd change my mind and help them out. I refused, no longer feeling obligated to serve my tormenters. The Bureau would just have to wait.

Our appeal with the Justice Department was rejected. We were unable to convince the department that they'd made a mistake. Unwilling to accept the un-indicted co-conspirator label, I declined immunity and I was never charged with a crime). The trial was drawing closer, and none of the defendants had entered a plea agreement.

I wondered whether the defense also doubted the government team's trial skills. Jarrell, Whiteside, Neeb, and Dick were ready to appear in court. The trial promised to be a big story. The media was already speculating on the likely outcomes and their potential effects on the healthcare industry. The courtroom would be filled to capacity. The show was ready to begin.

CHAPTER SIXTEEN

Trial Opening

It was hard to imagine that three years of hard work by government investigators and me would finally culminate in a criminal trial. It was even more difficult to grasp that the trial would pit federal prosecutors against four of my former colleagues. When I had begun working at Columbia/HCA in 1993, I feared and respected all four men. Now, on the first day of the trial—May 4, 1999—my feelings were mixed and unresolved. There was sadness coupled with regret, yet I felt genuinely hopeful that a flawed and broken system could be repaired.

Billed as the FBI's largest healthcare fraud investigation, the high-profile trial would be closely watched throughout the industry. U.S. District Judge Susan Bucklew would preside over the Tampa courtroom as the defendants—Jay Jarrell, 43; Robert (Bob) Whiteside, 48; Michael Neeb, 36; and Carl Lynn Dick, 54—accompanied by their legal teams, faced Assistant United States Attorneys Bob Mosakowski, Kathleen Haley, and Tony Peluso. Even though the trial focused on the alleged wrongdoing at only one of Columbia/HCA's hospitals, Fawcett Memorial, the government warned that it could call as many as sixty witnesses to the stand. Although I desperately wanted to watch the proceedings, as a witness in the case I was prohibited from attending the trial for fear that my testimony might be influenced by what I might hear in court.

While every minute seemed like an eternity 1,200 miles away in Milwaukee, I tried to concentrate on my job. That evening, Meagher told me about the trial's opening arguments. His recitation seemed so real that I felt I was there in the overcrowded federal courtroom buzzing with excitement. He said that as the jury entered, a hush fell over the jittery crowd. Judge Bucklew broke the silence as she cleared her throat and instructed Mosakowski to begin his opening statement on behalf of the government.

Mosakowski rose and said, "This case is about a group of business executives who conspired to exploit weaknesses in our government's audit procedures and defrauded three federal programs designed to provide healthcare services to the elderly, to the indigent, and the family members of the armed forces out of close to $3 million."

Slowly, he recounted the "Fawcett interest meeting" I had attended and methodically explained the core of the government's case. He related the history of Fawcett Memorial's mortgage loan, the first auditing mistake in the hospital's 1984 cost report, and the subsequent oversights and errors of the Medicare auditors. He told the jury about the first prosecution witness, Steve Dudley, and his account of what took place during his employment with BAMI. He told them that the fiscal intermediary, Blue Cross & Blue Shield of Florida, made its first mistake under Dudley's watch, and later Dudley, Dick, and Jarrell collectively agreed to remain silent, taking advantage of that auditor's error. Mosakowski then introduced the names of two other key witnesses, Larry Bomar and me, and summarized the testimony the jury could expect to hear from us.

Concluding his opening statement, Mosakowski said, "Blue Cross/ Blue Shield made a series of mistakes. The defendants found them, recognized them, exploited them, and enriched their company and furthered their careers to the tune of $3 million belonging to the United States of America."

Peter George, Jarrell's counsel, stood after a short pause and said that his client's defense was simple and straightforward: Jarrell always believed that the entire interest expense was a capital expenditure and therefore, Fawcett Memorial Hospital was entitled to claim 100 percent of the Medicare reimbursement it obtained.

"He believed it in 1986, when the issue first arose, and he believes it to this day," George proclaimed. He explained that Jarrell was not an expert and trusted and relied upon colleagues and experts more knowledgeable in the specialized area of Medicare cost accounting. George said that even though Jarrell became immersed in the Fawcett interest issue, cost reports were not his job or area of expertise. Then, as predicted, George painted me as a disgruntled employee. He said that because I had not received a promotion, I quit, hired a lawyer, and filed a multimillion-dollar lawsuit. George admonished the jury members to consider my motivation when weighing my testimony.

"You heard earlier today that he'll come in and tell you he has some financial interest in the outcome of this case—not just some financial interest, ladies and gentlemen—multimillions of dollars he's seeking in this case," George stated, emphasizing the size of the fortune allegedly driving my actions.

He also asked the jury to remember that after I'd left Columbia/HCA and filed my *qui tam* lawsuit, I returned to work for the company as a government informant who deceived my co-workers and colleagues. He called me devious because I didn't tell my employers at Columbia/HCA that I was a confidential witness. He went on to accuse me of stealing documents as I copied them for the FBI.

"Steve Dudley and John Schilling expect to derive a personal benefit. And what is that personal benefit? We talked about Mr. Schilling," he said. "What about Mr. Dudley? Mr. Dudley has bargained with the government." He paused dramatically. "He has immunity from prosecution for things that he may have done."

Neeb's attorney, David Geneson, rose next to address jurors. "For Michael Neeb," he said, "this case is about trust, whether he trusted wisely or unwisely, whether he trusted well. Whether he trusted properly in his fellow men and women as a man of faith and whether he made good judgments based on trust." Moving on, Geneson began to attack my credibility, telling the jury, "He was a secret agent sent back to get the government information. Schilling stands to gain millions if the lawsuit was successful."

By the end of the day, all the defense attorneys had denied that their clients had committed any crimes. They said the case really hinged on honest differences of opinion over complex billing issues. These were misunderstandings, the defense assured jurors—honest mistakes, but not crimes. They warned jurors not to believe the government's three main witnesses, Bomar, Dudley, and me.

On day two, prosecutors then called the first key witness, Steve Dudley, to the stand. His testimony would last several days. I had been worried that Dudley might not prove the best witness for the government because of his troubled relationship with the truth, which could compromise his credibility. He hadn't cooperated with the government at first, and I believed both the government and the defense counsel would make him squirm on the witness stand. His testimony would not be painless and would not pass unchallenged. Dudley had already admitted to lying, not only to the FBI but before the grand jury when he was first questioned. It seemed clear to me that he was not motivated by honesty or integrity. I wondered why the government opened such an important trial with the testimony of a man who had been dishonest and even obstructive. However, my feelings mattered little to the Criminal Division of the Justice Department.

Dudley said he understood Medicare rules and regulations. He knew how capital expenditures were treated on Medicare cost reports, explaining that capital expenditures included hard assets, such as buildings and equipment, but didn't encompass day-to-day business operations, such as payroll, maintenance, and utilities. Dudley explained that problems already existed at BAMI hospitals before he joined the company. Once onboard, he began researching earlier cost reports and discovered that the 1987 and 1988 cost reports had been filed incorrectly and claimed 100 percent of the loan's interest expense as a capital expenditure.

He said the Medicare auditors had appropriately adjusted the 1986 cost report, allocating the loan's interest expense between operations and capital, which meant the hospital received a smaller reimbursement. Dudley recalled that sometime after the 1986 audit, Dick and he had speculated how the auditors would approach the 1987 cost report, since it differed from the 1986 report. Knowing that auditors normally rely heavily on the prior year's work papers, he speculated that the fiscal intermediary would adjust it consistent with the treatment in the 1986 report. Dudley then sent a memo to Dick and Jarrell about the final results of the 1986 audit, explaining that the interest had been split between capital and operating expenses. While Dick was happy that the hospital was able to claim a portion of the interest as capital expense, Jarrell was peeved that Fawcett couldn't claim the full amount as a capital expenditure.

The Medicare auditor compounded the problem when she audited the 1987 and 1988 cost reports, mistakenly allowing 100 percent of the interest expense as a capital expenditure. This audit mistake benefited the hospital by $500,000 annually.

Dudley said he and Dick discussed the audit mistakes, liberally repeating the term "windfall." He said the hospital would accept the payment but omit the windfall from the hospital's financial records to remove any potential red flags that might alert auditors. If the auditor did discover the error, they decided the hospital would include the interest issue as a "reserve item." This reserve cost report, meant for corporate and hospital internal use only, would account for all the issues the executives knew were incorrect and had concealed from the fiscal intermediary. Dudley and Dick agreed that there was little chance the auditor would uncover the mistake.

At this point in Dudley's testimony, Haley interjected, "Mr. Dudley, did the question ever arise during your conversations with Mr. Dick that you had an obligation to tell the fiscal intermediary it had made a mistake?" Dudley said they never discussed disclosing the error to the auditor.

In the summer of 1990, Dudley said, BAMI hired public accounting firm KPMG to prepare its cost reports, further complicating the matter. BAMI gave KPMG not only copies of all the interest expense documentation but also the prior years' work papers from former consultant Price Waterhouse. Dudley said that even though the KPMG consultant had reviewed the correct documentation, the firm did not want to jeopardize BAMI's favorable treatment of the capital interest expense when preparing the 1990 cost report. He said KPMG also would claim 100 percent of the interest expense, including that from Fawcett Memorial, as capital expenditures on the 1990 cost report.

Contrary to what he told the 1997 grand jury in Fort Myers, Dudley now confirmed that after reviewing Fawcett's internal records, he believed that the 1990 cost report again had been filed incorrectly. He said his memory had been unclear on the day when he told the grand jury otherwise. Since then, he'd had the opportunity to review documents and refresh his memory.

Dudley said Dick suggested that the hospital obtain a third party to review the issue and obtain a legal opinion. One month later, Dick asked Dudley to draft a letter summarizing the high points of the Fawcett interest issue to send to an attorney. Dudley said Dick instructed him to be general, not specific, in recounting events, hoping to mislead the attorney to obtain a favorable legal opinion.

Dudley and Dick believed Medicare auditor Thuan Tran might present the last obstacle in ensuring that Fawcett's claim of 100 percent interest expense as a capital expenditure was allowable for all those cost report years. Dudley worried that the properly filed 1989 cost report, splitting the interest expense between capital and operating expense, would attract Tran's attention. He and Dick agreed there was a good chance that Tran, the auditor during the past two years in which the capital-related interest expense was incorrectly allowed, would mistakenly adjust the correctly filed 1989 cost report allowing the total amount to be claimed. But Dudley also feared Tran might discover the mistake and correct the previous cost reports, jeopardizing the hospital's multimillion-dollar windfall.

Dudley testified that during the 1989 cost report audit, he took matters into his own hands. At his request, the accounting manager at Price Waterhouse forwarded him a blank set of cost report work papers. Dudley created a duplicate of the interest expense schedule Price Waterhouse had originally prepared, changing some of the numbers under the "capital-related" and "purpose" portions of the form and leaving other areas incomplete. The original work paper divided the interest expense into 39 percent capital-related and 61 percent operating, while Dudley's fabricated work paper did not. Without telling anyone he'd created a document designed to deceive the auditor, Dudley sent it to the fiscal intermediary. In his grand jury testimony, Dudley had said that Dick and he had discussed the fraudulent work paper and that Dick had told him to send it to the FI. But in subsequent conversations with FBI agents, Dudley confessed he'd lied then. He said Dick knew nothing about the fraudulent document and they'd never discussed it.

Dudley told the jury that Jarrell and Dick knew that the cost reports fraudulently claimed the full interest expense as capital-related. Dudley also said several times during his testimony that he feared losing his job if he disclosed the information.

The defense couldn't wait to attack him. Each of the four defense attorneys had been licking his chops to cross-examine Dudley. Jarrell's attorney, George, entered Dudley's immunity agreement into evidence, then handed the document to Dudley on the witness stand to identify, driving home to the jury the message that Dudley would have done anything to avoid prosecution. George then attacked Dudley's testimony, questioning why he initially lied to Agent Joe Ford about the 1989 cost report audit. Driving to the heart of his defense, George portrayed Dudley as a deceiver and reminded the jury that Dudley, not Jarrell, submitted the fraudulent documents.

Bill Jung, Dick's lawyer, followed George in cross-examining Dudley and quickly hammered him about falsifying documents he sent to the

Medicare auditor. "Mr. Dudley, why didn't you just send in the Price Waterhouse work paper instead of cooking one up and telling them that it was a Price Waterhouse work paper? Why?" Jung asked.

"I did it to mislead them," Dudley answered.

"You did it to mislead them. You intentionally did it to mislead Tran, correct?" "Yes sir."

Jung accused Dudley of falsely implicating Dick, recanting his testimony to the grand jury, and omitting the information he told the FBI.

Dudley completed his testimony before noon on the fifth day of the trial. He'd stumbled through the cross-examination, but his points were made. Although he confessed to criminal behavior himself, he also implicated the defendants and supported the indictment charges in the case. His damaging testimony backed up the government's claim that the defendants knew about the fraud scheme and failed to intervene.

Meagher called me the evening of the fifth day of the trial. "Dudley's testimony is over, and it was enlightening," he said. "Even though he was hounded, he refused to back down under cross-examination. His testimony backs up your charges. They all knew about the Fawcett interest issue. It will come down to your testimony."

The next two weeks felt like two years, and the prosecution still was not ready for me to take the stand. Several witnesses testified after Steve Dudley, and thirty others were scheduled before me. In order to minimize confusion in a very complex case, the prosecution was careful to maintain the order of evidence.

Having listened with trepidation as Meagher recounted Dudley's ruthless cross-examination, I halfheartedly agreed to travel to Tampa for final witness preparation. I boarded a Tampa flight on May 15, after Alex's Little League team had posted its first victory in the season opener. I was one of the coaches, and during the flight, my thoughts drifted to the next practice and the next game. As the plane bumped to the ground in Tampa, I was jolted back to reality.

The next morning, I walked the two blocks from my hotel to the Mercantile Bank Plaza to meet with FBI Agents Michele Yaroma and Tim McCants. Poring over documents, they asked the same questions I had been asked numerous times before. My answers remained the same as we reviewed documents seized in the raids or recently obtained with subpoenas. Meagher and Judy Hoyer arrived and listened to the questioning.

After a lunch break, Mosakowski and I met for his final witness preparation. "Don't worry about the cross-examination," Mosakowski said. "It's my job to come back to you under redirect and clarify any issues." After redirect, he explained, the defense would have one final chance to cross-examine me again. Upon completion of the re-cross, my testimony would end. Since there was a possibility that I could be called back as a witness, however, I would still be barred from attending the trial after testifying.

Mosakowski asked the questions he expected to ask me during his direct examination in the courtroom. He didn't pause long before moving from one question to the next, taking notes as I responded. I'd answered these same questions many times before, so we plowed through them quickly. By 3:30 P.M., Mosakowski completed his session and passed me on to Peluso, who portrayed a mock defense attorney. Peluso rapidly fired questions designed to rattle me. Finding that technique ineffective, he then grew argumentative and hostile. I remained calm, though, ignoring the insults and answering his questions. Peluso fired away at me for three hours, unable to wear me down. I knew it was his job to see what would make me crack. His efforts failed. I wasn't shaken.

The next morning, I returned for round two of the final witness preparation. I met first with FBI Agent McCants, discussing my undercover recordings. Then Mosakowski and McCants took turns cross-examining me. By 1 P.M., the government was satisfied with my preparation. Anticipating that I could be called to testify the following Wednesday or Thursday, the government asked me to return on the weekend, only days away. They wanted me in Florida in case I was summoned early. They wanted no surprises.

With little time between me and the witness stand, I grew fearful. To assuage those worries, Meagher and Al Scudieri took me to the new federal courthouse in downtown Tampa. As we drove along Florida Avenue looking for a parking spot, Scudieri pointed out the seventeen-story stone-and-glass courthouse completed only eighteen months before. U.S. Marshals vehicles occupied the courthouse parking places, so we parked at a meter two blocks away. Scudieri explained that the courthouse was named after Sam Gibbons, a Tampa native and Democrat who served thirty-four years in Congress, chairing the powerful House Ways and Means Committee in 1994 and 1995.

As we approached the building, I noticed several older men milling about in blue blazers bearing the insignia of the U.S. Marshals Service. The federal court security officers, mostly retired policemen, observed the flow of foot traffic around the courthouse and checked identification. We entered the sleek building through the metal detectors and passed through a five-story glass atrium to a bank of stainless steel elevators. Avoiding the Columbia/HCA trial on the fourteenth floor, we exited the elevator one floor up. Scudieri found an empty courtroom, which we entered. The courtroom featured cherry paneled walls, a vaulted acoustical ceiling, and a large judge's bench with a black marble top. Meagher pointed out the tables on opposite sides of the aisle, where the prosecution and defense would sit, and the raised jury section, consisting of two rows of six chairs. Finally, he showed me the small platform surrounded by a wooden railing: the witness stand.

"Remember," Meagher reminded me, "When you take the stand, give concise answers and make eye contact with the jury. You'll do just fine." "I hope so," I responded.

I slowly paced the eerily quiet courtroom, familiarizing myself with the layout until Meagher interrupted the silence. "There will be a great deal of media coverage when you testify. Several reporters have already requested an interview with you when your testimony is complete," he said. I was already nervous about testifying, and with the media chronicling everything I said, I knew I'd be much less comfortable than when I addressed the grand jury. *I'm dreading this,* I thought.

CHAPTER SEVENTEEN

Anticipation

The door opened and FBI agent Bill Estevez burst into the makeshift conference room. It was 3 P.M. on May 26, 1999, and I'd been patiently waiting in the Mercantile Bank Plaza for five hours. I entertained myself reading grand jury transcripts for the hundredth time and scanning a newspaper. My attorneys were already at the courthouse monitoring the trial.

Startled, I dropped the newspaper I'd been reading and warily glanced up at Estevez. "John, hurry up, pack up your things. I've got to get you over to the courthouse," he commanded.

"Am I getting on the stand today?" I stammered. "I'm not sure, but Joe Ford called and said you're the next scheduled witness. Joe and Kathleen want you there. We can't have any interruption in witnesses or the judge may require us to rest our position," he responded. *That would be okay with me,* I mused.

I had grown increasingly nervous as the day wore on. My stomach growled and my throat became tight and dry. I grabbed my suit coat, tightened my tie, and rushed out ahead of Estevez to his car. We wove through the crowded downtown streets the half-mile to the courthouse and found an empty U.S. Marshals parking spot on Polk Street. Then we paced briskly to the entrance of the courthouse, barely pausing for Estevez to flash his shiny federal badge as he whisked me through security. *That was easy,* I thought. *I should always have an FBI escort when entering a federal building.*

As we ascended to the fourteenth floor in the stainless steel elevator, time seemed to pause for a brief instant. This was it. I wasn't happy or excited but sad and anxious that I was in this position. At least I knew that I was doing the right thing. The elevator bell announced our arrival on the fourteenth floor where Judge Bucklew presided. Just outside of the courtroom entrance was a witness waiting area, a small room with a long conference table, fabric-covered chairs, and a few newspapers and magazines strewn about. Estevez motioned to one of the chairs.

"Have a seat," he suggested. "They'll call you when they're ready." I took a seat and waited. I'd become accustomed to waiting. Sometimes it seemed like waiting was my real occupation.

Only four days earlier, back in Wisconsin, I'd coached Alex's Little League team to a 12–8 win. I was proud how well the team was working together. After the game, I'd flown to Tampa and the next morning joined my legal team of Stephen Meagher, Chris Hoyer, and Al Scudieri on what we hoped would be our last walk to the Mercantile Bank Plaza. We met with agents Joe Ford, Michele Yaroma, and Tim McCants. I clarified several new trial documents and then authenticated some of my undercover tape recordings.

Ford and McCants shared tips on testifying. They advised me to carefully listen to each question and allow each attorney to fully complete his thought before answering. They told me to answer concisely and to ask questions if something was unclear. "Do not get argumentative with an attorney," Ford reminded me. "It is the defense attorney's job to get you agitated and make you look irrational in front of the jury," McCants added.

Later that day, Bob Mosakowski joined us. He sat across from me, looked me in the eye, and said, "John, just tell the truth. Be yourself. Tell your story. Don't think you have to help us out. It is our job to win this case. It's not up to you. What happens, happens."

Meagher, ever my champion, suggested to Mosakowski that the government try to wrap up my testimony this week. "This has been a burden on John and his family. Let's get him on the stand so he can get back home to his family."

"I can't make any promises, but I'll try," Mosakowski replied. He vowed to keep me in the predetermined witness order but said that my testimony would not begin until at least Wednesday, May 26. "You are free for the next two days, but you have to stay in Florida," he said.

On Monday, I rented a car and drove south along the coast to Fort Myers. I wasn't going to just sit and wait in Tampa. I had lunch with my dad, who asked if he could attend the trial while I testified. Although I appreciated the support, I knew it would make me very uncomfortable to testify in front of him and asked him not to come.

"It won't be pretty," I said. "I don't want you to hear the garbage the defense is going to sling at me." Wishing me luck as I left, dad said he understood. "You did the right thing," he said. "I'll be watching the news."

I stopped to visit our friend, Eva Pomarico, who was home with her son, Mark, when I rang the bell. Eva welcomed me with a hug. She and her husband, Frank, had been supportive throughout our ordeal, despite our seemingly odd behavior. Unlike some others, they had backed us even after my story and name became public. The couple, who inspired me with their high moral values, had applauded me for standing up against the odds. As I departed, Eva said she was praying for me and urged me to hang in there.

The drive north to Tampa again gave me time to think about my family back in Wisconsin. Ultimately, I knew that by setting the example I had, I was teaching my children honesty and integrity, even if they were too young to understand. Alex, now eight, understood that by telling the truth I was helping the government. He was more interested, however, in my travel schedule. Would I attend his baseball practices or games? Would I show up for his school play? When would Stephen call again? Abby, who was four, and Austin, at three, could not grasp what was happening. Hopefully, someday, they would appreciate the sacrifices.

When I returned to Tampa, Meagher recapped the day's events in the courtroom. Only three witnesses had been called. "You might not get called this week if things continue at this pace," he lamented.

Just then, my cell phone rang. It was Kirsten. "No emergency," she said. "I wanted to tell you that I am flying to Tampa tomorrow." I couldn't refuse her because she had already purchased the nonrefundable ticket.

The next morning, May 25, Meagher and I separated. He headed to the courthouse and I went to the airport to pick up my wife. Even though I hadn't wanted her to come to Tampa at first, I was glad she joined me. We drove to St. Petersburg and stopped at The Pier, a downtown landmark. The mile-long boardwalk ends in an inverted five-story pyramid building housing shops, restaurants, and an aquarium. We enjoyed a leisurely lunch and browsed through the stores. Later, we sat on the observation deck watching the boats bobbing in Tampa Bay. The afternoon offered a pleasant diversion from the weightier realities of my coming testimony.

After lunch, Kirsten and I drove to Chris Hoyer's office, where I introduced her to my Florida legal team of Hoyer and Al Scudieri. Also, for the first time, Kirsten met my part-time therapist and full-time attorney, Stephen Meagher. Happy to finally connect the face with the name, Kirsten was impressed by Meagher and the contingent of confident, knowledgeable, and enthusiastic attorneys backing me. Kirsten timed her visit well. While the endless waiting in recent weeks had been excruciating for me, the last few days felt interminable. It was wonderful to see her and she took my mind off my obligations and the onslaught awaiting me.

Sleep was elusive that night. Images of movie courtroom scenes flashed in my thoughts as my stomach tumbled in distress. By now, all I wanted was to finish testifying and return to my normal life in Wisconsin. Although she offered, I asked Kirsten not to sit in the courtroom. Instead, she offered encouragement and promised to meet me after court ended that afternoon. I kissed her good-bye with trepidation.

After relocating from the Mercantile Bank Building in the late afternoon of Wednesday, May 26, Estevez and I sat in the courthouse witness room passing the time until I would be called. He excused himself, vowing to return in a few minutes. I waited patiently. I waited and waited, mulling over Meagher's prediction that I wouldn't be called until the next day. Estevez appeared several times to make sure I hadn't left, and by 5 P.M., I realized I wouldn't be called. *Oh well*, I sighed, *another sleepless night.*

Suddenly the door opened, and Mike Meagher (no relation to Stephen Meagher) entered the room, having just testified. Meagher, a former Columbia/HCA Medicare cost report consultant, was now a government witness. I greeted him and when we shook hands, I thought that he might not want to speak with me. After all, I was the reason he was testifying as a government witness. Politely, I inquired about his day on the witness stand.

"Are you finished with your testimony?" I asked. "Almost, but I'll have to return tomorrow," he replied. Stephen Meagher later said that Mike

Meagher's testimony wasn't very effective or convincing and that he frequently answered, "I don't recall." (I think he was frightened and just playing possum.) Shortly after this, Estevez returned to dismiss me for the day.

Media accounts of the trial until this point portrayed it as lackluster and dull since Steve Dudley had testified a few weeks earlier. Trial analysts predicted that my testimony would enliven the trial. Stephen Meagher arranged a meeting with *Modern Healthcare* reporter Mark Taylor after Wednesday's testimony had been completed. While I was present Meagher wouldn't allow Taylor to interview me yet, he answered questions from the reporter, who also photographed us for his article.

As Kirsten and I parted the morning of May 27, another drama was unfolding in the courtroom. The defense had objected to a cassette tape I'd recorded that the prosecution wanted to admit into evidence. It was a tape of one of the many conversations I'd had with Columbia/HCA personnel regarding the Fawcett interest issue. This marked the first of many defense attempts to suppress evidence in the case.

Tony Peluso asked Judge Bucklew to admit the tape, denying the defense team's assertion that I had recorded the tape to improve the chances of my *qui tam* lawsuit. Peluso said it was inconsistent to think that I'd brought the issue to higher levels of management at Columbia/HCA in order to maximize my lawsuit. "When the court analyzes the tape in context and the court analyzes the testimony, I think the court's going to see that Mr. Schilling's intent in discussing this with Ms. Reid, for example, is completely inapposite to someone who wanted to maximize the potential for a *qui tam*," Peluso pleaded. (In a blow to the prosecution, the court would later rule that the tape was not admissible as evidence and I was instructed not to disclose it to the jury. I could, however, testify about the meeting and what was said.)

Dressed conservatively in my dark blue suit, starched white shirt, red tie, and black wing tip shoes, I saw the apprehensive faces of Meagher and Scudieri when I got to the courthouse. "How are you feeling, John?" Meagher asked with concern. "Nervous," I replied. "You have nothing to worry about," he reassured me. "Just be yourself."

In the courthouse, Meagher and Scudieri went to the courtroom while I stayed in the witness waiting room. My stomach churned like a high-speed blender. There, I saw Mike Meagher seated at the table. We chatted about our families for a few minutes until a bailiff summoned him into the courtroom to complete his testimony. I wished him luck and returned to my current occupation and avocation—waiting.

At 10:30 A.M., Estevez entered the room. "John, are you ready? You're up," he beckoned. I gulped and, with my heart racing, and my stomach churning, I stood and followed him out the door.

CHAPTER EIGHTEEN

Testifying

As I entered the courtroom on May 27, 1999, I looked straight ahead at Judge Susan Bucklew, who seemed dwarfed by her large, black leather chair, and awaited her instructions. "Sir, if you would come forward to be sworn," she ordered sternly.

I walked up the center aisle past the packed gallery, around the lectern to the witness stand on the left. I entered the stand and adjusted the water pitcher and glass near my right hand as my heart pounded. Charles Lembcke, the attorney for my former manager Bob Whiteside, glared at me. I looked away, refusing the bait. The defendants sat no more than 20 feet from me on the opposite side of the room. Their proximity was jarring. Jay Jarrell, and his attorney, Peter George, were in the front row. Behind them were Whiteside and Lembcke, as well as Michael Neeb and his attorney, David Geneson. Carl Lynn Dick and his counsel, Bill Jung, occupied the third row.

Bob Mosakowski began his direct examination, asking questions regarding my work and educational background. These familiar questions, designed to put me at ease, worked. Feeling more comfortable, I poured myself a glass of water, which soothed my throat and calmed my nerves. I located Stephen Meagher and Al Scudieri among the spectators, two beacons of support in a sea of unknown or hostile faces.

I was sure the defendants wanted to leap across the tables separating us and strangle me. But I knew I could do this. I just needed to ignore the silent daggers the defense team hurled my way whenever our eyes met.

Mosakowski questioned me about the period when I first worked at Columbia/HCA and my responsibilities there. He asked specifically about my working relationships with Jarrell, Whiteside, and Neeb. Next, he moved into the Fawcett interest issue. As I had so many times before, I explained receiving the phone call from Medicare auditor Thuan Tran, the discussion during which Whiteside told me "jobs could be lost if this gets out," and the subsequent meeting at Fawcett Memorial Hospital with Whiteside, Neeb, and Jarrell. Throughout his direct examination, Mosakowski introduced numerous exhibits that included financial work papers, memoranda, and correspondence. I discussed the notes I took from this "conspiracy" meeting and the to-do list I was ordered to complete, which included diverting Tran away from the Fawcett interest issue.

I testified that Jarrell ended the meeting by suggesting, "If all else fails, we should offer her a job." Prosecutors then introduced into evidence a copy of Neeb's handwritten notes with the entries "pick other hospitals to load up work on" and "hire her."

Mosakowski probed the aftermath of the alleged conspiracy meeting. I explained that while the office became extremely tense after the meeting, Whiteside apologized to me about his behavior several weeks later. He told me that I needed more seasoning and, with more experience, would learn when to keep quiet. I testified that after several months, I reported back to Neeb and Whiteside that the auditor had never again questioned the interest expense at Fawcett.

I returned to the stand after lunch. Mosakowski asked me to explain my attempts to disclose the Fawcett interest issue. I told him I'd sought help from my new superiors at that time, Larry Bomar and Trish Lindler. I said that Bomar felt the same way I did but couldn't convince Lindler, his boss, to act.

Finally, Mosakowki prodded me to talk about the action I did take. I told the jury I contacted an attorney in February 1995 to determine my legal exposure and explore my options. After attempting to work within the company's hierarchy up the corporate ladder and finding no avenues to report compliance problems, I began collecting evidence. When I left Columbia/HCA in August 1995, I took copies of specific documents and detailed notes. My *qui tam* lawsuit was not filed until June 1996. I explained to the jury that by filing a *qui tam* lawsuit, I was eligible to receive a portion of any successful recovery. If my suit failed, I would receive nothing. In either case, my career in healthcare finance was ruined.

Next, with permission from Judge Bucklew, the seal of my *qui tam* case against KPMG was lifted. Mosakowski asked if I'd filed a *qui tam* lawsuit against any other company besides Columbia/HCA. "Yes," I responded. "And who's the defendant in that action?" he asked. "That's KPMG Peat Marwick," I replied.

Mosakowski then asked me to detail my work with the FBI and my cooperation with Joe Ford's investigation. I described my consulting arrangements and employment with Columbia/HCA while I was a cooperating witness.

At 3:30 P.M., Mosakowski ended my direct examination. It hadn't been difficult. There were no surprises. I felt confident I'd done well.

Now the defense attorneys would cross-examine me. I felt trapped and had no place to hide. I reminded myself to listen to the questions carefully before answering. Just let the prosecutors do their job, I thought to myself. When the prosecutors had prepared me to testify, they warned me about the commonly used defense attorney tactic of interrupting witnesses in mid-sentence and preventing them from completing their thoughts. I hoped the prosecution would object if the defense didn't let me answer fully and hoped I'd remember not to act insulted or become argumentative.

Charles Lembcke, representing Bob Whiteside, launched the defense attack. Lembcke began by asking if I recognized his client in the courtroom. Turning, I looked at Whiteside and identified him. Then Lembcke began his assault. His line of questioning seemed designed to distance his client from the reimbursement responsibilities in the Fort Myers division office. He attempted to overstate my authority and responsibilities. He suggested that during the period of the alleged crimes, Whiteside was no longer involved in the decision making in Fort Myers because he was relocating to Nashville. Only an hour into Lembcke's cross-examination, Judge Bucklew, citing other court business, adjourned for the day. She reminded me not to read any media reports or discuss my testimony with anyone, including FBI agents and my own attorneys.

On the drive to the hotel, Meagher said Bucklew's instructions were improper. While he urged me to comply with her instructions, he said that if I was concerned about the substance of any particular aspect of my testimony, I could discuss it with him. He believed her admonition violated the constitutional right to counsel and was an intrusion into the attorney-client relationship. Meagher said if Bucklew held him in contempt for discussing the case with me, he'd be happy to deal with it. He told me I was doing well on the witness stand and encouraged me to keep my composure.

When I got back to the hotel, Kirsten was waiting for me. "How did it go?" she asked. "It wasn't bad, but I'm glad it's over for the day. I got through the government's direct examination and about forty minutes of cross-examination with Whiteside's attorney. He tried to intimidate me by staring me down when I first entered the courtroom, but his line of questioning just seemed disorganized."

"What were you asked?" Kirsten said. "I am not at liberty to discuss my testimony." "Oh, come on!" she exclaimed.

"I'm serious. That was my instruction from the judge. You'll have to get tomorrow's paper and read about it. There were reporters from almost every major newspaper in the courtroom."

"I guess it'll give me something to read on the plane tomorrow."

That evening, Kirsten and I had dinner with Meagher and Scudieri. I stepped aside for a while so the three of them could discuss my testimony. She later told me that Meagher said I was holding up amazingly well. He told her I was one of the best witnesses he'd ever seen and credited me with completing the day on the stand with no mishaps. Meagher also said he was happy she'd flown to Florida to support me, which contributed to my successful initiation on the witness stand.

The alarm rang at 5 A.M. the next day, Friday. Kirsten had booked an early flight back to Wisconsin. Unable to sleep any longer, I rose with her, even though court wouldn't convene for four more hours. Still a little nervous, I hoped that this would be my last day of testimony and that I could join her and the kids back home that night. Kirsten kissed me, wishing me luck as she left the hotel. Ordinarily I would have read the local newspaper, but I was afraid to because of Bucklew's admonition. The headlines were sure to trumpet news of the Columbia/HCA trial. Instead, I watched the sports highlights on ESPN as I dressed for court.

Meagher and Scudieri escorted me to the courthouse, offering encouragement. They scurried to the courtroom and I headed to the witness waiting room. After about an hour Estevez entered and announced, "You're on, John." I followed him into the courtroom past the gallery full of reporters, note pads in hand, awaiting my testimony. I could feel their anticipation. Most, I suspected, wanted and expected to see fireworks, to watch the defense rip me apart. I felt like a gladiator in ancient Rome battling fierce, hungry lions to the applause of the spectators. I wondered if they ever fed accountants to the lions in Rome.

Lembcke, who had not finished his cross-examination the day before when court was adjourned, continued his questioning this morning. Wary that he would try to trick me into saying something untrue, I listened carefully to his questions. Today his strategy was unclear. Was he confused, or was he trying to confuse the jury? His questions were rambling and disorganized, and he often interrupted me. Some of his jumbled questions prompted objections from the prosecution. He still hadn't completed his cross-examination by the lunch recess, and I knew then that this would not be my last day on the stand. At first, Lembcke had impressed me as a slick used-car salesman. But there was nothing slick about him now, and he wasn't making the sale to the jury.

Lembcke plodded through his remaining questions that afternoon. It appeared that his strategy was to show that Whiteside was not a decision maker during the period in question. Since he was transitioning into his new Nashville position, he no longer participated in any business decisions in Fort Myers. Lembcke tried to blame me for the problem, noting that I had had many chances to alert the different auditors working on the cost reports but failed to do so. He asked the jury to believe my motive for not disclosing the Fawcett interest issue was that I wanted to file a *qui tam* lawsuit and win a multimillion-dollar jackpot settlement.

Contradicting him, I told the jury that I had hoped that my superiors would do the right thing and disclose the error. While I had contacted a *qui tam* attorney prior to leaving Columbia/HCA, I had agonized for sixteen months before filing a lawsuit.

Around 3 P.M., Lembcke relinquished the floor to Neeb's attorney, David Geneson. Geneson appeared kinder and gentler than Lembcke had been. At first, his questions floated gently through the air-conditioned courtroom. Unlike Lembcke's approach, which sometimes reminded me of the crazy tactics of the TV detective Columbo, Geneson took an almost amiable tack. His thoughts were organized and he did not jump from one subject to another. He actually seemed likeable. I could almost imagine being lulled into complacency by his soft-spoken demeanor.

That ended in a flash when he started to badger me about my relationship with Agent Ford and the FBI. It seemed that he hoped to show that the government—specifically, Ford—had directed me to return to Columbia/HCA as a spy. "The undercover role, forced on you by the government, was something you did not tell anyone about," he said.

Quite the contrary, I responded, I was not forced into working again at Columbia/HCA. It was my choice to become a cooperating witness and help the investigation. Geneson ended the day proclaiming that his client had relied upon me for my expertise and skills in the complex, specialized arena of Medicare cost reimbursement.

Dismissing the jury, Bucklew addressed me before we left. "Mr. Schilling," she said, "I'm going to give some of the same advice to you. We're going to be on a recess now, a rather extended recess, until June the 7th. That is a week from next Monday, and we will resume the trial at that time. Obviously, you're in the middle of your cross-examination. So I would ask you, just as I've asked the jurors, not to discuss the case, not to discuss your testimony with anyone, including friends, including attorneys, including witnesses, including parties, including agents, anyone at all. Do you have any questions about what I might have said?"

"No, your honor," I sighed.

Excused from the witness stand, I left the courtroom and stopped in the witness room where Estevez was waiting to escort me to the airport. Concerned about my safety because the defendants and their attorneys were flying out around the same time, the FBI offered me protection at the airport. I declined, realizing how unlikely it would be for the defendants or their legal teams to threaten me. I imagined they each wanted to return home to their families as quickly as possible.

My flight back to Wisconsin was uneventful. Exhausted both mentally and physically, I slept on the plane and dreamed that my testimony and the trial were over. Another flight to Tampa and time away from my children was painful; they were growing and evolving in many ways while I focused on the lawsuit and trial.

The plane landing in Milwaukee jolted me awake. I remembered my last impression from a dream as I awakened. It was seeing a compass on a ship. Funny, how the mind works. That compass must have appeared for some reason. I thought then about how this entire mess could have been avoided if my bosses had followed their moral compass. But a compass can only point toward the right direction. It cannot transport the traveler to that destination. At that moment, my destination awaited me at the gate: Kirsten, Alex, Abby, and Austin.

It was frustrating being unable to read press accounts of the trial. Kirsten, however, reassured me that the coverage was mostly positive. She said the press reported that I had cut through the fog of healthcare regulations and made the case a simple one of committing and hiding fraud, characterizing my testimony as perhaps the most damaging yet in the criminal trial.

That weekend, Alex's Little League team remained undefeated, clobbering a rival by a score of 14–5. Coaching baseball was therapeutic for me, totally transporting me from the stress of the trial. I wasn't just mentally drained but also showed physical symptoms of stress. I was uncharacteristically nervous and found my patience wearing thin. I slept poorly, and my body felt sluggish and much older than that of a thirty-seven-year-old ex-fireman.

I boarded the plane back to Tampa a week later. I hoped this would be my final visit. Flying to Tampa had become routine, but I was eager to complete my testimony. I couldn't wait for it to end. Seeing a light at the end of the tunnel, I envisioned stepping off the witness stand for good in a day or two.

On Monday morning, June 7, 1999, Meagher and Scudieri again accompanied me to the federal courthouse. In the quiet witness room, I removed my jacket, poured a glass of water, sat down, and waited. Again. The endless waiting had moved far beyond deja vu. I felt trapped in the repetitive rinse cycle of waiting.

As I waited in the witness room, the defense teams moved for a mistrial in the courtroom, arguing that the defendants knew nothing about my secretly taped conversations of co-workers during the investigation. They requested that my testimony be stricken from the court records. Judge Bucklew met with the prosecution and the defense in a sidebar (a private conversation between the judge and the opposing counsel to discuss legal points outside of the earshot of jurors). During the sidebar, Carl Lynn Dick's attorney, Bill Jung, pleaded, "Would you hear me briefly, Judge? I'm just flabbergasted. Did I just hear that John Schilling had fifteen tapes? Your Honor, is that not impeachment, that he went around with a bug on fifteen or twenty times and surreptitiously recorded people?"

Jung, who claimed to be speechless, then went on to make a speech, denying he'd known about the secret recordings until this late period of the trial. He demanded to know where else I'd gone and what else I'd done. "He's the most important witness in this case and we're told in the middle of his cross that there are fifteen tapes . . . ," he moaned.

Prosecutor Tony Peluso responded. "Even before we admitted that Mr. Schilling had worked for the government in continued investigation as a confidential source, the defendants well knew about it," Peluso stated. "And if the court reviews all the pleadings in this case, . . . the fact is that the defense depicted Mr. Schilling as a spy. That was the word they used. The defense well knew that Mr. Schilling was engaged in surreptitious conversations in a confidential or undercover capacity for many months. So we have not hidden that. . . . Mr. Jung is just wrong, flat-out wrong as a matter of law and a matter of equity. He's not entitled to a mistrial." Peluso denied that the prosecution had done anything wrong. "The government is not required to expose the rest of its investigation in detail to these gentlemen, just because they want it," he concluded.

It wasn't until after my testimony that I learned that the tapes I had secretly recorded with FBI approval had complicated the criminal trial.

At 10 A.M., unaware of what had transpired in court without me, I confidently returned to the witness stand, drew a deep breath, and sat down for a long day of grilling. I steeled myself against the defense team's unsubstantiated attacks. David Geneson continued his cross-examination, battering me with questions delivered with a sneer. He asked me to explain my "cooperating witness" arrangement and detail the secret tapes I'd made. He introduced many documents into evidence and asked me to recall the Fawcett interest issue meeting five years earlier with Whiteside, Neeb, and Jarrell. Geneson intended to convince the jury that my motive was greed. After all, I'd filed not just one but two *qui tam* lawsuits against huge international corporations.

"There's a big bounty for the relator, for the person who comes to the government in secret," Geneson pointed out. "You can get between 15 percent and 25 percent of whatever money the government gets, right?"

"That's correct. That's the way the law is," I answered.

"And you've also brought a *qui tam* suit against KPMG Peat Marwick, right?" Geneson said. "That's correct," I responded.

"That's another one of those secret suits. As a matter of fact, the first time it was public was in this courtroom, right?" "Correct," I said plainly. I couldn't deny that I had filed the lawsuits. Geneson's attack, while tedious, was designed to make one specific point: that unlike anyone at Columbia/HCA, my actions were driven by greed.

As he wrapped up his cross-examination, Geneson made one final attempt to tarnish my character. "Mr. Schilling, is it not true that it was your idea, not Jay Jarrell's, to hire Thuan Tran, if necessary, to divert her from the Fawcett interest issue?"

Shocked by this blatant lie masked as a question, I took a deep breath. Regaining my composure, I chuckled softly. *You've tried throwing me a curveball, Mr. Geneson,* I thought. *But you just gave me a hole to smack that ball through.* Mulling the question over for a minute, I nearly laughed out loud at his nonsensical assertion. I was the low man on the totem pole and the least likely to have masterminded such a plot. I had no authority and possessed absolutely no hiring abilities at Columbia/HCA.

I replied vehemently that it was not my idea to hire the auditor, nor would I have been able to. I told him he was completely wrong. With that, Geneson concluded his cross-examination.

It was late afternoon when another member of the defense tag team—Jarrell's attorney, Peter George—came at me swinging. Unlike Lembcke or Geneson, George was tall and intimidating, like Jarrell. Of the three lawyers so far, he appeared to be the most confident and ruthless, almost like a schoolyard bully. He began cross-examining me about the two *qui tam* lawsuits I'd filed and my role as a governmental cooperating witness.

Holding my resume in his hand, he inquired about my consulting arrangement with Columbia/HCA. "And you sent this resume in to Ms. Gaffney after you had been meeting with the FBI for a period of time?" he asked, referring to Robin Gaffney, Columbia's reimbursement reporting manager in Winter Park. "Correct," I stated.

"You also didn't put on the resume that you had agreed to come back to Columbia with the approval and blessings and urging of the FBI, did you?" "No."

George began questioning me about each employee I'd supposedly deceived when rehired at Columbia/HCA. Irritated by this line of questioning, Mosakowski objected. "Now we're going to go over a litany of the list. It's just a waste of time, Judge. If he says I taped seven people I worked with. . . . Writing it on the board just seems a huge waste of large amounts of time. . . . Judge, I object."

George responded, "Now, this is a key witness in this case. And I believe, with all due respect to Mr. Mosakowski, that I'm entitled to show this jury every single time he has deceived somebody, whether he wants to call it that or not, to show the extent of his duplicity in this case. And it's not a waste of time and it's key to our defense."

"Well, let me tell you," began Judge Bucklew, "when you repeat again and again, it is a waste of all of our time. And not only do I find it a waste, I'm sure the jury does, too. And some of these things have been asked by your brethren here who have cross-examined this witness before. We've been over some of the same things with at least Mr. Geneson and I was going back to see if it was perhaps Mr. Lembcke, too."

Finally, when the legal bickering had subsided and I was given the opportunity to respond, I answered George. I reminded him that under the law I had not been at liberty to disclose my *qui tam* to anyone while it was under seal. Then, addressing George's claim that I had stolen thousands of documents from Columbia/HCA to help my lawsuit, I said, "I thought I needed to copy information to show there was fraud."

George further questioned why I hadn't disclosed the Fawcett interest issue to the auditors, even though I had had plenty of opportunities. I said that I feared losing my job. "I thought by bringing it up to my superiors, they were going to disclose it." At 5 P.M., George wrapped up his cross-examination and Judge Bucklew dismissed the jury for the day.

Excused from the witness stand, I walked out of the courtroom and stopped in the witness room to wait for Meagher and Scudieri. Twenty minutes later, amid congratulations on surviving another day, they whisked me out of the courthouse.

Back at my hotel, I called Kirsten to recount another day of bruising cross-examination without giving her any details. She and I both hoped that tomorrow would be my last day on the witness stand. That glimmer of hope kept me focused and moderately sane. "I love you. Remember how proud I am of you," she said.

I woke the following day to a sense of relief mixed with apprehension. Today was my last scheduled day on the witness stand. Outside the sun was just peeking through the buildings across the street. *Just one more day of testimony*, I thought. At 8 A.M., Meagher and I relished what we hoped would be our final drive to the courthouse together.

While I waited in the witness room, Judge Bucklew addressed the defense motion for a mistrial. "There is no reason the tapes should be turned over and there is no reason for this court to grant a mistrial due to the government's failure to turn the tapes over," she said, explaining her ruling to the assembled attorneys. "Furthermore, there's no reason to strike Mr. Schilling's testimony—absolutely none."

Meanwhile, back in the witness room, I was abruptly startled from my reverie thinking about Alex's Little League team. Amy Ciampa, the controller at Southwest Florida Regional Medical Center, entered the room and glanced quickly at me. She took a vacant seat across the table from me.

After I had resigned from the hospital, I was told that Ciampa had fingered me as the whistleblower. The irony of the situation did not escape me as we sat across from each other, alone in the room. She was right. I was the whistleblower. We made polite small talk, revealing nothing of importance, until I was called into the courtroom.

Glancing at the defendants as I entered the courtroom, I felt glad I wasn't in their shoes right now. Judge Bucklew reminded me I remained under oath as I took my seat. There were no surprises in Mosakowski's short redirect. *This is a piece of cake,* I thought, coming after yesterday's onslaught. But it wasn't over yet.

The defense quickly took the floor. Judge Bucklew warned Lembcke several times that his questions, which the judge said introduced information not discussed in Mosakowski's redirect, were out of the scope of his re-cross. But Lembcke, like a windup toy programmed with only one direction, was undeterred and continued. Annoyed, Judge Bucklew had enough.

She bellowed, "Please approach sidebar. I just need Mr. Lembcke and Mr. Mosakowski. Now, I've about had it. This is outside the scope and you know I'm very strict about re-cross and none of this was asked on his redirect, so don't push me or I'm going to tell you to sit down in front of the jury. Mr. Lembcke, this is outside the scope. And you either ask a question on the redirect or don't ask questions. Otherwise, I'm going to tell you to sit down." Shortly after his reprimand, Lembcke wrapped up his lengthy re-cross.

Geneson and George then took their turns. Each painted me as an aspiring instant millionaire who filed two *qui tam* lawsuits. They claimed that I didn't disclose the problems to government auditors because I was motivated only by money, not righting a wrong. They finished around 11 A.M. and I breathed a controlled sigh of relief, even though I wanted to leap off the witness stand and dance out of the courtroom to celebrate. But I remained composed—I am an accountant, after all—and carefully strode down the aisle and out the courtroom door. Before I entered the witness room, Joe Ford who had sat at the prosecutors table during my testimony grabbed my arm and ushered me down the hallway. "Great job, John! You did well. Kathleen is so pleased with your testimony," he gushed. "Thanks," I responded.

Always the FBI agent, Ford blurted hurriedly, "I can't talk now, but we will be in touch." "Okay. Good luck with the rest of the trial," I muttered quickly as Ford returned to the courtroom.

I turned to find Scudieri at my elbow. "Congratulations! Job well done, John. Let's get your paperwork done so you can get out of here."

Guiding me to the government's witness coordinator, I completed official-looking forms so I could be reimbursed for my travel expenses and paid the $40 per day fee for testifying. That didn't go smoothly. For almost thirty minutes, the witness coordinator questioned every expense I'd incurred. Finally convinced that my expenses were legitimate, she approved the paperwork, sending me to the U.S. Marshal's office to procure a check. It took another forty-five minutes to collect the check.

"Be ready at 6 P.M. Stephen and I are taking you out for a celebratory dinner tonight," Scudieri reminded me.

Relief swept over me when I entered the hotel room. My fingers dialed my home phone number and Kirsten answered. "It's finally over! I am done testifying," I excitedly told her. "How did it go today?" she asked.

"It was short. I was only on the stand for two hours. I can't tell you how relieved I am. I can't wait to be home. Maybe now the civil cases can begin to move. You know Stephen previously told me the criminal trial has slowed the civil case way down. There's no action right now. Columbia/HCA was waiting to see the outcome of the trial before it made its next move."

"Well, don't hold your breath. In any case, we can't wait to see you tomorrow," Kirsten replied.

Happy to be shedding my suit, I pulled on shorts and a T-shirt. The boardwalk beckoned from below my hotel window. The tropical sun warmed my skin on this typical June afternoon. The courtroom always felt cold to me, with the ventilation system blasting arctic air. After being in that artificial environment, it was a pleasure to walk along the board-walk bordered by mangrove trees and imagine the tropical wildlife beyond my view. As I approached the end of the boardwalk, I felt like I had stumbled into a kind of natural nirvana. The air was still, fragrant, and peaceful. Heron, ibis, and other exotic birds scanned the tall grasses for food.

Then it hit me how truly naive I'd been when I started working for Columbia. The truth had always hidden just beyond my view. I was disheartened to find men whom I respected lying and cheating. The truth seemed clearer to me now. The men sitting in the courtroom today, with whom I'd worked and socialized, had been motivated by dishonesty, ignorance, and greed. There had been so many choices in the past six years. I chose to tell the truth and chose to right a wrong. They hadn't. Whatever the trial's outcome, I knew I could live with the choices I'd made. I wondered if they could.

That evening, my legal team and I celebrated at legendary Bern's Steakhouse. We toasted the end of my testimony with a 1979 bottle of Clos des Papes, Chateauneuf du Pape, a great French wine I could barely pronounce and couldn't yet afford. I was told that as the prosecution's lead witness, I'd scored many points against the defense. Meagher was confident that my testimony had been very damaging to the defendants. He complimented me on my composure throughout the ordeal.

Meagher told me that my friend and former confidant, Larry Bomar, had taken the witness stand as the government's last witness that afternoon. His testimony was consistent with mine. He also claimed that his job would have been at stake if he were to have disclosed the Fawcett interest issue.

(According to trial transcripts, Bomar testified that Whiteside entered his office one day in casual clothes while saying his farewell to his Florida colleagues before departing for Nashville and his new corporate position. "And he walked in the office and he was standing by the door, the door was wide open, and he was—kind of had his arms at his back just kind of leaning against the wall like this," Bomar explained, demonstrating Whiteside's body language. "But [in] his parting words . . . he basically told me that if the Fawcett interest issue was ever discovered under my watch, I would probably lose my employment with Columbia/HCA."

In the end, it was this little piece of innocuous testimony and Bomar's description of Whiteside's body language that would convince one juror that Whiteside was guilty. Bomar confirmed that Jarrell suggested that Columbia/HCA should hire Thuan Tran if she ever uncovered the Fawcett interest issue.) Court ended that day while Bomar was midway in his direct examination, Meagher related.

Our last supper was fabulous and the celebration ended with dessert upstairs in the famous Harry Waugh Dessert Room. Meagher and Scudieri congratulated me again as we left. Full and jubilant, I was looking forward to finally going home.

Once I arrived home, my family eagerly asked about the trial. I told them I was relieved it was over. Testifying in the criminal trial was not only stressful but also physically and emotionally challenging. I hoped it was a once-in-a-lifetime experience, an experience I never wanted to repeat. I described the court proceedings and the atmosphere of the crowded courtroom.

While the trial had been serious, there were some odd questions and lighter moments. One stood out and I related it to my family. Whiteside's attorney, Lembcke, once accidentally addressed me as "Mary" during his cross-examination. My family chuckled, just as the courtroom gallery had. At the time Lembcke stumbled, I paused, scrunched up my eyebrows, and asked myself if I'd heard him correctly. Lembcke quickly realized his mistake, apologized, and moved on.

I'd been barred from reading press accounts of the trial during the period in which I was under oath and testified. And while the government and my legal team were pleased by my performance, I told my family that I was anxious to discover what reporters wrote and how the trial played in the media.

That evening, as I read one of the many articles about my testimony, I received a call from my friend, Jim Alderson. He said he was closely monitoring the trial while receiving updates from Meagher. "You should be proud, John," Alderson said. "From all accounts you held up well. I give you a lot of credit for what you did."

His observations paralleled what reporters wrote in the articles I read that night. The media called me a reliable witness with a compelling and believable story. They observed that my testimony had damaged the defense, yet the trial was far from over.

CHAPTER NINETEEN

Defense and Closing Arguments

It was a relief to be home with the stress of the trial behind me. Yet when asked about it, I found it cathartic to rehash the gauntlet of cross-examination I'd endured. My family and co-workers were interested in what it was like to testify in federal court. Before long, though, things returned to normal at work, and with the help of my colleagues, I was able to focus on developing new healthcare fraud cases at United Government Services.

At home, baseball was the primary topic of conversation around our dinner table. Alex's Little League team was still undefeated.

Stephen Meagher reported to me on how the trial was progressing. He said that Larry Bomar had been an excellent witness for the prosecution. His testimony was consistent with mine. Meagher said that Bomar also testified about the June 1995 meeting with Bonnie Reid to discuss the Fawcett interest issue. AUSA Kathleen Haley asked if he remembered what occurred at that meeting.

"Was some decision made with respect to disclosing this issue to the intermediary?" Haley asked.

"Yes," Bomar said. "Bonnie Reid made the determination not to disclose it, to file the '94 as the previous several years."

"Did you agree with that determination?" Haley asked, to which Bomar replied, "No, I did not." Bomar explained that the proper course of action would have been to disclose the error to the intermediary.

While Bomar and I were only two of the forty witnesses called by the government, our testimony had most severely damaged the defense. "If the prosecution succeeds in this case," Meagher predicted, "the investigation into Columbia/HCA will only intensify. Hopefully, it will result in a quicker civil settlement."

After the prosecution rested its position, the defense team began to call witnesses in the trial. Jay Jarrell's attorney, Peter George, called character witnesses, experts, and finally Jarrell himself, who began his testimony by denying all of the charges in the indictment. After denying guilt on each count, Jarrell said, "From the first time the Fawcett debt issue came to my attention, I concluded without any doubt in my mind that the debt was completely capital-related. That was my opinion then and that is my opinion now."

George asked Jarrell, who described himself as a Hoosier who grew up in a small Indiana town, to discuss his background and work experiences. George also asked Jarrell to explain his responsibilities at Columbia/HCA. In his direct testimony, Jarrell tried to distance himself from the alleged fraud. "I didn't review cost reports. I wasn't involved with the preparation of cost reports," he said, while acknowledging that he was responsible for supervising the reimbursement department. He didn't recall participating in the Fawcett interest issue meeting in the spring of 1994 or remember the discussion about which Bomar had testified.

Jarrell also denied suggesting the company "hire the auditor" at the meeting I'd attended in Port Charlotte. Recalling my testimony, he exclaimed, "There is no way I would have said what he said I said."

Even under prosecutor Tony Peluso's cross-examination, Jarrell repeatedly failed to recall the Fawcett interest meeting or the conversations Bomar and I had had with him about hiring the Medicare auditor. He maintained his innocence, denying that he'd participated in fraud. "There is no way Columbia or I would do anything fraudulent or illegal related to $3.5 million or any other amount. This issue, despite this trial, was not a focused or major issue to Columbia. . . . It was a reserve item out of a thousand reserve items, which everybody in the company in the financial reimbursement area probably knew about and could see," Jarrell said.

While his testimony didn't hurt him or the government, his confirmation that the Fawcett interest issue "was a reserve item out of a thousand reserve items" corroborated my allegations in my civil lawsuit. This company had prepared thousands of reserve cost reports, some legitimate, but probably some illicit.

Once on the stand, Mike Neeb's defense attorney, David Geneson, asked him routine background questions about his education and CFO responsibilities and then asked him to recall the Fawcett interest meeting in April 1994. Neeb said that during the meeting, "Jay explained that the legal opinion did not require us to disclose any inconsistency that the FI may have had in the treatment of this interest, and that it allowed us to continue to file the interest at 100 percent."

Courtroom trial transcripts show Neeb relating a contrasting version of the meeting, accusing me of suggesting ways to divert the attention of Medicare auditor Thuan Tran. And while admitting that there was a to-do list, including the "hire her" notation, Neeb said that no one had been assigned any of the tasks.

Contradicting himself minutes later, he said, "No. Jay specifically said we're not going to do any of these things. We're going to wait and see if she calls back. And in the meantime we're going to go out and do all these to-dos so we'll be ready to defend our position." The truth was that he had suggested items for the list while I took notes, and later he repeatedly contacted me to update the status of the to-do items assigned to me.

After hearing about his testimony, I concluded that Neeb couldn't distinguish the truth from lies. I had already testified that it was Neeb, not Jarrell, who wanted Bob Whiteside and me to review the 1993 cost report to make sure the reserves allocated for this issue were correct. Neeb had told us he didn't want to take a financial hit at a hospital he led.

Bob Mosakowski cross-examined Neeb, who feigned any prior knowledge of the meeting's purpose or who'd requested it. He didn't remember discussing the interest issue with anyone, including Whiteside, before the meeting. Nor did he remember asking me to repeat the conversation with Tran before Jarrell joined us at the meeting on the phone. In fact, he said he didn't know why the meeting was even called. He agreed that I was Whiteside's assistant, but recalled that most items on the to-do list were suggested by me, even though I was the low man on the totem pole.

Mosakowski didn't score many points in his cross-examination of Neeb, whose story differed so dramatically from mine that it was difficult to discern the truth from the lies. Though he was the hospital CFO at the time, Neeb tried to portray himself as a mere observer, rather than a participant. Who was the jury to believe?

Charles Lembcke took the floor next, calling his client and my former manager, Whiteside, to the stand. Lembcke asked Whiteside what was the most important thing he wanted the jury to know. "I want this jury to know and I want the judge to know and I want everybody to know that I haven't done anything wrong. And this is the first chance I've had to tell anybody that, other than the defense team," Whiteside said.

He denied having the conversations that Bomar and I had testified about and painted a very different picture. "If I had the slightest inkling there was anything fraudulent about it, I would have told everyone in that room," he told the jury.

When it was her turn, Haley stood and addressed Whiteside. "Mr. Whiteside, isn't it fair to say that the ultimate decision as to whether or not a fiscal intermediary should be contacted and told about this problem, this interest issue at Fawcett Memorial Hospital, was Mr. Jarrell's?" she asked. "I don't believe so," Whiteside replied. Haley responded, "You didn't go out—you didn't volunteer any information to the fiscal intermediary, did you?"

Though he once was director of reimbursement at the Fort Myers division office, he was still trying to distance himself. He responded, "In the April meeting we found out we didn't have all the information and we asked Mr. Schilling to gather that and forward the information up to Trish Lindler. I expected that if an issue would come up, Ms. Lindler would follow up on it. She had done that in the past."

"Mr. Whiteside, I asked you, you never contacted the fiscal intermediary about this, did you?" Haley said. "No, I did not. I didn't have the information," he answered.

"You never called the OIG [Office of the Inspector General] hot line about this, did you?"

"No, I did not."

"You never dialed Columbia's compliance number and talked to anybody about this, did you?"

"No, I did not."

Whiteside downplayed the significance of the issue, indicating that it was one of thousands of issues, and the amount due back to Medicare would have been relatively minimal.

Haley continued, "So your superiors at Columbia would have been just thrilled if all of a sudden they had to come up with $3.5 million?"

"Three and one-half million dollars to a $20 billion company is not very much. They would not have been upset because it would have no bottom-line impact," Whiteside responded.

Whiteside testified that because he was taking a promotion and moving to Nashville, he was no longer my supervisor, further removing himself from the issue. He said, falsely, that he had urged me many times to contact my new supervisor, Lindler, about the issue.

Whiteside also described the Fawcett interest issue as not seeming "like a big deal to me at the time," but noted that "I did make sure that Mr. Schilling had it on his list to talk to her [Lindler] about it." Trying to pin him down, Haley pointed out that, "One little call from you and she would have been aware of the issue, isn't that right?"

"She was aware of the issue in '94. It was on the list of issues given to her," Whiteside explained.

"By whom?" she asked.

"By Mr. Schilling."

"You just said he didn't reach out and contact her."

"Uh, in June of '94 she did come down to Fort Myers and they sat down and met. He told me before I left that it would be on the list. I cannot swear that it was on the list when he gave to it her."

"Didn't you just testify that you told John Schilling to let Trish Lindler know about it, and that he did not? . . . ."

"I know he met with her in June, because later on I saw a memo that said the issue was brought up in a June meeting with Lindler." While he couldn't remember the date of his last day in the Fort Myers office and swore he'd never met with Lindler there, in reality, Whiteside had joined Lindler in our office that day as well.

At times during the intense three-hour cross-examination by Haley, Whiteside grew testy and argumentative. Haley had scored several points for the government, while Whiteside was unsuccessful in dodging her blows.

The last defendant to testify was Carl Lynn Dick. His attorney, Bill Jung, asked Dick to describe the Fawcett interest issue. Dick's version differed slightly from the story that Steve Dudley had told. Dick called Dudley the executive making the reimbursement decisions, not him. Jung asked, "Who was the go-to guy at BAMI on Medicare?" "Uh, go-to guy would be Mr. Dudley," said Dick, "and if he didn't have the answer, why then we would go to the outside consultants."

"When was the first time that you were aware that Steve Dudley had counterfeited a Price Waterhouse work paper and sent it to an auditor to deceive the auditor?" Jung asked. "About three months ago," Dick replied.

"In your entire life, have you heard of such a thing?" Jung asked. "Uh, no, I haven't."

Peluso's cross-examination of Dick was like a lopsided boxing match, and Dick seemed unable to recover from Peluso's punches. At one point, Dick became confused and stumbled with his response.

Peluso asked, "Is it your testimony before this court now in June of 1999 that in May of 1989 you did not know that the fiscal intermediary, in addressing the 1985 and 1986 cost reports, had determined that the capital treatment should be reduced from 100 percent to 39 percent? Is that your testimony?"

Dick responded, "In, uh—in May of 1999 I believe that the intermediary had, uh, done their work, uh, and had, uh, in March proposed adjustments on the 19—uh, uh, that '86 cost report. That's—that's—that's my recollection."

Throughout his testimony, Dick refuted many of Dudley's statements and specifically denied that Dudley ever told him the cost report claims were suspect. Dick claimed Dudley knew more about Medicare reimbursement than anyone else in the company. After wrapping up Dick's testimony, the defense rested its case.

That evening in our phone conversation about the trial, Meagher confirmed that Dick fared poorly under the rigorous cross-examination. He said the government was pleased with how the case was proceeding and would not call me back to the stand. That news relieved us both. Prosecutors intimated to Meagher their confidence in trying the case. Closing arguments now represented the last opportunity to persuade the jury.

It was June 28, 1999, and once again, Judge Bucklew's courtroom was overflowing. The case would go to the jury for deliberation immediately after closing arguments. The twelve-member jury would decide the fates of the four men charged with Medicare fraud.

Mosakowski presented the government's closing arguments. "Basically, the defendants exploited weaknesses in the auditing system of Blue Cross/Blue Shield, found a mistake, covered it up, and continued to file false cost reports to conceal that money, keep the money that the auditors mistakenly permitted them to have, and to claim falsely more money in the future," he summarized. He recounted the government's case against the four defendants and why the jurors should find them guilty. The importance of the witnesses' testimony and the evidence that had been presented could not be overlooked, he told the jury. Of specific importance was the testimony and actions of three key witnesses.

"Now, you saw Mr. Dudley. He's sort of a mousy-type guy up here. Do you think he made this decision on his own? How many times did he tell you he's not going to keep his boss informed? He's going to call the shots? Uh-uh," Mosakowski answered, shaking his head. "And Mr. Dudley is scared he's going to lose his job."

Then in vivid detail he recalled for the jury my story of what had happened. He explained how I was hired in July 1993 and had been at Columbia for less than a year when I spoke with the Medicare auditor, Thuan Tran, who was charged with reviewing Fawcett's cost reports for her employer, Blue Cross & Blue Shield of Florida, the Medicare fiscal intermediary. Mosakowski told how Tran was conducting an audit of a 1991 cost report and asked in passing if I knew anything about a reopening of a 1980s cost report from Fawcett. Mosakowski reiterated that I didn't, but offered to look into it for her.

"At that point she's asking him the question. And Mr. Whiteside's not around, so he calls Jim Burns and asks him. And Burns, the controller over at Fawcett Memorial Hospital, says, 'Gee, you know, it probably has something to do with all those big reserves, those interest reserves we have on the books.' So, Whiteside comes back and Mr. Schilling asks him about it," the prosecutor explained.

"And Mr. Whiteside says, the fiscal intermediary, the auditor, made a mistake in the past. Don't do anything about it, just let it lie. And Mr. Whiteside, by that time, knows enough about it. He's been talking to Mr. Jarrell on the reserve issue. Mr. Jarrell knows there's a mistake, which we just looked at. That's where Mr. Whiteside got it. The intermediary made a mistake. Let it lie," Mosakowski recapped.

Mosakowski also recounted when Whiteside came into my office the next day hopping mad. "He says, '. . . I don't appreciate being put on the hot seat with Neeb.' He talks about the issue, says gather up some information. We got to go to a meeting tomorrow. People could lose their jobs if this got out. . . . We're talking three-and-a-half million dollars if the intermediary gets wind of the mistake."

Mosakowski told how Whiteside and Neeb downplayed the significance of the Medicare overpayment within the large corporation. "Now, during their testimony, Mr. Whiteside and Mr. Neeb said, yeah, but you know, Columbia's worth $20 billion, it doesn't matter if we have to pay three-

and-a-half million dollars—nothing. Like it's a joke, you know, half-a-million here, half-a-million there, pretty soon you're talking about real money. But, you know, you heard the testimony of Mr. Neeb. He got up there to tell you about it on his direct testimony and he wanted to tell you about his family and he wanted to tell you where he went to school and he told you he went to Jesuit High School. . . . And one of the things he tells you about is how he saved the company $50,000 one year. Fifty thousand dollars was important enough to him to tell you about it while he's on trial and wants you to get to know him. . . . Fifty thousand dollars . . . in that story was a lot of money to him." The prosecutor pointed out that Neeb was very proud of the commendation and letter he received for saving the company that $50,000.

He went on, ". . . Three-and-a-half-million dollars means a lot to a publicly held for-profit company. That's how they get $20 billion, because they keep making money and not throwing it away. It would mean a lot to them to have to call up and say, we need this money. And it's just silly to say it's not—that it doesn't."

Summarizing the Fawcett interest meeting, Mosakowski continued, "According to Schilling, they were worried about reopenings and one of the first things Mr. Jarrell talks about is this legal opinion. . . . What does the legal opinion do for them, other than provide some sort of shield if these draconian penalties are going to be attached?" He suggested that the effort to obtain a legal opinion was a cynical ploy to cover their tails if the problem was uncovered and things went bad. "That's what this opinion says. That's all it says. Not much of a shield at all, except [for] fraud penalties. . . ."

Mosakowski described the men panicking over the possibility that the Medicare auditors would find out about the cost report overpayment. "Why the panic? Mr. Schilling told you why. Because they were scared they were going to reopen. And when they reopened, at a minimum there was a good chance that the money would be taken away for years while they have to appeal it. And actually they'd never get it back because there's nothing in the books and records."

Mosakowski discussed the conspiracy of diverting the Medicare auditor. "So, they want to make sure she doesn't discover it. So they come up with suggestions on how they're going to divert her. Now, Mr. Jarrell, of course, once again, doesn't recall this. 'I don't even recall the phone call, but I wouldn't have done that because I wouldn't do anything illegal.' So he knows it's illegal to divert an auditor, but we have two other individuals say he said hire her, three—Mr. Schilling, Mr. Neeb, and Mr. Whiteside. These guys are all auditors, former auditors. Two of them worked for the fiscal intermediary. All CPAs. They know you're not allowed to divert her," he said. "It's against the law. They know that."

Mosakowski then summarized Bomar's testimony and Whiteside's job threat. "Mr. Bomar was down at Port Charlotte and he's standing there in the office and Mr. Whiteside comes in to say good-bye and says, 'You could lose your job if the interest issue gets out.' Now, Mr. Whiteside is a friend of Mr. Bomar, who helped get him a job. Why would Mr. Bomar come in and make that up? What reason does he have to come in here and make that up? Mr. Jarrell talks to Mr. Bomar about reopenings. Mr. Bomar says Mr. Jarrell heard about the reopening involving Tran. We were talking about it. He says, can we hire her? . . . Mr. Jarrell can't remember that."

In his final attempt to sway the jury, Mosakowski shored up my testimony, which had been attacked by the defendants. "Now, Mr. Schilling filed a *qui tam* suit, no doubt about it. You'll hear a lot about it in the next couple of hours, I'm sure. But you saw his demeanor. You heard him testify. It's entirely consistent. He's corroborated by other documents in the file. It's corroborated by Mr. Bomar. And he told people before he left he tried to get this fixed," he recapped.

"No, he didn't call the IG [Inspector General] or the internal auditor, but he told his bosses. He told Larry Bomar and Bomar tried to fix it. They told Trish Lindler. They told her in January. He didn't go see a *qui tam* lawyer until February of '95, in January he went to Lindler. He put together a list in a memo to her and [Jerry] Glather in January before he saw . . . the lawyer."

He described other actions I took, including my letter to management disclosing my concerns with the Fawcett interest reserve and other inappropriate reserves. "Now, he's got a lawsuit. Maybe he should have reported it somewhere else, maybe he shouldn't have filed, but you know, it was his right under the law. It's a statute. If you don't like the law, talk to Congress," Mosakowski said. "He filed the lawsuit. But, you know, if they had listened to him in January of 1995, he wouldn't have had a lawsuit. Because if Trish Lindler hadn't retired in February, along with Helen Cummings [the vice president of reimbursement], and Glather hadn't been transferred, if somebody said, hey, this is nonsense, pick up the phone and call the fiscal intermediary, we'll write them a check, because $3.5 million isn't a big deal to Columbia, he wouldn't have a lawsuit."

He related my final meeting with Bonnie Reid before I left the company and how the company failed to report the overpayment. He recounted how I worked for the FBI, filed my suit, and told the agency about the fraud. "Did he report it to anybody? He reported it to the government, the Federal Bureau of Investigation, because it's a crime. And he filed his suit. They had an ongoing investigation of fraud and they asked him to cooperate with them and go undercover," Mosakowski explained. "Now, if you think that hurts his credibility because he assisted the United States government law enforcement authorities in an ongoing investigation concerning Medicare and healthcare fraud, then there's nothing I can say to really help you on that issue. But, ladies and gentlemen, he's corroborated anyway, and there's nothing wrong with helping the country ferret out crime. He's supposedly a liar because he didn't tell people he was wearing a wire under instructions from the FBI. Well, he wouldn't be very good as a covert individual . . . if he put on an FBI raid jacket and said, 'Speak into the mike' when he talked to them. . . . You'll have to decide if that impairs his credibility in any way."

He explained that the verdict in this case wouldn't directly affect me financially. "He's not suing these guys, he's suing Columbia," he said. "This isn't the only issue. The investigation he helped wasn't only this issue. . . . Would he be in a better position with a verdict of guilty in this case? Probably. Probably. You can assess that when you look at his credibility. But he's juxtaposed with the testimony of Bomar and all the documents."

Wrapping up his three hours of closing arguments, Mosakowski addressed the jury for the last time. "Ladies and gentlemen, they [the defendants] walked a line and they went over it real far. I submit, ladies and gentlemen—the government submits that the government has proven its case beyond a reasonable doubt. The defendants are guilty on all counts and all that remains if you . . . go back in the deliberation room and remember the testimony, look at the documents, apply your common sense and then say so."

Defense attorney George spoke next. "You must give Mr. Jarrell the benefit of the doubt and find him not guilty in this case unless the prosecutors' proof to your satisfaction is so convincing that it excludes any reasonable doubt, so convincing that it eliminates any real doubt, so convincing that you would act upon it and rely upon it in the most important of your own daily affairs without hesitation."

He told jurors that they must decide whether the government had met its heavy burden of proving that his client acted willfully with criminal intent. "Jay Jarrell always had a genuine good-faith belief that Fawcett Memorial Hospital was entitled to a 100 percent reimbursement from the time he first looked at it in 1986," George explained. "He believed it then and you heard him testify in this courtroom he believes it now. And he explained it to you and why he believed that."

He conceded that Jarrell suggested hiring the Medicare auditor. "But he said it . . . in a derisively joking manner," George added.

He portrayed me as a man with an incentive to lie, calling me, "the Lotto man . . . seeking to hit the jackpot . . . and become a multimillionaire before he turns forty. Now, would he . . . embellish, would he perhaps tell something other than the full truth if it would help him to get multimillions of dollars?" he asked.

He said Mosakowski wrapped me in the American flag as a wonderful person who wanted to help FBI Agent Ford. "He was helping himself more than helping Joe Ford. He was helping himself from being prosecuted, from being taken away from his family, from being arrested. He was helping himself on a whole lot of things because if anybody did anything wrong, Schilling was the one who was responsible for these things," he stated.

George described to jurors a deal he imagined I had made with the government. "I'll deceive my co-workers. I'll deceive everybody. I'll wear a wire, I'll steal documents," he theorized me thinking. "It was pretty easy and consistent with his own personal interest. And we know what he does when it's in his interest to do something. He tells half-truths, he misleads, he doesn't tell his co-workers what he's doing. . . . What it shows you is Mr. Schilling is capable of successfully deceiving," George said, describing how I allegedly lied to co-workers and secretly stole 12,000 documents.

"He got away with it. He was good at it. He's good at deception. He's good when it's in his interest at telling the half-truth, ladies and gentlemen, so factor that in when you think about John Schilling and what really went on at that meeting in 1994," he said, nearing the end of his ninety-minute closing statements.

He cited government mistakes in the case and asked jurors to question the motivations of people like Steve Dudley who were given immunity to testify. "Think about that. Think about when you tell someone okay, I'm not going to prosecute you, I'm not going to take you away from your children. And you saw they all said, well, I got immunity if I tell the truth," he said, hoping to plant doubts in jurors' minds.

He reminded jurors that Judge Bucklew would instruct them to consider the testimony of witnesses who were given immunity (Dudley and Bomar) with great caution. "They're not normal witnesses. They didn't bring you witnesses who have no reason, who have no bias, who have no interest in the case. Those are their key witnesses, ladies and gentlemen," he concluded. "Those are their key witnesses."

Neeb's attorney, David Geneson, didn't waste much time before attacking my credibility and version of the Fawcett interest meeting. "He becomes an important witness because it's his testimony that sort of makes this case," Geneson said, suggesting I exaggerated the importance of that early meeting to support my lawsuit. "If there's nothing bad going on at that meeting, it's just another meeting. . . . They would have you believe that meeting was evil."

Geneson painted me as a skilled, well-trained witness who lied for money. "Mr. Schilling needed a bad meeting, so he created a bad meeting," he said. "Ladies and gentlemen, Mike Neeb had a good basis of reliance; he had a good basis to trust." But he said Neeb was never offered a chance to explain his version of events. "Ladies and gentlemen, I'm going to ask you to go back in the jury room and deliberate and send this man home, . . . make him free of this two-year nightmare. Send him home to his family, to his wife and his children."

Whiteside's attorney, Lembcke, followed. The government he explained was prosecuting an innocent man who had no responsibility for any crimes committed. "And in this case, the government argues that Bob Whiteside should have done things that were not part of his job, that were not part of those responsibilities, that he should have done things that other people were required to do," Lembcke said. "And that's unfair. That's not right."

Lembcke again related Whiteside's version of events. Lembcke rationalized that other cooperating witnesses and I may have feared for our jobs because of Columbia/HCA's many mergers during that period. "People become afraid of their jobs," he said, adding that Whiteside "never told

John Schilling he would lose his job because he wasn't going to lose his job. If he took it that way, that's fine."

He said if I had discovered fraud, Whiteside would have told me to report any fraud. "And you are to report it with sufficient clarity and with sufficient information to enable the company to go and to work on that and to find out the fraud," Lembcke recounted what Whiteside would have said.

Lembcke also attempted to shift jurors' attention away from the criminal charges against his client to my *qui tam* lawsuit. "He didn't go to a lawyer in Fort Myers or Port Charlotte. He didn't go to a criminal lawyer because he was concerned. He didn't go to a civil lawyer just because he wanted some information. He called Washington, D.C., for a *qui tam*, a very specific lawyer," he said, trying to tarnish my motivation.

Lembcke asked jurors to find his client not guilty. "He was a good director of reimbursement, a prospective, operational reimbursement person. He addressed the issues. He relied upon the people around him and he handled them appropriately. I've showed it to you repeatedly throughout here, he handled it appropriately," he concluded. "And when you look at all the evidence, conclude that Bob Whiteside is not guilty of each and every crime that he's charged with."

Finally, Dick's attorney, Bill Jung, tried convincing the jurors one last time. "I am telling you this man is innocent. If you convict Lynn Dick, you have convicted an innocent man," Jung said, noting, "Mr. Dick—he's not slick, he's not a glib talker, fast talker, stammered to my questions, stammered to Mr. Peluso's questions, but he got on the stand and told you the truth. The truth—the sound of the truth isn't the sound of slick, glib, fast talk."

Jung tarred the chief witness against his client, Steve Dudley, as a man who had created a false document. "He knew it was false and he didn't want anybody to find out about it, but he was afraid that it would lead to his trouble. And you know what was Mr. Dudley's motivation?" he asked jurors. "May the 7th he testified without objection that he didn't want to be indicted, facing felony counts with five-year prison terms, and he didn't want to go to prison." He implored jurors to acquit his client. "Lynn Dick's life and that of his wife is in your hands. I pray to God that you see the truth. He is not guilty."

AUSA Haley addressed the jury for the government's rebuttal, answering the attacks made by the defendant's counsel. She began by acknowledging my interest in the outcome of this case. "He's got a lawsuit," she said, quickly adding, "Each and every one of these defendants has an interest in the outcome of this case. And it doesn't have anything to do money, ladies and gentlemen."

She posed questions to jurors to help them assess the credibility of the witnesses they had heard. "Did the witness impress you as one who was telling the truth? Did the witness have any particular reason not to tell the truth? Did the witness have a personal interest in the outcome of the case?" she inquired. "I respectively submit to you, ladies and gentlemen, that these defendants definitely have a personal interest in the outcome of this case. Did the witness seem to have a good memory? Some people remembered more things than others. Mr. Jarrell didn't remember much. Did the witness have the opportunity and ability to observe accurately the things he or she testified about? Did the witness appear to understand the questions clearly and answer them directly?"

She recounted how Geneson told jurors that his client, Neeb, looked them right in the eye and told his story. "Well, you looked at him. Was he looking you right in the eye in cross? Were these defendants looking you right in the eye on cross-examination? Contrast the polished, I would suggest, rehearsed testimony you heard on direct examination, and then look at what the defendants did on cross. Poor Mr. Whiteside was so nervous he spilled water. He was a wreck. The demeanor is something . . . you could take into consideration, ladies and gentlemen. And finally, did the witness's testimony differ from other testimony or other evidence? The defendants chose to take the stand. They chose to take the stand and they can be judged the same as any other witness."

She said that in today's society when problems occur, everyone is looking for somebody else to blame. "You need to be accountable for your own actions. I'm going to ask you . . . to do the right thing," Haley instructed. "Hold these individuals personally accountable. Find them guilty of what they're charged with."

With that, the landmark trial ended after two months. Judge Bucklew carefully walked the jury through their instructions, and at 2:39 P.M. on June 29, 1999, the jury exited the courtroom to begin deliberations.

If convicted, Whiteside, Jarrell, and Neeb each faced maximum prison sentences of thirty-five years and $1.75 million in criminal fines and penalties. Dick faced five years in prison and a $250,000 fine.

It was disturbing to read their versions of what had happened and how they tried to distance themselves from any wrongdoing. They all described themselves to jurors as honest, law-abiding citizens who would not do anything wrong. They blamed me for the problem, saying they relied on my expertise. I was angry, but knew I couldn't do anything about it and hoped the jury would not believe their fabrications. (Years later, it was even more troubling to read the trial transcripts and see the lies the defendants told under oath.) If they truly were the honest, religious individuals they purported to be, why couldn't they take responsibility for their actions, I wondered.

While the defendants did not slander me, their attorneys had personally attacked me. I was warned, but it still stung. They called me thief, liar, snitch, mole, Lotto man, and a greedy, disgruntled employee.

Now that the trial had ended, I was free to follow news reports and speak with my attorneys. "Read the papers," Meagher suggested. "Every news organization was there."

Checking online often, I eagerly awaited the verdicts. My legal team was confident the government would secure the convictions they sought. Columbia/HCA and the hospital industry nervously awaited the outcome. It was up to the jury.

CHAPTER TWENTY

Convictions

The airports were crowded with holiday travelers as I flew back home to Wisconsin from a business trip on July 2, 1999. Dinner was on the table when the phone rang at 5 P.M. Groans resonated around the table. It wasn't Stephen Meagher, though. It was my dad calling from Fort Myers.

"John? The TV news just broke the story that Whiteside and Jarrell were convicted," my father said loudly, above the television noise in the background.

Surprised, I exclaimed, "Already?"

"Neeb," my dad continued, "was acquitted and the jury was hung in regard to Dick."

Just minutes before in Tampa, Judge Susan Bucklew's courtroom had quieted as the jurors entered at 4:43 P.M. They had deliberated for three and a half days. Clearing her throat, Bucklew prepared to hear the verdicts. "Madam Clerk," the judge was quoted in the trial transcripts, "I'm going to ask you to publish the verdicts and they're in order by indictment. Mr. Jarrell, sir, we're going to start with you. If you will rise. . . ."

The deputy clerk read the first verdict. "In the case of the United States of America versus Jay A. Jarrell, verdict: We, the jury, find the defendant Jay A. Jarrell as to Count 1, the offense of conspiracy: 'Guilty.' " The courtroom reverberated with both groans and sighs of relief.

The deputy clerk continued to read each count regarding Jarrell. The guilty finding was read after each count, except the seventh, of which he was found not guilty. Each time a guilty verdict was read, Jarrell shook his head, finally burying it in his hands. His wife, surrounded by friends, sobbed softly. A shell-shocked Jarrell slumped into his seat after hearing the final count read.

Judge Bucklew then asked Mike Neeb to rise. The deputy clerk pronounced him not guilty on every count. Neeb sighed and silently mouthed "thank you" to the jury.

Judge Bucklew then asked Bob Whiteside to rise. The clerk continued, reading the jury's finding of guilty of all but the seventh count. Whiteside appeared stunned but showed no strong emotion except to hang his head as he took his seat.

Finally, the judge asked Carl Lynn Dick to rise and addressed him, saying, "Mr. Dick, the jury has been unable to reach a verdict as to Count 1, the offense of conspiracy." (Two months later on September 16, 1999, Dick entered a plea agreement with the government. Although the details of the agreement were not made public, legal analysts speculated that he would cooperate with the continued investigation into Columbia/HCA if the government agreed not to retry him.)

The courtroom stirred as reporters scurried out to file their stories or go live on the evening news with the verdicts in this drama.

Judge Bucklew immediately scheduled a sentencing hearing for October 15, 1999, allowing Jarrell and Whiteside to remain free on bond until then. As the courtroom cleared, Jarrell's wife, eyes red from crying, confronted prosecutor Tony Peluso in the hallway. "Are you happy? Are you proud of what you've done?" she snapped. Peluso left without replying.

Back in Menomonee Falls, Kirsten and I discussed the news. It felt like I'd been vindicated. The jury had agreed that the men needed to take responsibility for failing to take action. I asked Kirsten to put dinner on hold so I could telephone Meagher. He had also heard the report and offered congratulations. Though it was only a partial conviction, he considered it a victory for the government.

"And you were a big part of their victory, John," he told me. "It shows that a jury that doesn't know the first thing about cost reports could figure it out. The jury understood the defendants got money they weren't entitled to; they knew it and they tried to cover it up. It shows people can be convicted of Medicare cost report fraud even though cost reports are complex."

He called it a landmark healthcare verdict. "This is the first time there has been a ruling from a jury that says if you get Medicare reimbursement to which you're not entitled and you know about it, you can't just sit on it and cover it up," he explained. "You've got to give it back."

Meagher predicted that other indictments would come. In addition, new criminal indictments should no longer delay my civil *qui tam* lawsuits, he said. In fact, the convictions could speed up a settlement. "This has a chance of unlocking what had been a gridlock in resolving the case," he reasoned.

Eight days later, the *St. Petersburg Times* published juror Kelly Permenter's account of the tense days of jury deliberations. Overwhelmed by the magnitude of evidence and testimony they'd witnessed, Permenter said, the jury floundered at first. Permenter recounted the jurors' frustrations with the amount of material they had been presented with. It seemed overwhelming. The jury struggled with Jarrell's inability to remember key events and Whiteside's professed lack of responsibility in the Fort Myers divisional office. During his testimony Larry Bomar had described Whiteside leaning against a wall as he issued Bomar a warning. During Whiteside's own testimony he leaned casually against the jury box in the same manner. That tidbit was enough to help the jury find the key witness (Bomar) credible. Permenter commented that the defendants should have considered their own families before perpetrating crimes.

The convictions bolstered speculation among news outlets, which consulted industry insiders and stock analysts to predict what the convictions meant to the company, HCA's stock, and the hospital industry. Some forecast more arrests and trials. Others believed that the convictions strengthened the government's position in the civil *qui tam* lawsuits, improving its bargaining position. Some speculated that HCA would settle for more than $1 billion.

Charles Wilson, the U.S. Attorney in Tampa, proclaimed, "The verdicts will have widespread implications for how healthcare providers will do business with the government," adding, "I think the verdict will make people think twice about cheating Medicare."

In press releases, Columbia/HCA expressed disappointment and sympathy for the families of the defendants, downplaying the significance of the criminal convictions by isolating the conduct to a single issue at one hospital and denying any company role in the incident. Furthermore, the company press release hypothesized that the jury verdict would not impact the ongoing settlement discussions between Columbia/HCA and the government. (In hindsight, I believe that Columbia/HCA manipulated the defendants as pawns in its legal chess match against the government. If the defendants had been able to defeat the government in this criminal trial, I think HCA believed that the civil *qui tam* lawsuits would lose steam and eventually disappear.)

The convictions exerted a chilling effect on the healthcare industry. Already, the industry was being more careful in its dealings with Medicare. The inspector general of the Department of Health and Human Services reported that stepped-up enforcement of Medicare laws by government regulators, increased funding and resources targeting fraud, and growing compliance by hospitals and other providers combined to slash improper Medicare payments by almost 50 percent from 1997 to 1998. Many experts in the field believed that industry fears about government investigations compelled healthcare companies to become more cautious in submitting their reimbursement claims. While the convictions would not stop all Medicare fraud, the government's victory sent a powerful message to healthcare providers. Jim Alderson and I believed that the massive investigation into Columbia/HCA's business practices convinced many providers that the risks weren't worth the rewards for committing healthcare fraud.

On December 3, 1999, Judge Bucklew sentenced Whiteside at a hearing in a virtually empty courtroom. Only a few reporters and a small contingent of family and friends and attorneys from both sides attended.

The judge asked Whiteside if he wished to speak. "No, ma'am," he responded quietly.

"Alright, Mr. Lembcke?" Charles Lembcke portrayed his client as a good person and pleaded for a light sentence.

Then Kathleen Haley addressed the judge. "Your Honor, obviously no one is really happy to do this to anyone. . . . However, we would like to point out that this defendant, together with his co-conspirators, actively chose to steal money from programs that have been set up by the government to assist the indigent, the elderly, and the members of the families of our armed forces," Haley said, noting that Whiteside knew the rules and regulations concerning reimbursement.

"And it was almost a game to them, your honor," Haley continued. "You heard the testimony: 'Well, if we get caught, we'll pay the money back.' And it was a joke that they were going to divert the auditor. I don't really believe that the defendants and Mr. Whiteside took this seriously until they actually got here. And it is a serious matter. . . . He actively chose to break the law, and he should be punished for it."

Judge Bucklew then asked Whiteside to stand at the podium, where she sentenced him to serve two years in prison and pay $645,796 in restitution and a fine of $7,500. She also sentenced him to probation upon release.

After court was dismissed, the few reporters waited patiently while Whiteside was photographed and fingerprinted. As a convicted healthcare felon, he would lose his CPA license and be barred from working in jobs funded by federal healthcare dollars. Columbia/HCA, which had placed him on paid leave throughout the investigation, would cut him from the payroll but continue to pay his legal fees during the appeal process. Lembcke vowed that Whiteside would appeal the conviction and requested that his client remain free pending appeal. "The judge was as fair and compassionate as she could be," Whiteside told reporters.

Later that month, on December 22, 1999, Jarrell appeared before Judge Bucklew to hear his fate. For three hours, Jarrell's attorney, Peter George, and the prosecutors—Bob Mosakowski, Haley, and Peluso—argued before the judge.

"Mr. George, is there anything that you would like to say, or is there—would Mr. Jarrell like to be heard regarding sentencing, either as to where I should sentence in that range, or anything else?" Judge Bucklew asked.

"This case, of course, has and will continue to bring grief to Mr. Jarrell and his family," George said. "And he is the sole breadwinner, if you will, in the family. He's already lost a great deal of his reputation. He will be losing his employment tomorrow. And I would only ask that the court sentence him at the lowest end of that particular guideline that we're at right now, Your Honor, so that he's not kept from his wife and children for any longer than is necessary. Thank you."

Looking straight ahead, Jarrell declined Judge Bucklew's offer to speak, saying in a monotone, "No, Your Honor, Mr. George has spoken for me."

However, Haley accepted the judge's offer to speak. "There's been much talk here today about how this is so different from a drug kingpin or a mob boss, but the bottom line is, this is money that is earmarked for individuals who are elderly, who are indigent, who are veterans and their families. And when these defendants, including Mr. Jarrell, agreed to participate in programs that would reimburse the hospitals that they ran, they made a promise to the United States that they would abide by the rules of the program," Haley said.

"In fact, each and every cost report that was filed on behalf of Fawcett Memorial Hospital contained a certification that it was accurate and correct and that it was based upon the books and records of the hospital. And further, that they would be subject to penalties if there was something in that report that was incorrect, and here we stand today. The jury has found these individuals guilty of filing fraudulent cost reports. They broke their promise to Medicare and to Medicaid. . . . I believe the industry is watching."

Haley described what she considered a prevailing "anything goes until they're caught" attitude endemic in the hospital industry, an industry closely watching the verdicts and sentencing. She mentioned another Medicare cost report case, cautioning providers against playing cat-and-mouse games with Medicare. "I believe in terms of a deterrent it's sending a message to the community, to the provider community, that it's important to sentence Mr. Jarrell to incarceration," she said.

Then Judge Bucklew summoned Jarrell and George to the podium before her, read each count and jury verdict, and sentenced him to serve thirty-three months in prison, pay $1.68 million in restitution, and pay a $10,000 fine. Jarrell showed no emotion.

Jarrell and his attorney quietly left the courtroom without comment. While free on bond, Jarrell too would lose his CPA license and his Columbia/HCA job and paycheck, and be banned from working in any federally funded healthcare organization. Both Whiteside and Jarrell were ordered to report to the Federal Bureau of Prisons on January 12, 2000, to begin serving their sentences.

But Judge Bucklew later granted Jarrell and Whiteside a reprieve, delaying their prison reporting date and allowing them to remain free on bond, pending their appeals.

The U.S. Court of Appeals for the Eleventh Circuit, in Atlanta, would most likely take at least one year to review the case, a development Meagher assured me would not hinder the settlement discussions on my *qui tam* lawsuit already in progress.

CHAPTER TWENTY-ONE

Partner in Crime

Once the verdicts were announced, the media began prowling for follow-ups. Healthcare industry trade magazines and newspapers, including my hometown *Milwaukee Journal Sentinel,* interviewed me. It was therapeutic to finally be able to discuss the stress and sacrifices my family and I endured for the last five years. My story made the front page of the *Milwaukee Journal Sentinel* on Sunday, August 8, 1999.

The headline read, "FBI mole dug up huge Medicare scam." Reporter Joe Manning described me as a bookish-looking CPA who ". . . may have done more to curb Medicare fraud than all the hard-nosed, steely-eyed federal agents in the country." The last line read, "He blew the whistle, and health care giants rocked." For the first time in more than three years, I was able to publicly share my belief that rampant and profitable healthcare fraud hurt not only the healthcare system but impacted every American because it drained state and federal resources intended for the poor and elderly.

My family was pleased with the article, and our neighbors and friends were quite surprised to see my picture on the front page. At work the next day, colleagues approached me offering congratulations and asking about the details. My *qui tam* case and the criminal trial also provided a platform to discuss healthcare fraud at several training seminars when the FBI and U.S. Attorney's Offices asked me to conduct cost reporting fraud training seminars for their staffs.

But the increased exposure spurred more paranoia in our family. Kir-

sten and I carefully watched our children and grew suspicious of everyone. I began to check under my car for loose wires or cut brake lines
before driving. Prank phone calls we'd been receiving continued to fan
our fears. Eventually, the calls stopped, but we never determined the
source. Earlier, Joe Ford handed me a scribbled sheet with his pager number on it. While unlikely he had cautioned, it was possible I could be
threatened. If so, I should contact him immediately. He'd also suggested
telling Alex's school that I was a witness in a federal criminal trial and
allow no one but Kirsten or me to pick him up. Despite Ford's warnings,
though, Stephen Meagher and Peter Chatfield had assured us that our
feelings were unwarranted, the result of watching too many movies.

The summer of 1999 was nearly over, and Alex's Little League team,
the Brewers, were undefeated and had taken first place in season play.
With twelve victories notched, the team was destined for the postseason
playoffs. The Brewers faced a double-elimination tournament and were
marked as the team to beat. The team, however, suffered its first loss in
tournament play and lost its final game in a nail-biter. They were a dedicated group of ballplayers, and as one of their coaches, I couldn't be pro-
uder.

On July 19, 1999, Columbia/HCA suffered a major loss. The company's home healthcare management partner, Atlanta-based Olsten
Kimberly, pleaded guilty to three felony counts of conspiracy, mail fraud,
and violation of the Medicare anti-kickback statute. By entering the guilty
pleas, Olsten agreed to pay a $61 million fine and be barred from the
Medicare program. Unsealed at the same time was former employee Don
McLendon's *qui tam* lawsuit, which the government had joined. McLendon had been the company's vice president of client development and
marketing.

Two years earlier, Meagher and I had met McLendon and his attorney,
Marlan Wilbanks, in Atlanta. A judge had partially unsealed the lawsuit
because of a legal loophole involving overlapping claims between multiple
whistleblowers. That unsealing allowed us to meet the shadowy figure
that Agent Ford had alluded to when he prodded me to amend my complaint.

We met at Wilbanks's law office, Harmon, Smith, Bridges & Wilbanks.
McLendon had also filed a *qui tam* lawsuit alleging that Columbia/HCA
and Olsten submitted false claims to the government and cheated Medi-

care of millions of dollars. Our lawsuits claimed the companies had improperly reported the costs of home healthcare acquisitions on their Medicare cost reports. In the past, Columbia/HCA had paid millions of dollars to acquire home health operations. But in November 1994, the company purchased twenty-two home healthcare agencies from Olsten at costs far below fair market value.

This was not an industry standard. In exchange for the low sale price, Olsten had agreed to Columbia/HCA's offer to retain Olsten to manage the facilities and accept much higher than normal management fees. This deal was structured solely to disguise goodwill as management fees. "Goodwill," an intangible asset, is defined as the purchase price less the book value of assets acquired, or the premium one pays over the book value. Under Medicare rules, management fees are reimbursable expenses, while goodwill is a non-reimbursable cost. Columbia/HCA and Olsten had conspired to circumvent Medicare rules with this agreement. They both knew Medicare would not pay for goodwill but would reimburse management fees. Columbia/HCA had low-balled the purchase price for the Olsten agencies.

Both lawsuits alleged that Columbia/HCA retained Olsten to manage those agencies and fifteen others, agreeing to a lucrative management agreement. By structuring the acquisition in this manner, Columbia/ HCA illegally changed the non-reimbursable goodwill cost to an allowable management cost under Medicare's rules. Olsten officials told investors that the sale/management agreement would double or triple its operating profits, amounting to a realized profit of $55 million to $60 million. The scheme benefited both companies; not only did Medicare improperly reimburse Columbia/HCA for much of its acquisition costs, but Olsten gleaned illegal profits as well.

McLendon and I met in Atlanta with our attorneys to explore joining both cases. Since Jim Alderson and I had very successfully combined our cases on the reserve cost report claims, it seemed possible we could as well. McLendon, who turned out to be not as mysterious as I'd expected, explained that he had also worked as a confidential informant with Ford and had made secret recordings. He believed the government would soon obtain criminal indictments concerning illegal activities in the home health business and was sure that Columbia/HCA employees were likely targets. He said my former boss, Bob Whiteside, could be one of them.

"I got Bob on tape," McLendon said. "What did he say?" I asked.

"He made a joke about the home health acquisition arrangement. He said it was all about assets. If the government finds out, our assets will be in jail. That's not all," McLendon continued. "I heard that Jay Jarrell is in deep shit, too."

"Wow," I sighed. I too had heard rumors of home health indictments. My former colleagues seemed to be sinking deeper and deeper.

Our meeting was productive and we agreed to join cases. Meagher reminded us how media attention had helped our case and said the publicity could force Columbia/HCA to negotiate a settlement. "We can't let this case go along quietly," Meagher explained. "Since companies don't seek negative attention, the media is one of the greatest tools we have at our disposal."

Switching gears, Meagher warned us of the battles ahead. He cautioned that we might have to fight the government in relator share negotiations, the amount awarded to whistleblowers. "The Justice Department has been known to bite the hand that feeds it," he cautioned.

He reminded us that Ford's ultimate goal was to successfully prosecute criminal indictments by steering the criminal investigation in the right direction. And we needed the criminal case, which he called essential to the civil case's viability, to proceed unhampered. While I understood the criminal case's value, I was surprised when Meagher stated that Ford had little interest in the Civil Division's case. I was naive in the assumption that the Justice Department's umbrella was inclusive.

It was apparent that even though I'd filed my amended complaint two hours before McLendon, giving me "first to file" status, our cases were mutually beneficial. He and I agreed to split any recovery from Columbia/ HCA. McLendon would receive the entire amount from any settlement with Olsten Kimberly, as my lawsuit did not specifically name that company as a defendant.

While I was happy that McLendon's journey was nearly over, I couldn't help but envy how quickly the Olsten case had settled. His lawsuit had been filed and settled in little more than two years. I wondered how this development would help my case. After all, Olsten Kimberly's slick partnership with Columbia/HCA was the reason the company was now paying the government millions of dollars. Olsten also agreed to plead guilty to federal criminal statutes. Would Columbia/HCA as its partner now take responsibility and admit guilt? I was puzzled that even though the government had spent the last two years investigating Columbia/HCA and Olsten, prosecutors had issued no indictments. Two years earlier, McLendon had been positive that indictments would be forthcoming. After all, Ford and Kathleen Haley implied that employees from both companies were under investigation. We knew that Jarrell and Whiteside were deeply involved with the acquisition of the home health agencies.

The message to Columbia/HCA was unmistakable. They were next.

CHAPTER TWENTY-TWO

Partial Settlement

In January 1998, six months after the FBI raids, it was widely reported that Columbia/HCA had concluded its internal investigation. Dr. Thomas Frist, Jr., was quoted in articles saying that he was ready to hammer out a civil settlement with the Justice Department. My attorneys, Stephen Meagher and Peter Chatfield, told me that Frist hadn't even scheduled a meeting yet with the government, and they doubted that a quick settlement would occur. Rather than making a genuine settlement overture, more likely Frist was trying to appease shareholders, hoping to stave off a revolt. My attorneys commented that Frist played the media like a fiddle. They were correct. The media failed to acknowledge the obvious: that with so many hoops to jump through, a quick civil settlement was impossible, even for HCA's "white knight."

An entire year later, in January 1999, the Justice Department confirmed that it was finally involved in civil settlement talks regarding the Columbia/HCA investigation, now two-and-a-half years old. Kirsten and I believed the company was genuinely attempting to settle the lawsuits. But we soon realized that negotiators had made little progress in the civil settlement discussions. Chatfield, returning from yet another settlement meeting between the Justice Department and Columbia/HCA, phoned me with disappointing news. "It was a waste of time," he exclaimed.

Columbia/HCA wasn't as serious about settling as it claimed. The cases were unlikely to settle in the first quarter of 1999. The company repeated its insistence that the dual cost report practice was an accepted practice industry-wide and that its reserves were not fraudulent. The company also refused to employ a statistical sampling to determine the amount of damages its business practices had caused the government, the actual cost of the fraud. Since each hospital was unique, the company said, it was impossible to find a true sample. Furthermore, Columbia/HCA officials complained that with their limited manpower, they were incapable of conducting self-audits on each hospital Medicare cost report for every year in question. Chatfield said the only proposal Columbia/HCA offered was to apply a benchmark approach, with the help of the (now defunct) Arthur Andersen accounting firm. The company's proposed plan was to measure the overall amounts Columbia/HCA hospitals claimed for various cost categories on their Medicare cost reports and compare them against industry averages. Then they would analyze the areas in which the company's hospitals were significantly above the norms. This method had little or nothing to do with the theory of my case. We also were concerned that the benchmarking approach would heavily favor Columbia/HCA because its hospitals would fall into the average category with few "excessive norms."

My attorney's believed that Columbia/HCA's alternative methodology might supplement the individual reserve damage analysis that both the Justice Department and Phillips & Cohen favored. For its part, the Justice Department left little doubt that it was uncomfortable with Columbia/HCA's methodology. The government refused to accept the benchmark methodology to assess the cost of the fraud.

The civil case remained on hold until long after the criminal trial of the four Columbia/HCA executives ended in July 1999. FBI activity markedly increased for several months after the trial. The criminal case against Columbia/HCA had picked up steam since the convictions. I was in continuous contact with the FBI, answering questions. It was apparent they were still focusing on home health issues and reserve cost report practices. By this time, twenty-six *qui tam* lawsuits had been filed against Columbia/HCA. None appeared to overlap the reserve cost report issues that Jim Alderson and I alleged in our suit. After the years we'd invested in the case, neither of us wanted a protracted battle with another whistleblower.

The home health violations that Don McLendon and I alleged were a different story, however. Several home health claims, although different in small ways, were similar in how they related to home health operations.

In an effort to avoid protracted litigation, McLendon and I had already struck a deal. Most of the twenty-six relators with overlapping claims chose not to form similar partnerships, and many ended up battling each other.

My legal team and I continued to work with Marie O'Connell, the Justice Department attorney, and the government's cost report experts to solidify our civil case. Meagher and Chatfield attended one of many meetings between the government and Columbia/HCA and reported that the company was deliberately stalling. In June 1999, the government had presented hundreds of improper cost report reserve issues, and months later the company had addressed only 10 percent of them. At this rate, it would take years for the company to respond to everything the government had presented. The two sides were miles apart.

The news wasn't all bad, however. It appeared that Columbia/HCA and the Justice Department were closer to settling the home healthcare claims. News organizations reported that the two sides would no longer attempt to settle all twenty-six *qui tam* lawsuits in one global settlement, but sought to negotiate through a series of smaller settlements categorized by five general classes of alleged wrongdoing. Those categories included Medicare cost reporting, home healthcare, laboratory billings, physician kickbacks, and diagnosis related group (DRG) upcoding. (Upcoding is billing for a more expensive service than the one actually performed.)

Optimistically, Meagher predicted that a partial settlement on the home health claims was near. After all, he said, Columbia/HCA's partner in crime, Olsten Kimberly, had already pled guilty. But having been jolted by the expectation roller coaster so many times before, I didn't bet my house on his prediction.

A nervous nation watched as the clock struck midnight on December 31, 1999, ushering in the new millennium. There had been no Y2K computer crashes and the stars had not collided. Buried in the holiday news cycle was the news that the U.S. Attorney's office in Miami, which had led the exhaustive two-year criminal probe into the allegedly fraudulent business practices of executives from Columbia/HCA and Olsten, was dropping the case. The five individuals targeted in the criminal investigation, including Jay Jarrell, were told that the government would not file any charges. Though we were disappointed that Joe Ford's hard work developing the case had ended without criminal indictments, Meagher and I speculated that this action cleared the path for the partial settlement.

The pressure on Columbia/HCA was escalating. The government had hired cost reporting experts, and for months they compiled cost report reserve data for each Columbia/HCA hospital. My attorneys also hired their own cost report experts to compile cost report reserves and develop settlement strategies. We learned that Dan Anderson, an attorney with the Justice Department's main office in Washington, would lead settlement negotiations with O'Connell. Anderson, who had recently executed the Olsten Kimberly settlement, was described as the "deal closer" in the Justice Department. My legal team and I were grateful for the change. After years of working with the hesitant and indecisive O'Connell, it was time for some new blood and fresh ideas.

Alderson and I were heavily involved, assisting our attorneys and experts wherever needed. In March of 2000 the FBI asked me to fly back to Tampa to meet with the agents assigned to investigate the criminal acts relating to Columbia/HCA's cost reporting practices. I spent a full day with Ford and several other agents analyzing documents in the Tampa Mercantile Bank Plaza. The questions continued for hours, but it was more relaxing than the trips to Tampa the year before. This trip also alerted me to the areas in which the agents were focusing.

That same week, the government presented to Columbia/HCA the initial findings from their experts' compilations. Meagher, who attended the meeting, was incensed by Columbia/HCA's stubborn resistance as their attorneys argued each issue, continuing to deny the company was at fault. While Meagher believed that Columbia/HCA's tactics would ultimately benefit our case, the company's arrogance infuriated the Justice Department, thus strengthening its resolve. Unfortunately, the parties would need to develop a new settlement strategy, since they were far from agreeing on the reserve cost report issue.

Meanwhile, friends and family members routinely asked, "Isn't that lawsuit settled yet?" That question haunted us wherever we went. The seventeen months that the case had been public had seemed to drag on forever to outsiders. But Kirsten and I had battled the emotional juggernaut for nearly five years at that point. One moment our spirits soared on news of progress toward settlement, but soon after our expectations crashed as talks failed or detour signs went up.

On May 18, 2000, I was at my desk when I saw Bloomberg break the news online. With no advance warning, I was shocked to find that a deal had been struck. Several tension-filled weeks had finally culminated in a partial settlement agreement between the government and Columbia/ HCA. After more than one year of negotiations, a handshake agreement was announced, pending court approval and approval from top Justice Department officials. In the partial settlement, Columbia/HCA was slated to pay $745 million. The civil settlement would cover some of the home health claims that McLendon and I had filed.

I reread the story several times before calling Kirsten. Controlling my excitement, I read the story to her. Our happiness was tempered by the reality that the settlement would not be finalized for months. That was not soon enough for us. Since we'd moved back to Wisconsin, we'd struggled to pay two mortgages (since we still owned our house in Florida) and care for three young children. Finances were tight. I had hoped that this settlement would relieve some of the pressure. The reality was that the deal wouldn't be final until it was final. We had no reason to celebrate until the final "t" was crossed.

The partial settlement created big news for most newspapers and trade publications. It was by far the largest civil healthcare fraud settlement ever signed by the government. Covering civil claims relating to diagnosis related group (DRG) upcoding, laboratory billing, and home health issues, the settlement was contingent upon several events. Most important, the government agreed to complete its home health criminal investigation by December 31, 2000, or Columbia/HCA could terminate the deal. This condition worried my attorneys and me. Could the government complete their investigation in time? If not, we worried we'd have to return to square one.

Columbia/HCA tentatively settled without admitting wrongdoing, and Dr. Frist beamed when he told the press, "We are pleased to have reached an understanding on these issues, and today's announcement signals that a significant step in this process is complete."

Even though the news was positive, it was important for us to focus on what was omitted from the settlement. Meagher pointed out in an interview, "Columbia/HCA has not agreed to pay one dime on the oldest and largest claim in the book." The reserve cost report allegations were not resolved by the partial civil settlement.

The press, erroneously assuming the five-year-old drama was nearly over, championed Frist as an effective leader who had successfully refocused the company, restored its tarnished reputation, and returned it to business. What the media failed to recognize was that the alleged fraud included in the reserve cost report issues that we'd brought forward alone surpassed the entire partial settlement amount.

While the partial settlement won praise on Wall Street, Representative Pete Stark (Democrat of California) called the deal "gentle." He told reporters, "I absolutely feel somebody has to go to jail. There's no question there was wanton criminal activity at the highest level, and I see no reason they [Columbia/HCA] should continue to treat Medicare patients."

When finalized, the partial settlement would make us multimillionaires. It would be months before McLendon and I would know how much money we would share, but we believed it could exceed $20 million. Alderson and I knew, however, that the reserve cost report issue was much larger.

In anticipation of the financial independence the partial settlement would confer on our family, Kirsten and I decided to move back to Florida. We had missed both the sunshine and the friendships we had nurtured there. While living in Wisconsin had served us well and we'd made many more wonderful friends, we'd always regretted leaving the Sunshine State. The people who had been renting our Fort Myers home had recently moved out, so the timing couldn't have been better.

The long road trip to Florida was fun as we anticipated the moment when we'd drive into our Three Oaks neighborhood. Our dear friends, Frank and Eva, and their children, Sarah and Mark, greeted us after we pulled into our driveway. Once back home, it felt on the surface as if very little had changed. We were in our old home with our old neighbors and everything just felt right. But everything had changed. Kirsten and I had changed: No longer did we cower or fear the future. We felt secure knowing that soon I'd be relieved of the burden of being a whistleblower. And soon we'd be financially independent, even able to retire young, allowing us more time with our children.

The transition from Wisconsin to Fort Myers went smoothly. The new school year was fast approaching, and Alex and Abby would attend school at Three Oaks Elementary, just around the corner. We enrolled Austin in a morning preschool program. My employer, United Government Services, allowed me to telecommute from home, so Kirsten and I again created a makeshift office in our bedroom. All the pieces seemed to fit into place.

Since the partial settlement had been announced, we had awaited news about my relator's share of the recovery. We speculated it would take no more than a few weeks, possibly months, to find out how much it would be and when we would receive payment. But Columbia/HCA still stubbornly denied guilt while continuing to change and manage the public's perception of the company. It surprised no one in 2000 when the Frists changed the name of the company, returning to the original brand name and logo the family had given the company when they founded it in 1968. The company came full circle, renaming itself HCA: The Health Care Company.

As the months passed, my cases progressed almost imperceptibly. The partial civil settlement, while agreed upon, had not been finalized. It seemed that the Justice Department was in no hurry to complete its criminal investigation by the December 2000 deadline. McLendon and I prayed the deal wouldn't crumble. I reminded myself that the government would certainly look foolish if it blew a $745 million settlement.

Since we had spoken at length the night before, I was surprised to hear Meagher's voice when I answered the phone on December, 14, 2000. "John, congratulations are in order! HCA and the government officially consummated the deal today. The total partial settlement is $840 million, including criminal fines and civil damages. [The value of] McLendon's and your claims amounted to $140 million of the total," he said. "And HCA pled guilty to several [criminal] charges of cost reporting fraud."

I calculated the numbers: *15 percent to 25 percent of $140 million—why, that's a staggering $21 million to $35 million that McLendon and I would split,* I figured. Wow!

It had taken HCA and the Justice Department seven months after announcing the joint partial settlement to remove all the conditions, clearing the way for payment. Those seven months had felt like an eternity.

I breathed a sigh of relief. "God, Stephen, that's great!" I responded, my mind racing. "When are the relators going to be paid? Do you know what percentage the government is going to offer McLendon and me?" I asked.

"I hope to know very soon. Let's take it one step at a time. The judge has to approve it first. It's important that the partial settlement and pleas pave the way for a resolution on the remaining claims."

Attorney General Janet Reno announced the settlement, saying, "This investigation has been the largest multi-agency investigation of a healthcare provider ever undertaken by the United States and reflects our commitment to vigorously pursuing all types of healthcare fraud schemes." Reno lauded the whistleblowers who alerted the government to the malfeasance. The settlement details indicated that HCA would pay $745 million to resolve five civil issues, $95 million to resolve allegations of outpatient laboratory billing fraud, $403 million related to DRG upcoding, $50 million to settle non-reimbursable home health marketing and advertising costs disguised as community education, $90 million related to non-reimbursable costs associated with the purchase of home health agencies disguised as management fees, and $106 million for improperly billing for home health visits.

In addition, the company agreed to pay more than $95 million in criminal fines and signed an eight-year corporate integrity agreement, which required the company to agree to certain auditing and compliance measures and more government scrutiny. Two nonoperational HCA subsidiaries, Columbia Homecare Group and Columbia Management Companies, pled guilty to fourteen charges of criminal conduct, including cost report fraud. The plea bargain did not involve prison sentences for any company officials and effectively allowed HCA to remain in business. Had HCA itself pleaded guilty to the criminal charges, the company would have been barred from receiving Medicare and Medicaid funds, a financial kiss of death that surely would have crippled it.

Dr. Frist's carefully worded statement about the settlement was designed to mislead the general public. "Today's action represents one of the last steps needed to put the Columbia investigation behind us and allow us to move forward maintaining our focus on providing quality patient care," Frist said in the news release. He implied that the worst of the company's legal and financial troubles were behind it and those remaining were insignificant. This overlooked the fact that many of the civil investigation allegations were unresolved by the settlement.

News of the settlement barely budged HCA stock down 22 cents per share, indicating that investors also believed the settlement was old news. Some Wall Street analysts seemed to agree with Frist. Others surmised that the agreement carried political undertones. Did the Justice Department need to cement the deal before the Clinton administration left office? Would the incoming Bush administration expand the focus on healthcare fraud or hinder it?

Meagher continued to beat the drum. "The government can still spend years going after the individuals on this. The FBI people that I've talked to tell me there's no plan to disassemble the investigation," he said. "The cost report and kickback issues could get this to $2 billion." Shrewd journalists reported that since much of the civil investigation remained unresolved, the case was far from over.

Still feeling the financial squeeze, Kirsten and I finally saw a light at the end of the tunnel. The announcement was like an early Christmas present. All that was needed now was approval from U.S. District Judge Royce Lamberth. In the meantime, the Justice Department would work with each relator's attorneys to determine their share. We'd previously agreed that McLendon and his attorney would lead the negotiations with the government for our relator's share.

Encouraging news continued to trickle in on the HCA partial settlement. In February 2001, McLendon and his attorney, Marlan Wilbanks, negotiated a $25 million relator's share with the Justice Department. Since we'd privately agreed to a split months before, we only needed the judge's approval before dividing our relator's share. Though we couldn't celebrate quite yet, Kirsten and I now knew that we soon would be millionaires. It was just a matter of time.

We still didn't realize how long it would actually take or how much squabbling occurred between other whistleblowers and their attorneys. Quite a few of the other cases overlapped, and we had ringside seats for the relator battle royale. Many other cases, deemed frivolous or unsubstantiated, were formally dismissed.

On August 20, 2001, I was in the bedroom when the phone rang. I excitedly answered since I had been expecting this call.

"John, this is Janice at SunTrust Bank. Your wire arrived. Congratulations!"

I couldn't believe it. "Janice, that's great. Thanks for calling."

I almost jumped up from my chair, phone still in hand. I bounded out of the bedroom to find only Alex at home. He said Kirsten had gone grocery shopping with Abby and Austin. He must have thought I was crazy as I picked him up and hugged him. I told him I just received the first multimillion-dollar payout from my lawsuits. Alex, then 10, had lived through the tumultuous and stressful times our family had experienced in recent years. Jumping to his feet, he chanted, "We're rich, we're rich, we're really, really rich."

Although I wanted to join him, I refrained, content to watch him, beaming with excitement. I didn't explain that my lawyers and I had much more work ahead of us.

Shortly thereafter, the garage door opened and Kirsten hustled Abby and Austin into the kitchen. Alex, unable to contain himself, raced into the kitchen to share the news. As she set down the grocery bags, I told Kirsten that our first settlement payment had arrived while Alex tried to explain it to his little sister and brother.

Just two weeks before, on August 7, 2001, Judge Lamberth had approved the $745 million civil settlement and $95 million criminal plea announced in December. He also approved the payment shares for the whistleblowers. Although the settlement had been reached back in May 2000, it took fifteen months of legal negotiations between the Justice Department and HCA, and eventually the whistleblowers and their legal teams, before the deal was finalized.

Even now, that day seems a bit surreal. In today's technologically advanced era, when a person becomes instantly wealthy, a Brink's truck does not pull up and dump stacks of bills in your front yard. Instead, one bank electronically wires the money to another bank and prints a paper receipt. I've kept that little white bank receipt, the only tangible connection we have to that magical day.

Wanting to celebrate and make a lasting memory of that day, we invited Frank and Eva out for dinner. It wasn't an extravagant affair—just a quiet, joyous evening with friends.

We had missed our Three Oaks neighborhood while we were living in Wisconsin, and that first year back in Three Oaks was wonderful. But over a period of time, our neighborhood school had slipped from being an excellent school with fine teacher-to-student ratios to an overcrowded school with lower than average test scores and growing academic problems. Because Kirsten and I volunteered there frequently, we witnessed the deterioration and declining standards. We agreed that our children would be better served in a different academic environment. After researching schools in our area, we chose a challenging private school located in nearby Naples.

But the thirty-minute commute to the school soon grew difficult, so we decided to move closer to their new school and purchased a newer, larger home in Naples. We'd outgrown our three-bedroom house in Three Oaks and could now afford a more spacious home that would allow office space for me and more room for our family. While we missed living next door to the Pomaricos, we were still nearby and remained close.

The Schillings weren't the only ones to bask in the success of the investigation's outcome. The Justice Department honored the Assistant U.S. Attorneys and FBI agents in Tampa for their roles in recouping $840 million in civil and criminal payments from the HCA case. Janet Reno bestowed the U.S. Attorney General's Award for Exceptional Service to FBI Agent Joe Ford and to AUSA Kathleen Haley—who had married Ford and now went by the name of Kathleen Haley Ford.

The attorney general also honored Assistant U.S. Attorneys Tony Peluso and Bob Mosakowski for their work in the case. Reno and the FBI bestowed the FBI Director's Annual Award for Excellence on the different FBI agents involved in the case: Ford, Tim McCants, Bill Estevez, Michele Yaroma, Kenneth Walsh, and Michael Wysocki.

CHAPTER TWENTY-THREE

The Slaying of KPMG

The government still had not joined my *qui tam* lawsuit against KPMG, which had been filed in April 1998 and subsequently unsealed during the HCA executives' criminal trial in May 1999. In December 1999, seven months had passed since its unceremonious unsealing in open court, KPMG still denied wrongdoing. To bolster my case against KPMG, I agreed to review forty-six boxes of documents for the government. By now, the Federal Express driver and I were on a first-name basis, and while I'm sure he wondered what the boxes contained, he never asked. Kirsten and I sometimes speculated what the neighbors thought about all the constant deliveries.

Marie O'Connell, assigned to prosecute the KPMG case for the Justice Department, again seemed slow to develop the investigation. Rather than deciding to join the case, in January 2000 she instead requested an extension. The government and KPMG had met several times to discuss my lawsuit, and Peter Chatfield reported that the company had a weak legal position. Chatfield said the government would be foolish not to intervene.

While working at UGS, I was astounded to read that Medicare's own policy-making arm, the Health Care Financing Administration, had awarded KPMG a contract to perform audit quality reviews of fiscal intermediaries. The government, while fully aware that KPMG was accused of cost report fraud, nonetheless had chosen the company to review fiscal intermediaries performing cost report audits. Alarms went off in my head. How could that be? *Someone has ignored a huge conflict of interest,* I thought. Hoping to rattle some cages, Stephen Meagher quickly contacted O'Connell and the government's General Accounting Office (now called the Government Accountability Office, but still known by the acronym GAO) about this imprudent HCFA contract. Subsequently, in September 2000 the contract was revoked.

On October 31, 2000, the GAO issued a blistering report chastising the HCFA, saying its officials should have known about the pending civil and criminal actions against KPMG before extending its contract for another year. "Moreover, these same officials knew or should have known that, as an audit quality review contractor, KPMG would be responsible for re-viewing transactions that were of the same type of transactions about which KPMG had advised Columbia/HCA," the report found. In fact, the report revealed that the HCFA contracting officer responsible for the contract with KPMG knew about my civil suit against KPMG alleging "serious and credible allegations of fraud related to KPMG's work for Columbia/HCA, yet did not advise her supervisor . . . or retain relevant documents in the contract file."

Later, this HCFA contract officer found a copy of the still sealed *qui tam* complaint against KPMG on her desk. Instead of notifying her super-visor, the contract officer violated the law by contacting KPMG officials, according to the report.

I was infuriated when I read the report. The contracting officer had not only violated the law by disclosing a sealed lawsuit to the defendant, but she chose not to consider the allegations as serious. Why would HCFA hire the fox to guard the henhouse? Maybe for the same reason it chose to hire an incompetent contracting officer: lack of money. HCFA didn't pay competitively and wasn't always able to hire the cream of the crop. In addition, the agency was so out of touch with current industry practices that it seldom saw how providers exploited Medicare's vulnerabilities. I am sure the agency was embarrassed that Jim Alderson and I had to point out how rampant cost report fraud was plaguing the industry to the very people paying the bills, who should have uncovered this scheme them-selves.

The media had a field day reporting the GAO findings. While the story embarrassed KPMG, the HCFA also suffered a black eye. How could the Medicare policy maker continue to employ KPMG? Both the HCFA and KPMG declined comment.

Delivering another blow to KPMG was the Justice Department's decision to intervene in my lawsuit against the firm on December 4, 2000. Tipped off weeks earlier by the government, Phillips & Cohen had prepared a news release, titled "Government charges that KPMG helped HCA commit Medicare fraud; joins whistleblower lawsuit." The release noted that this was the first time the federal government had sought to hold an accounting firm liable under the False Claims Act "for aiding and facilitating Medicare fraud committed by a client." It described my lawsuit and alleged that KPMG knew the annual cost reports HCA submitted were false. "The government's decision to join our case puts outside accountants and consultants on notice that they may be held liable if they knowingly assist their clients in submitting false claims," Meagher pointed out in the release.

Major newspapers and trade journals reported the government's agreement to join the lawsuit and recounted the allegations against KPMG, announcing that consultants and providers alike would be held to the same standards. KPMG vigorously denied any wrongdoing and said the services it provided were appropriate. The suit won praise from Representative Pete Stark of California, who said, "This is the public's money. It's not just there to be dipped into. I'm pleased to see the suit go forward."

Jim Moorman, the president of Taxpayers Against Fraud, also cited the historic precedence of the suit. "There hasn't been a prominent case in this field like this," Moorman said.

Not only were dishonest providers called to account for their actions, but consultants were also on notice that they too faced legal liability if they aided or ignored clients committing fraud. Meagher's original pitch to the feds regarding KPMG had been successful. He'd argued, "If you know that a client is submitting a false claim to the government, you can't be silent. You have certain responsibilities." At last the government proved that it agreed with us.

Nine months later on September 11, 2001, just before we closed on our new home in Naples, the world changed forever. Four hijacked planes attacked our nation and its psyche. We sat riveted to the television, watching the first plane strike the north tower of the World Trade Center. Like millions of other Americans, Kirsten and I watched in horror as a second plane dove into the south tower of the World Trade Center. Time froze for a moment. We watched the chaos that ensued as a third plane struck the Pentagon. On the last plane, passengers fought back against the hijackers, causing the plane to crash into a field in Pennsylvania. The terrorism altered our view of the world forever. Thus began our first week in Naples, indelibly marked forever.

The news in the United States understandably shifted in the next few weeks. Terrorism had landed on U.S. soil. The media explored the emotional tidal wave of the 9/11 disaster in New York City and covered the subsequent tumbling of the stock market. Newspapers, television, and radio captured this horrific period of American history. Soon, federal resources from most of the same agencies charged with investigating healthcare fraud would be diverted to investigate and fight terrorism. Our national security depended upon it, but it impacted federal efforts to fight fraud.

The news in my corner of the world was more hopeful. I had scored a second victory on October 23, 2001, when KPMG agreed to settle with the government. "KPMG Peat Marwick to pay the United States over $9 million for preparing fraudulent Medicare & Medicaid cost reports" headlined one newspaper. The firm had settled the case when it became clear that the government held more than one smoking gun—the multiple reserve cost report documents prepared by KPMG employees. The evidence was so overwhelming that had the company gone to trial, it could have faced certain treble damages and far greater fines than the $9 million it paid. Still denying any wrongdoing, the company claimed it had settled to "avoid the costs of litigation."

Seven months earlier, KPMG and the Justice Department had reached an agreement in principle. One condition was that none of the involved parties would disclose the settlement publicly until all the terms were met. The announced settlement was the first of its kind. Never before had the federal government held a "Big 5" accounting firm or any consultant liable under the False Claims Act. In its press release, the Justice Department not only announced the $9 million agreement to settle allegations of preparing false hospital cost reports submitted to Medicare and Medicaid, but also highlighted KPMG's alleged misconduct.

"The government alleged that KPMG, acting as a reimbursement consultant and preparer of the cost reports, knowingly made claims for repayment on behalf of its client hospitals that were false, exaggerated, or ineligible for payment and concealed errors from government auditors enabling BAMI and HCA to illegally retain Medicare funds," the Justice Department explained. "At the same time that KPMG prepared the reports that were actually filed with Medicare, the financial services company also prepared 'reserve' cost reports used to estimate the impact on a hospital's reimbursement that would occur in the event that the non-allowable expenses and allocations in the filed reports were detected on audit by Medicare's fiscal intermediaries."

Robert D. McCallum, Jr., the assistant attorney general of the Civil Division, said, "This settlement demonstrates the United States's commitment to protecting federal funds from fraud and abuse and to holding accountable not only those who receive ill-gotten gains, but also those who facilitate the submission of false claims to federal programs."

In Phillips & Cohen's statement, Meagher observed that "KPMG's participation in the fraud proved costly." Chatfield added, "KPMG evidently was more interested in client relations than the integrity of its work. If outside accountants help their clients perpetrate Medicare fraud, 'just following the client's orders' is no defense."

Sweet justice, I thought. Just the year before, KPMG had balked at the Justice Department's initial demand. Originally, KPMG had offered roughly $200,000 to settle the case, slightly more than it received as consulting fees from BAMI. When the lawsuit was unsealed, KPMG publicly attacked me and my motives, telling the *Wall Street Journal* that "The only false claims we are aware of are those apparently being made by Mr. Schilling." The company also told the *Journal* that my lawsuit was a gross exaggeration.

Now, with the settlement announced, Chatfield retorted, "Who showed more integrity: Mr. Schilling, who exposed the fraud, or KPMG, which went along with it? KPMG's settlement demonstrates that HCA's fraud—and KPMG complicity—have not been exaggerated."

CHAPTER TWENTY-FOUR

Battling the Justice Department

After the KPMG settlement was consummated, Stephen Meagher reminded me of the warning he had given me years before. He'd said that in the end, my toughest battle could be against the Justice Department. I hadn't taken his admonition to heart after the years I'd invested in educating, developing, and wholeheartedly assisting federal prosecutors and investigators. It was very disturbing and ironic to realize that government resources that should have been directed to fighting fraud were now being spent contesting my relator's share.

Quorum Health Group, the HCA hospital management company spinoff that had fired Alderson ten years earlier for refusing to participate in the company's dual cost report scheme, continued to vehemently deny wrongdoing. Like the Columbia/HCA lawsuit, Alderson's Quorum suit alleged that the company included costs that were not reimbursable by Medicare when filing its annual cost reports. Quorum routinely kept a reserve or dual cost report that specifically identified the improper claims so the funds would be readily available if Medicare auditors ever discovered the improper claims.

But on October 2, 2000—ten years after his battle began with Quorum—Jim Alderson's persistence finally paid off. Quorum announced the settlement it had agreed to three months earlier after lengthy mediations with the Justice Department. Alderson and his Phillips & Cohen attorneys had worked diligently for years against enormous odds, sometimes even fighting their alleged ally—the Justice Department's Marie O'Connell—to keep the case alive.

The results were staggering. Alderson's *qui tam* lawsuit against Quorum settled for $77.5 million. In addition, Quorum also agreed to pay Phillips & Cohen's legal fees of $2.5 million. Quorum's legal expense for defending itself was estimated at $10 million.

The government had delayed Alderson's case for years, unconvinced of its merits and unable to grasp the systematic fraud scheme mired in the complex regulations governing Medicare cost reports. In a 1997 effort to derail the lawsuit, O'Connell had even told Phillips & Cohen that she would not recommend intervening in the case that had dominated Jim and Connie Alderson's lives for years. Calling his lawsuit "a dog of a case," O'Connell had claimed the lawsuit contained little substance. Without Phillips & Cohen's foresight and the Aldersons' unyielding persistence, the Justice Department would never have pursued the case and intervened. But recognizing the benefits of government intervention, the Aldersons and their attorneys had reluctantly agreed to innumerable seal extensions.

Even after the government finally agreed to intervene in the case, Quorum's stance did not change. The company may have been emboldened by the government's hesitancy and lack of resolve. In fact, the company was buoyed when the American Hospital Association (AHA) filed an *amicus*—or "friend of the court"—brief defending Quorum's dual cost reporting practice. The message seemed clear to me: The AHA was more interested in protecting its own than in reforming illegal cost reporting practices endemic in its industry.

Quorum President James Dalton Jr., rationalized paying the 2000 settlement, saying it made "business sense" and was in the best interest of the company and its shareholders. Dalton defended his company, saying it had acted in a proper and ethical manner.

When questioned about the announced settlement, HCA spin doctors adamantly denied that the Quorum settlement would impact HCA's negotiations with the government (which were still going on). Phillips & Cohen took a different approach on the matter when issuing its release. Peter Chatfield boasted, "James Alderson's lawsuit exposed a practice in the hospital industry that was draining Medicare of hundreds of millions of dollars a year." John Phillips added, "The Quorum settlement shows that nationwide cost-reporting fraud cases against large providers can be resolved. Perhaps HCA will get that message." Alderson and I hoped so.

Though Phillips & Cohen boasted broad knowledge and experience, the firm had anticipated the rough legal battle ahead with HCA. Thus, the firm retained well-known litigator and former Assistant Attorney General Gerald M. Stern to bolster our team. Stern was first brought into the firm as a consultant early in the case and then full time in 2001.

The settlement offered sweet vindication for the Aldersons. Kirsten and I were as happy for them as they had been for us when the Columbia/ HCA partial settlement had been announced several months earlier. I called that evening to congratulate Jim on the news. Financial relief finally seemed near for him and his family. He also had uprooted his family and depleted his savings to finance the long, protracted legal battle. After being blackballed within the hospital accounting industry, he also had accepted lower paying jobs. While both Alderson and I eagerly anticipated returning to normal lives, the subsequent months proved that our battles were mere skirmishes compared to the war we'd wage against our own government—a fight for justice against a federal department that failed to live up to its name.

I'd seen how the Justice Department—even when bolstered by longstanding criminal investigations, ironclad evidence, and corporate pleas—lacked the backbone to pursue additional indictments and demand higher civil penalties. Like Alderson, I'd experienced the government's shortsightedness and unfairness to the whistleblowers who helped them make their cases and helped them recover hundreds of millions of dollars.

Taxpayers Against Fraud published The Justice Department's Relator's Share Guidelines in their *Quarterly Review*, Vol. 11, January 1997. The guidelines state that when the government intervenes in a lawsuit, a relator should receive at least 15 percent, but not more than 25 percent, of any recovery resultant from the action. Legislative history suggests that the 15 percent should be viewed as the minimum award—a finder's fee, the starting point for determining the proper award. The 10 percent difference is based on the value added to the investigation—the legal and other assistance the relators and their attorneys provide.

Those guidelines suggest that increases in relator's shares could be awarded if the fraud is reported promptly or if the relator, upon discovering the fraud, tried to stop it or reported it to supervisors or the government. The guidelines also explain that whistleblower shares could be increased if the lawsuit or ensuing investigation caused the defendant to stop the fraudulent practices or the suit warned the government of a significant safety issue. Relators were also entitled to larger percentages if they provided extensive, firsthand details of the fraud to the government. Other factors to consider include whether the government knew about the fraud and the level of the relator's cooperation during the investigation or pretrial phases. If the case went to trial, the level of assistance and cooperation by the relator's counsel and whether the relator was an excellent, credible witness could also be weighed. The government could also increase the relator's share if filing the complaint caused adverse impact on the relator, and if the false claims recovery was relatively small.

On the other hand, relator's shares could be reduced if the whistleblower participated in the fraud, delayed reporting the problem or filing the complaint, or violated certain False Claims Act procedures, such as publicizing the lawsuit while it remained under seal and stating material facts without evidence. The government could also reduce the relator's share if it determined that the whistleblower actually had little knowledge of the fraud or if that knowledge was based on publicly available information. Shares could be cut if the relator learned of the fraud through a government job, if the government already knew about the fraud, or if the relator and his/her attorneys didn't help after filing the complaint or unreasonably opposed the government's position in litigation. The government also has flexibility in lowering the relator's share when the case requires substantial government effort to develop, when the case is settled quickly, when the case requires little discovery, or when the settlement is relatively large.

In summer 2001, prior to the KPMG settlement announcement, I was insulted when the Justice Department initially offered my attorneys a 15 percent relator's share. I did not hesitate to reject it. The Justice Department insinuated that my attorneys and I had contributed little to the case. Meagher also felt slighted by the offer. He told me that while the Justice attorneys enjoyed their safe government jobs with secure pensions and generous benefits, they envied successful relators.

I grew frustrated after several months passed with little progress toward agreeing on an acceptable relator's share. The government increased its offer to 17 percent but was unwilling to go any further. We were at a stalemate. Since my attorneys and I had been cooperating with the government for years, we knew we deserved more than Justice was offering. I'd received some money from the partial settlement of the Columbia/HCA case, so I wasn't desperate to settle this matter quickly and could hold out longer. It was with great regret that I informed Phillips & Cohen that I was ready to let a judge decide the matter.

At the same time I was negotiating my relator's share with the government, Alderson found himself in the same predicament with his Quorum settlement. The Justice Department initially offered him the same 15 percent relator's share, which rose to 17 percent when the two sides arrived at an impasse. Alderson, a bulldog on principle, was unwilling to back down. Instead, he asked Phillips & Cohen to request a hearing and let a judge decide what constituted a fair relator's share. In May 2001, Alderson and his legal team took on O'Connell and the Justice Department in the courtroom of U.S. District Judge Steven Merryday. Both Jim and Connie Alderson took the stand. It was reported later that Judge Merryday found Connie most persuasive. She described the hardships that her family had suffered over the last decade. Particularly convincing was her assertion that she and Jim had always done what they felt was right for their community and country. She expressed her disappointment with the Justice Department's lack of appreciation for what her family had endured.

In an unprecedented move at the end of the hearing, Judge Merryday stepped down from the bench and personally thanked Connie. Then he apologized on behalf of the government and agreed that they should have worked together as a team. The Aldersons and their attorneys were encouraged by the judge's heartfelt candor, which boded well for his ruling.

As for my share, in a last-ditch effort to avoid drawn out litigation, Chatfield drafted a letter to the Justice Department's Civil Division offering a best and final offer of a 20 percent relator's share. He wrote: "It is beyond dispute that the quality of the information provided by Mr. Schilling at the commencement of the action was exceptional. The documents detailing the creation of reserve cost reports by KPMG were unusually comprehensive and clear. This was not a case where further investigation uncovered additional claims. Every reimbursement issue in every cost reporting year at every hospital in the case was detailed from the outset in the documents Schilling provided."

He went on: "Apart from the quality of the documentary evidence he brought forward, Schilling's assistance in the FBI investigation was also crucial. Mr. Schilling spent literally hundreds of hours assisting agents and investigators in their efforts to understand the reimbursement issues detailed in the reserves created by KPMG. With the encouragement of the FBI, Schilling returned to work in the Southwest Florida Division of Columbia/HCA in order to assist the investigation. The evidence he produced about reimbursement issues concerning the hospitals involved in this case formed the basis for the government's subpoenas and interviews of KPMG personnel."

Chatfield also noted that while the relator's share guidelines lack the force of law, "Schilling clearly meets the overwhelming majority of the factors identified as justifying an award at the high end of the scale." The Justice Department did not respond to the letter for weeks.

After researching Alderson's case for five months, Judge Merryday issued a blistering opinion critical of the Justice Department. In October 2001, Judge Merryday ordered the Justice Department to award Alderson a 24 percent relator's share. The judge recognized the critical role Alderson and his attorneys had played in the investigation, rating them a 9 out of 10 extra percentage points on the Justice Department guidelines. Judge Merryday noted in his decision, "The record establishes that Alderson's counsel contributed significantly in both quality and quantity and at certain moments crucially to this case. That contribution deserves manifest and telling weight in determining the relator's award."

He acknowledged that some might consider the relator's share excessive or inequitable. "However," he explained, "Congress has chosen a mechanism calculated to encourage potential relators to undertake the risk and enervating hardship often attendant to litigation. Alderson took up the risk of litigating against prohibitive odds, persevered with his case under excruciating circumstances, and performed a distinctive and admirable service to his country, precisely as Congress intended in the False Claims Act."

The victory couldn't have come at a better time for Alderson and me. We knew this ruling would set a precedent if and when the HCA lawsuit settled. Within days of Merryday's ruling, the Justice Department accepted my 20 percent relator's share proposal in the KPMG case, and I was awarded an astounding $1.8 million as my fee from the $9 million settlement. The financial rewards were starting to mount.

Now financially independent, Kirsten and I agreed that I should resign from my fraud investigator's job at United Government Services so I would be able to dedicate all of my time to the looming litigation between HCA and the Justice Department. Even though I enjoyed my employment with UGS, I officially retired in October 2001 at age 39.

The holidays seemed more festive than in the past years now that we were finally financially secure. Kirsten and the kids gave me a present that I quickly put to use: a platinum Cross Medalist pen engraved with the word "Truth." With Kirsten witnessing, on January 2, 2002, I signed the KPMG settlement release with my new pen. The government required my signature on the agreement and release before it would officially transfer my 20 percent relator's share. With no fanfare, the money would be wired to my bank account within the next two weeks.

While it was more money than any of us had imagined at the beginning of this odyssey, Alderson and I expected an even bigger reward months or years in the future when HCA finally settled our reserve or dual cost reporting claims. Now that the KPMG and Quorum cases had been resolved, we were prepared to help Phillips & Cohen and the Justice Department in the looming showdown with HCA. The end was growing near.

CHAPTER TWENTY-FIVE

Poker, Anyone?

In January 2001, Judge Royce Lamberth intervened in my five-year-old Columbia/HCA reserve cost report case and ordered the Justice Department to file monthly status reports updating him on the progress of all the *qui tam* cases. While the reports were designed to clarify settlement progress, they generated huge amounts of stress for me every month. Deadlines came and went. Status reports came and went, most un-encouraging. In February 2001, the status report detailed an impasse between the government and Columbia/HCA on the physician kickback allegations, but reported that negotiations continued on the cost report reserve issues. The status reports were our only gauge of the negotiation process. My attorneys and I hoped settlement negotiations were progressing smoothly, but the reality was that Columbia/HCA and the Justice Department were squaring off on both issues.

Weeks after the December 2000 partial settlement agreement was reached, Columbia/HCA named Jack Bovender, a twenty-year HCA veteran, as its president and chief executive officer. Dr. Thomas Frist, Jr. remained chairman. I wondered if Frist was stepping aside believing the worst was behind him. I speculated that HCA wasn't genuinely interested in settling the cost report issues quickly. Rather, it seemed that the company's strategy was to stall as long as possible. The company had outlasted the Justice Department officials, including Attorney General Janet Reno, from the Clinton administration. Now we were in a Republican administration, which was presumably friendlier to business, with a new attorney general, John Ashcroft.

The changing political winds concerned me for several reasons. President George W. Bush had nominated Michael Chertoff of the firm Latham & Watkins to head the Justice Department's Criminal Division. Chertoff had been HCA's lead outside counsel and had directed the lengthy negotiations in the December 2000 partial settlement. Disappointingly, Bush also nominated hospital industry lobbyist Thomas Scully to head the HCFA. Scully, the president of the Federation of American Hospitals—of which Columbia/HCA was a member—would be appointed administrator of the agency that administered Medicare. I believed these two appointments could impact my case in significant ways, and probably not in my favor.

On March 15, 2001, the Justice Department boldly moved to file an amended complaint. This document included 1,000 pages of exhibits detailing a vast scheme of fraud in the reserve cost report lawsuit brought by Jim Alderson and me. The Justice Department's press release said, "The government has alleged that HCA and its predecessors engaged in a pattern and practice of knowingly including unallowable charges in cost reports, unlawfully shifting costs from hospital departments [that are] paid flat rates set by Medicare to departments reimbursed on cost." Prosecutors also alleged in the amended complaint that HCA committed a variety of other accounting improprieties designed to extract from Medicare and other government programs money to which the HCA hospitals were not entitled. Many of these schemes were known to HCA management and were documented on internal documents.

The Justice Department projected that the cost report claims would involve more than 14,000 items on 3,460 cost reports. For example, the government's amended complaint revealed details of HealthTrust's 1987 spinoff from HCA, when Dr. Frist was HCA's chairman, president, and CEO. Then in 1995, HCA reacquired HealthTrust. In a March 29, 2001, article in the *Tenessean*, Clayton McWhorter—the former HCA president and chief operating officer and the former HealthTrust CEO—said his finance people assured him the Medicare billings were proper. McWhorter maintained HealthTrust's innocence, stating, "I can assure you we never made a decision that was not appropriate. We did everything we could to make sure what we did was appropriate, ethical, and legal."

He didn't mention that he'd profited greatly from the deal and Health-Trust's subsequent success, which was partially fueled by the company's "aggressive cost reporting practices." In 1995, McWhorter's annual compensation reached $14 million, mostly from maturing stock options. That year, he was one of the best paid executives in the United States. The complaint asserted that HealthTrust (once again part of HCA) intentionally defrauded Medicare of more than $100 million of the cost of this spinoff. Now, it was obvious that Frist wasn't the white knight the company had portrayed him as, after Rick Scott's ouster. The entire reserve cost reporting scheme did not originate with Scott solely as a product of the Columbia era, but was prevalent within HCA during Frist's reign in the 1980s.

Alderson and I staunchly supported the Justice Department's gutsy move. The lawyers at Phillips & Cohen were confident that filing the amended complaint would speed settlement talks. Issuing its own press release, Phillips & Cohen cited the government's analysis that HCA established reserves from reserve cost reports worth more than $400 million over a ten-year period from 1987 to 1997 to cover claims that they knew were not reimbursable under Medicare. If the cost report case resulted in a victory at trial, HCA could be forced to pay triple damages, as much as $1.35 billion.

Seeking to defuse the adverse publicity, HCA chose to downplay the significance of the amended complaint, restating that the allegations were nothing new. In response, Stephen Meagher was quoted in news accounts saying, "These are new claims. To those who say there's nothing new here, they're burying their heads in the sand. The breadth of the allegations and the detailed calculations of Medicare's losses are a clear signal that Columbia/HCA's problems with the government are far from over."

One month later, I was disgusted when HCA countered the government's amended complaint with a lawsuit on April 12, 2001. The suit sought to force the government to review and release more than 1,000 Columbia/HCA Medicare cost reports that had been suspended since 1997. The HCFA had not paid Columbia/HCA for those reports because of the fraud investigation. Columbia/HCA alleged that the government wrongfully suspended cost report payments and sought back payment with interest, expenses, and legal fees. In its suit, HCA claimed that the government demands for settling the cost report fraud allegations exceeded a reasonable range. And instead of settling, the company vowed to fight our lawsuit in court. "A stall tactic designed to put pressure on the government to resolve all of HCA's outstanding cost reports at one time," Meagher surmised.

Meanwhile, the company's in-house counsel, Steve Hinkle, threatened that if the case went to court, HCA would compel the government and my attorneys to separately prove every one of the 14,000 claims of alleged fraud—a voluminous task that could take years to complete. This was a serious threat. The Justice Department had already invested much time and money developing the case and was severely out-staffed. With millions of his firm's dollars and countless staff hours invested in this case, John Phillips was not about to let that happen. He agreed to secure whatever additional outside attorneys and additional support staff might be necessary to succeed. Once again, I entrusted my future to the Justice Department and Phillips & Cohen.

The settlement talks between HCA and the Justice Department had stalemated since April 2001, with neither side willing to budge. Each was preparing for a civil trial. The stakes would increase considerably if the case went to trial. If it lost, HCA could pay triple damages, which could be more than $1 billion. As far as I was concerned, the Justice Department was already offering a bargain to settle the cost report issues.

Industry observers likened it to a poker game in which neither side is willing to blink. Both sides were gambling that they held the high cards. Responding to a request from the Justice Department's Marie O'Connell, my firm engaged a tremendous amount of legal firepower. Assisting in trial preparation were some of the best litigators in the business, roughly seventy attorneys, thirty-five of them working full time. A number of elite law firms were involved. The attorneys represented the elite law firms of Heller, Ehrman, White & McAuliffe; Hennigan, Bennet & Dorman; Irell & Manella; James, Hoyer, Newcomer & Smiljanich; and Boies, Schillier & Flexner. High-profile attorney David Boies of Boies, Schillier & Flexner, who represented the Justice Department in the Microsoft Corporation antitrust lawsuit and Al Gore in his presidential election recount in Florida, topped the marquee. With the addition of the Justice Department's five full-time attorneys, the government and Phillips & Cohen were prepared for the potentially long and costly endeavor. The combination of the additional fire power and HCA's stall tactics were working in our favor. Daily our team was unearthing additional evidence and HCA counsel Latham & Watkins, one of the country's largest law firms, could barely keep pace.

My "retirement" in October 2001 had been short-lived. On a part-time basis, I now spent my days as a consultant developing civil and criminal fraud investigation cases for several law enforcement agencies. One case involved two brothers, Amjad and Iftakhar Khan, who owned and operated a home health agency and an outpatient physical therapy company in suburban Detroit. They had become quite adept at cheating Medicare. In a twenty-count indictment, the U.S. Attorney in Detroit alleged that they bilked the Medicare program for more than $2 million. For example, while neither of their spouses worked at either company, the brothers intentionally misreported the women's salaries as expenses on their business's Medicare cost reports.

The two pleaded guilty in separate pleadings in late 2006 and early 2007, and in the summer of 2007 they were both sentenced to prison. It gave me some satisfaction to see two corrupt providers actually held accountable for their actions.

CHAPTER TWENTY-SIX

Clash of Giants

No trial date had been set for what some reporters and stock analysts were calling the "Business Trial of the Century," HCA's challenge of the civil *qui tam* lawsuit I filed. Court documents revealed that my army of attorneys intended to depose at least seventy-eight current and former Columbia/HCA officials, thirty-eight of them from the company's corporate level.

Depositions would start in January 2002 and were scheduled to end in June. The list of those to be deposed included Dr. Thomas Frist, Jr., the company's former CEO who'd retired in December 2001; the company's current chairman and CEO, Jack Bovender; former CEO Rick Scott; and former HCA Chairman Clayton McWhorter.

The Justice Department was rumored in press reports to have offered to settle the cost reporting case for $800 million, or double the alleged fraud damages. HCA had reportedly rejected the offer. HCA spokesman Jeffrey Prescott said, "We know what this case is worth." While he wouldn't identify the company's price tag for settling, it appeared that the company hoped to pay no more than one single year's earnings to resolve the allegations. He confirmed that HCA was pursuing a dual legal strategy, preparing for trial at the same time that it hoped for a settlement.

Why was HCA fighting this issue so hard? Did it think the $845 million payment from its earlier partial settlement would satisfy the government? Did the company believe it could outlast the government? Or did HCA officials believe that the change in presidential leadership in Washington would improve the outcome of its case? The company's only discernible strategy to the outside world was stalling. But even that strategy was costly. From 1998 to 2000, HCA spent another $224 million in legal, investigative, and accounting fees, the company reported in its securities filings.

Optimistic Wall Street analysts resumed rating HCA stock as a "buy," implying that its remaining Medicare claims risks were minimal. Some believed that the remaining cases would settle for between $100 million and $250 million, suggesting that the government had been unable to substantiate higher settlement demands. These analysts were optimistic, however. In reality, HCA was worried about the lingering Medicare liability. My attorneys and experts close to the case agreed that the low-range settlement figures that analysts touted were unrealistic.

On January 8, 2002, my attorneys began their two-day deposition of the first HCA official, Milton Johnson, the controller. Johnson's deposition did not help. He was frequently unable to recall statements and events, attorneys who attended his deposition said. After only a few depositions, the company pulled the plug. HCA attorneys unexpectedly canceled the remaining scheduled depositions and asked the Justice Department to disclose which former and current employees were still targeted in the ongoing criminal investigation. In a legal motion, the company asked Judge Royce Lamberth to postpone depositions until August 2002, seven months away. HCA argued that executives fearing criminal prosecution would be forced to invoke their Fifth Amendment rights and refuse to answer questions in depositions for the civil trial. The company feared that this would hurt its defense in the civil case. Spokesman Prescott defended the company's move, explaining, "We want people who don't have anything to worry about from a criminal standpoint to be able to talk."

The Justice Department called the move "a tactic for strategic delay," responding that disclosing the names of executives who faced charges could undermine the criminal investigation. Stephen Meagher viewed Columbia/HCA's move as an attempt to derail the litigation process. "They're worried," he said. "This is the first time senior executives are to be put under oath and questioned about their accounting practices."

In a February 27, 2002, article in the *Wall Street Journal*, Jim Moorman, the president of Taxpayers Against Fraud, observed, "You know what that says to me? All of a sudden they woke up to find that they've got a real problem and they panicked." In hindsight, I think he was right. The company realized that what began as a small annoyance had snowballed into a huge catastrophe.

In another court filing, HCA accused our attorneys of employing smear tactics. In the filing, it was asserted that, "A rash of press stories riddled with quotes from the relators' counsel have appeared in the media." The document also stated, "These misleading and baseless stories strongly suggest that an unseemly effort is under way to generate publicity aimed at influencing a matter submitted for the court's consideration."

In an April 15, 2002 *Tennessean* article HCA spokesman Prescott explained that whistleblower attorneys gave the impression that HCA was trying to shield their senior executives. "They tried to paint our original motion as being about senior executives. That, frankly, wasn't true," Prescott said. "The company's motive was to protect midlevel executives from legal uncertainty." John Phillips responded to HCA's claims, saying that the charge of fraud against HCA was huge and that HCA had already acknowledged guilt.

I was concerned that the lengthy battle with HCA was draining the Justice Department. I knew the FBI agents wanted to move on to something newer and more exciting. They were tired of poring over HCA cost reporting documents. After the 9/11 terrorist attacks, many FBI agents and other government enforcement staff had been transferred to fight terrorism. The routine phone discussions I'd regularly shared with them abruptly stopped. While nobody questioned the government's appropriate need to shift its focus to investigating and fighting terrorism, the vacuum those departures created left many fraud cases in limbo.

The collapses of Enron and Arthur Andersen also occupied the attention of the Justice Department's white collar crime investigators. Enron became a top priority, and Joe Ford, who'd been promoted within the FBI in recent years, took a lead role in that investigation. Even the Enron story seemed juicier to investigators than Medicare fraud. Based on my personal experiences, I knew it could take years for the government to fully investigate this newfound fraud.

I was confident that Phillips & Cohen and the team of big law firms they had engaged would not let Jim Alderson and me down. They were prepared to wage the fight against the healthcare giant at all costs. We also had Senator Charles Grassley of Iowa closely watching the case.

During a Senate hearing, Thomas Scully, the new administrator for the Centers for Medicare and Medicaid Services (formerly the HCFA), pointed out differences in legal opinions between the CMS and the Justice Department over the HCA case. Scully—who formerly headed the for-profit hospital industry's trade group—openly criticized the Justice Department's fraud investigation into HCA. I was not surprised by his comments. Though he then worked for the government agency administrating the Medicare program, Scully's true loyalties weren't to taxpayers but to the industry he had left behind. (Scully later rejoined the industry after brokering the biggest Medicare benefit increase in forty years, the prescription drug plan that proved a boon to managed care companies and pharmaceutical manufacturers. In December 2003, he became a lobbyist with the Washington office of Atlanta law firm and power broker Alston & Bird. Before Scully left, he came under fire for allegedly threatening to fire a CMS analyst if he revealed the true cost of the prescription drug plan. He also took heat for negotiating new jobs for himself while still leading CMS.)

Referring to comments made by Scully in a March 14, 2002, Committee on Finance subcommittee hearing, Grassley said, "The Justice Department is the nation's lawyer. As such, the Justice Department is responsible for protecting the taxpayers against fraud. CMS absolutely cannot undermine the Justice Department's ability to police healthcare fraud." Grassley said the CMS had a duty to cooperate with the Justice Department in the HCA investigation.

Then, in a letter addressed to Tommy Thompson, secretary of the Department of Health and Human Services, dated June 25, 2002, Senator Grassley wrote, "Recent comments by CMS Administrator Thomas Scully have given me great concern that there is an active, ongoing effort under way to change or modify FCA (False Claim Act) enforcement policy that in my view could significantly undermine the FCA . . ." His letter continued, "In testimony before the Health Subcommittee of the Senate Finance Committee on March 7, 2002, Mr. Scully said that DOJ's prosecution decisions regarding a specific FCA case were 'beyond comprehension.' Based on subsequent conversations with my staff, it became clear that Mr. Scully's comments were directed to the government's wide-ranging case against HCA . . ."

In Florida, our change in fortune allowed us to take a real family vacation for the first time since I had filed my *qui tam* lawsuit years earlier. Generally, our vacations had revolved around the twenty-four–hour drive to Wisconsin to visit our families. We'd never been able to afford anything more. For Christmas 2001, Kirsten surprised the kids and me with a Disney Cruise she'd scheduled for spring break 2002. Excitedly, we planned and packed for the three-night adventure aboard the Disney Cruise Line's *Wonder*. It was a fun-filled distraction from the daily stresses of the case. For the first time since I'd filed my lawsuit, I was able to relax with my family without any phone interruptions.

The answering machine was flashing when we returned home on Sunday, March 24, 2002. Pushing the play button, I listened as Meagher's familiar voice echoed in the kitchen. "John, it's Stephen. Call me on my cell phone when you get this message."

I dialed Meagher's cell number. After he answered, we briefly discussed the cruise. Then he said, "We had some bad news while you were gone." I took a breath, then asked, "What is it?"

"The Eleventh Circuit Court of Appeals in Atlanta overturned the Jarrell and Whiteside convictions. The three-judge panel said the U.S. government failed to prove they intended to defraud Medicare. In the ruling, the court concluded that competing interpretations of the applicable law are far too reasonable to justify these convictions."

"How could they?" My heart sank. "Is there anything the Justice Department can do?" "They can ask the Federal Appellate Court to reverse its decision. I don't know if they'd file a petition at this point."

The fantasy glow of the cruise faded quickly. I was flabbergasted. For six years, I'd worked with the Justice Department, the FBI, and other federal investigators to build the case that would eventually convict Jay Jarrell and Bob Whiteside. To have it instantly erased was unfathomable. My family and I had gone through hell, giving up years of our lives. Not only had I put my career on the line, but I'd exposed myself and my family to retaliation. How could I not be disappointed by our judicial system and the appeal court's decision?

With so much at stake, the question had to be asked: What did this mean for my civil case? Trying to put a positive spin on the news, Meagher replied, "Well, it's not so bad. The ruling won't hurt your case. The company has already pled guilty to cost report–related fraud; they can't ask for that guilty plea to be reversed. The appellate court focused on the lack of clarity in the regulations. The court's decision was only on the Fawcett interest issue, which is one claim out of 14,000. There are

13,999 others. This appeals court ruling could actually help speed up the civil settlement."

"How would it speed up?" I asked, still stunned by the news of the reversal. "I think it'll allow us to move forward with the depositions of their employees and executives," Meagher replied.

"I can't believe that three well-educated judges couldn't understand the black-and-white evidence before them," I told him.

Whiteside, who'd been free on bond, said he was grateful to HCA for supporting him during the ordeal. "I personally don't know of anything that anybody's done wrong," he told a Bloomberg News reporter. Jarrell declined comment. His attorney, Peter George, said, "This ought to be the end of the case." George also stated in the *St. Petersburg Times*, "This ruling should give the government pause before they charge someone with a crime when the regulations they are relying on are ambiguous."

After hearing news of the reversal, HCA, which had paid the legal bills for Jarrell and Whiteside, announced they could be rehired. Once again, providers were given fodder to complain that Medicare rules were complex and confusing. The healthcare industry celebrated along with Columbia/HCA spokesman Prescott. "Clearly, the wording in the opinion is very straightforward. This supports our contention that the Medicare cost reports are vague and confusing and open to interpretation," he said. Prescott would not speculate how the court ruling would affect the rest of the fraud case, though he did admit the decision introduced new information into the settlement talks, according to a Bloomberg story. HCA quickly filed documents with Judge Lamberth, overseer of the civil case, detailing the appellate court's ruling.

In a well-crafted paper, *United States v. Whiteside:* Granting a License to Steal? Peter Chatfield supported his contention that the appellate court erred in its ruling. Chatfield concluded, "While the opinion does not represent a triumph of justice or judicial insight, neither does it constitute a license to steal. And the prosecution itself, although ultimately reversed, no doubt has had a salutary effect on an industry that had let its obligations to report costs accurately to Medicare for taxpayer reimbursement digress into a cat-and-mouse game where Medicare was always the loser." (See Appendix B for the full text of Chatfield's paper.)

Four months after the Eleventh Circuit's reversal of the convictions of Whiteside and Jarrell, the ramifications of the three-judge panel's decision still reverberated. In an anticlimactic ending to the criminal case, the

U.S. Attorney in Tampa closed the office's criminal investigation of the HCA executives on July 16, 2002. Having begun nearly six years earlier with FBI agent Ford leading the way, the case concluded in one trial, two overturned convictions, and millions of dollars and hundreds of thousands of work hours spent. The government did secure company guilty pleas from Olsten Kimberly and Columbia/HCA.

But now, after all these years, there seemed little to show for that unprecedented show of government resources. Even though he'd moved on, I imagined that Ford was disappointed. He had expressed great expectations for the criminal case and once proclaimed that he wouldn't be happy unless many conspirators were sent to prison.

After the Whiteside/Jarrell trial, everyone involved with the case had expected further indictments and trials. They never materialized. In December 2001, the Justice Department ended its Columbia/HCA criminal probes in Miami and Dallas. The case may have grown too old. In addition, Columbia/HCA and its practices were viewed differently now, and the company had to some extent changed. Seven years earlier, when Rick Scott led the company, Columbia/HCA was widely feared in the hospital industry. As the company rapidly expanded, its corporate philosophy had rewarded hardball business tactics more than healthcare quality. Competitors found Columbia/HCA's management style intimidating and arrogant. After the investigation started in 1997, though, the corporation began repositioning itself within the industry. HCA was no longer gobbling up the competition. Instead, its machine had changed course to save face and keep the stockholders (who had been relatively uninformed of the truth) happy. The corporate priority became damage control.

With the new presidential administration operating in a post–9/11 world, we wondered which way the fraud-fighting pendulum would swing. Would all the government's resources shift to fight terrorism? Had the FBI tired of Medicare fraud? Did the Bureau now seek new criminal challenges? Enron, Global Crossing, WorldCom, and Tyco demanded attention. It was ironic, however, that while other cases involving corporate crime and executive misconduct yielded prison sentences, this one ultimately did not.

U.S. Representative Pete Stark of California vented his anger to *Modern Healthcare* magazine, saying, "These executives ought to be forced to pay back what they stole and serve jail time for the crimes they committed. They are nothing more than simple crooks who ought to join the growing photo of poster children for corporate abuse. Yet, no one is being held accountable."

What Stark didn't discuss were the strong Republican ties of the Frist family. Dr. Thomas Frist, Jr.'s brother, Senator Bill Frist (Republican of Tennessee), was ascending to the post of Senate majority leader and was touted as a future presidential candidate. Could politics have played a role in the Justice Department's decisions to drop the criminal investigations? Did the Bush administration exert its influence to spare the family embarrassment? The Justice Department was supposed to be immune from political influence. But as the investigations into the firing of U.S. Attorneys in Spring 2007 demonstrated, political influence sometimes permeated department actions.

Though Jarrell and Whiteside's March 2002 victory disappointed career prosecutors and investigators in the Justice Department's Criminal Division, Meagher saw a silver lining. "It's a turning point for the civil case," he explained. "As a result of the ruling, Columbia/HCA has withdrawn its motion and will make its executives available for depositions. The criminal investigation has been a thorn in our sides for a while. Now we are able to push ahead on discovery." I saw his logic and thought that maybe we were finally getting close.

The end of the criminal investigations put to rest HCA's objections that current and former employees could be targeted in the probe. Spokesman Prescott said, "That frees up everybody to give depositions without fear of personal criminal liability. As we've said all along, we're interested in letting these folks tell their story because we think it will benefit us." I didn't believe it, and I didn't think the company was serious.

Two months before, on May 8, 2002, the Justice Department had presented HCA with another settlement offer. Company CEO Bovender told shareholders at an investor meeting, "The proposal is before us. We're studying it now. We'll be back to the government and review that with them in a fairly short period of time." He advised investors to expect negotiations to continue throughout the summer.

Bovender also expressed to the investors that he wanted to see the case settled, but that the company was not willing to settle unless the settlement amount was in a "reasonable range." When asked when a settlement might be reached, he responded, "It is much better for us to get this settled than to litigate all these issues."

Bovender's earnest public comments belied the company's true private position. By July 2002, the company still had not responded to the government's May offer. That meant HCA was preparing for trial. (Later, I learned from a corporate insider that the company expected to pay one time its annual earnings to settle the entire investigation. The company still refused to tell the government the amount of their "reasonable range.")

For months, Phillips & Cohen's huge legal team had examined hundreds of thousands of documents. As team members dug deeper and deeper into the archived files, Meagher and Chatfield reported that the case was growing stronger by the hour. My attorneys found many smoking guns and identified and catalogued them all. They documented practices that would make top executives scheduled for depositions squirm. We never doubted that if HCA chose to litigate, we'd win.

Now that the path had been cleared to resume depositions, my legal team was ready to launch their very well thought out program designed to unearth relevant policies and practices employed by the company to defraud the federal government. Chatfield recalled that HCA's defense attorneys appeared surprised that our legal team understood the documents so well, never anticipating how the incriminating documents would compromise their clients.

In the middle of all this, on March 28, 2002, my attorneys and I were shocked to learn of an HCA agreement with the CMS. The CMS announced that HCA would "pay the Medicare program $250 million to resolve all cost reports that had been pending while the Justice Department investigates a healthcare fraud case." The agreement did not resolve civil issues or whistleblower lawsuits involving cost reports. We learned that the Justice Department did not negotiate or participate in this settlement, nor had it approved the agreement. How coincidental that Scully, the former head of the for-profit hospital industry's trade organization, was now on the inside negotiating a deal for HCA.

Without Justice Department consent, Scully had structured a sweetheart deal between HCA and the CMS. Justice Department officials publicly doubted the fairness of the settlement, calling it too low, much too favorable to HCA, and potentially damaging to the civil fraud case. Senator Grassley also questioned the settlement deal in a scathing, seven-page letter to Department of Health and Human Services (DHHS) Secretary Tommy Thompson dated October 17, 2002. Senator Grassley lambasted Thompson's department for failing to enforce the False Claims Act and blasted the CMS for failing to respond to questions he'd previously posed regarding the Columbia/HCA case. Frustrated by the lack of response from the department, he informed Thompson that "This is just not an acceptable way of doing business with Congress. I expect my questions to be responded to in full."

Grassley questioned whether DHHS officials misled him and demanded all the information the CMS relied on to make its settlement decision. "Clear language should leave no doubt," Grassley continued. "I am concerned that if press reports are accurate, CMS is looking to try and settle the HCA case for far below the possible loss to the taxpayers."

He concluded, "The publicly announced Columbia/HCA settlement by CMS is exactly the type of inappropriate action I fear. Too often in the past I have seen the False Claims Act goals undermined by agencies that put the relationship with their contractors before their duty to the taxpayers."

CHAPTER TWENTY-SEVEN

Millions of Dollars or a Lump of Coal

Checkmate. On December 18, 2002—just weeks before the deposition of HCA CEO Jack Bovender and former HCA Chairman Thomas Frist, Jr.— the company announced a tentative record-breaking Medicare fraud settlement. The agreement still required approval from U.S. District Judge Royce Lamberth and senior Justice Department officials.

HCA would pay a staggering $898.5 million to end the largest, lengthiest Medicare fraud investigation in U.S. history. The company agreed to pay $631 million to resolve all civil claims, including kickback and cost reporting issues. A separate $250 million payment was included in HCA's earlier agreement with the CMS on outstanding cost reports, and the company would pay $17.5 million to resolve Medicaid-related fraud allegations. The combined Columbia/HCA settlements recovered more than $1.7 billion for the government healthcare coffers and resulted in fourteen corporate criminal guilty pleas.

In true government fashion, federal authorities left Jim Alderson and me in the dark about the settlement amount attributable to our lawsuits. We hoped the Justice Department would remember Judge Steven Merryday's ruling in the Quorum case when it offered us our relator's share. Based on our Quorum and KPMG experiences, we expected a battle with the Justice Department. "We have standing in court to object to the settlement. We will object unless our share of the settlement is adequate and fair," Stephen Meagher assured Alderson and me.

In a press release from his office, Senator Charles Grassley cautioned,

"Until I see the math, I'll remain skeptical. This settlement can't be a Christmas gift to HCA and a lump of coal for the taxpayers."

The move to announce the settlement in December benefited HCA. Stock analysts and Wall Street investors responded appreciatively as the stock prices rose 3 percent on the news. In a written statement, HCA's Bovender said, "We are pleased to have successfully negotiated a settlement to the remaining two civil issues, cost reports and physician relations. Today we are a stronger company with a corporate integrity agreement, a corporate compliance initiative that has set the standard for many in our industry, and a culture that is focused on the delivery of quality patient care in the communities we serve."

My initial reaction was relief, but upon hearing the amount, I was disturbed. A close inspection of the underlying documents found that the amount of the settlement resolving fraudulent cost reports—$356 million—was low, based on the value of the fraud our team of lawyers and experts had discovered. The cost reporting issue alone was worth far more and could have fetched more than $2 billion. The government was entitled to seek triple damages but barely recovered the amount we estimated was stolen, amounting to single damages. Even so, Alderson and I could not deny it was a monumental settlement.

And it had taken a monumental effort. Phillips & Cohen, a law firm with a handful of attorneys, along with a well-assembled team of outside litigators and experts, had dedicated more than 75,000 hours and spent close to $30 million to help the government pursue the case. As the team worked, the case had grown exponentially. As attorney Gerald Stern pointed out, "The more we dug into the records and the more we deposed current and former HCA employees, the more substantiation we found of ways HCA had defrauded Medicare. It took a Herculean effort to recover this money for the government."

But the attorneys weren't the only ones working this case. Alderson and I had spent thousands of hours ourselves, working tirelessly to assist both our legal team and the government in advancing our cases. We always told the truth, we never lied, and we never fabricated a document. We relied on Columbia/HCA's own documents as evidence. Columbia/HCA spent more than $300 million in legal fees and investigation costs trying to mask the truth. In the end, the truth caught up.

The timing of the settlement was not accidental. It came at a pivotal point in the political career of Senator Bill Frist of Tennessee. The senator had recently surfaced as a leading candidate to replace Trent Lott as Senate majority leader, a point that didn't escape Meagher. "It would be difficult for a doctor to assume a leadership role in the Senate touting a desire to reform Medicare from the ground up, with his family the subject of a Medicare fraud case," Meagher observed. He speculated that Dr. Thomas Frist, Jr. and Jack Bovender feared questioning under oath in the depositions, and believed HCA preferred throwing in the towel rather than exposing its executives and founding family to potentially embarrassing or legally risky depositions.

Key among the many things that we'd learned over the previous six years was patience. Although Phillips & Cohen doggedly nipped at the Justice Department's heels after the December 2002 announcement, Alderson and I remained uninformed about our relator's share. Finally, John Phillips received a call from the Justice Department. Government authorities told him that the recently announced settlement required HCA to pay $356 million to resolve claims related to Medicare cost reports above the $250 million paid to the CMS as reported in March. The Justice Department offered a record amount as the relator's share. Alderson and I would share a whopping $100 million.

It took months to get our heads around the offer. Was it fair? Was it reasonable? Peter Chatfield said, "I understand the motives on both sides to shut it [the case] down, and as a matter of timing it was acceptable. I think the settlement is big enough to satisfy the public interest, and if it wasn't such a big and huge complex case, they [HCA] would have paid a higher proportion to what they actually stole."

He was right. It would be hard for the government to extract much more without years of costly litigation. The reality was that $100 million was a lot of money. It was also a record relator's share. There was no guarantee that a judge would agree to a higher amount. Ultimately, Alderson and I accepted the $100 million offer, ending a nearly decade-long fight for justice.

We both signed the deal and waited to be paid. Long ago, Alderson and I had agreed how we'd split the money. We had a gentleman's arrangement that we'd never put in writing, even though our lawyers strongly recommended it. But we had become friends, sharing a rare and unusual experience few others could understand. Even as events had spiraled out of our control, in a small way we'd been able to relieve each other's emotional stress, the feelings of isolation and the stigma of being whistleblowers. Separated by thousands of miles, but connected by phone and shared values, we trusted each other. Our relationship grew as we shared many of the same problems and rode the same emotional roller coaster. Both Certified Public Accountants, we'd both been forced to accept jobs that paid less than our experience commanded. Our families had survived on tight budgets and had needed to borrow from relatives to get by. We paid our bills, but had little else.

And now Alderson and I shared 100 million validations of our decision.

For years, Jim and I'd spent hundreds of hours coming up with strategies and discussing our cases by phone. He and his wife, Connie, had become an integral part of our lives, yet we'd never met in person. We finally had the opportunity to meet in 1999, when Jim asked us to come to Oregon in October. He told me, "I got us a speaking engagement with a professional trade organization to discuss our *qui tam* lawsuits at their conference. They're willing to reimburse both of us for our travel expenses." "That sounds like fun," I had responded. "Kirsten and I will be there."

When Kirsten and I arrived at the hotel in Eugene, Oregon, it had been overwhelming to finally shake hands with the Aldersons for the first time. Kirsten and I were able to share our experiences with two people who empathized completely. Independent of each other, Jim and I had each chosen the same path, risking everything by telling the truth. We each understood that if we'd failed, we would have lost everything but our pride. Neither of us regretted the decisions we made. "If I hadn't come forward, if I'd looked the other way, I would have been no better than the men convicted," I told the Aldersons.

It had taken the government a staggering fourteen months to process the relator's share from the partial settlement in 2001, but that wait was slashed to seven months for the second settlement. Just as in the partial settlement, no dump truck backed up to our front door to drop tons of bills on our porch steps. Without fanfare, the government quietly wired my portion of the $100 million relator's share to my bank on July 15, 2003. Of course, we were elated, but after everything we'd been through, actually receiving the money was somewhat anticlimactic. There was no White House invitation, no congratulatory call from the president or letters of commendation.

Just one politician, Senator Grassley, honored Alderson and me at a

Taxpayers Against Fraud event in April 2004. "These are patriotic Americans," he said. "They demonstrated extraordinary courage in the face of extraordinary adversity. They suffered and their families suffered greatly for sticking their necks out and committing the truth. It's extremely difficult to be a whistleblower. They are about as welcome as a skunk at a Sunday afternoon picnic . . . . Someday, I want to see the president of the United States honor whistleblowers with a Rose Garden ceremony and send a clear message that those who speak up—whether it's in government or from the private sector—about fraud against the taxpayers, will see rewards, not reprisals."

Grassley then presented Alderson and me with engraved golden whistles in small wooden boxes, saying the awards recognized "their integrity, independence, and tremendous sacrifices." The engraving on the box said, "John W. Schilling—In appreciation for having the moral courage to blow the whistle on fraud and helping save American taxpayers billions of dollars."

While our financial independence was ensured, I actually got far less than it first sounded. After Phillips & Cohen took its 40 percent contingency fee and 35 percent was deducted from what remained for income taxes, our share of the $100 million relator's fee had greatly shrunk in size. But the battle was finally over and the money was safely banked.

The dual cost report scheme had been practiced in scores of hospitals around the nation for many years. Hundreds knew about this "standard" practice in the healthcare industry, but Alderson and I were the only ones to report it. And only a handful of other HCA whistleblowers alerted authorities to other misconduct within the company.

The government bears some responsibility for allowing the fraud to flourish. In a revolving door scenario, industry insiders join government service and then return to the private sector, with little oversight or restriction. It's just the way things are done in Washington. No bright line exists between Medicare auditors and the private sector. People take jobs back and forth, just as I had done. How could such an open and blatant fraud scheme continue for so many years without challenges from the government? Why had it taken two whistleblowers and a persistent law firm to force the government to act? Perhaps federal authorities were loathe to concede that their system for detecting, preventing, and prosecuting fraud was ineffective and woefully in need of reformation.

I am proud that the False Claims Act worked as President Lincoln

intended when it was enacted during the Civil War. Since the False
Claims Act amendment in 1986, Taxpayers Against Fraud reported that
whistleblowers have helped the government recover more than $20 bil-
lion.

Years after the settlement had been signed and the dust settled, some
questions linger. Is HCA adhering to its corporate integrity agreement?
Could today's HCA manipulate Medicare as easily as it did in the 1980s
and 1990s? Does the company accurately self-report overpayments, or
instead, does it keep them? Has compliance transformed the company?

I am proud to say I am a whistleblower. When I joined Columbia/
HCA, I could not have imagined facing the moral dilemmas I did, nor
could I have envisioned the wealth I would glean for simply standing up
and doing the right thing.

Epilogue

Looking back, I am still astounded to have played a role in the history of this era and these landmark settlements. While I invested seven years of my life in these cases, I am not the only one who dedicated such time. I am extremely grateful to the talented attorneys at Phillips & Cohen for their diligence and unwavering support, and I'm thankful to the Justice Department for seeing beyond the fog of Medicare cost reporting. I am also proud to have played a role in returning $1.7 billion to Medicare. I would do it all again. The effect of those investigations cannot be measured solely by the settlement amounts. The lawsuits reverberated within the healthcare industry years after they were filed and became publicly known, spurring greater compliance with Medicare rules and healthcare laws and exerting a huge deterrent effect on healthcare providers.

The bias against whistleblowers is deeply engrained in U.S. culture. To many, the term *whistleblower* evokes negative images characterized by disparagements like rats or moles. I've been called "tattletale," "snitch," "disgruntled," and worse. Some people, however, believe whistleblowers serve an important role in our society: to report wrongdoing and corruption that would otherwise go undetected and unpunished. By standing up for what I believe in, I sacrificed a successful accounting career and was ostracized by the healthcare industry, but it didn't ruin my life. While I'm not a highly recruited commodity in the healthcare business world, I remain gainfully employed. Several years ago, I founded JWS Group, a forensic healthcare financial consulting business. I offer healthcare fraud prosecution litigation support to government agencies and *qui tam* attorneys involved in healthcare fraud cases. I bring expert testimony, damage analysis, and case review services.

I'm often asked whether my lawsuit impacted the healthcare industry or whether whistleblowers' actions lead to positive changes. Writing this eleven years after filing my lawsuit against Columbia/HCA in 1996, I answer a qualified *yes*. The subsequent investigation into the company and its business practices dramatically affected the hospital industry, both in the short term and over time. A comprehensive audit conducted by the Office of the Inspector General for the Department of Health and Human Services found that between 1996 and 1998, Medicare overpayments (including fraud, error, and waste) decreased from $23 billion to $12 billion, nearly a 50 percent drop of $11 billion. There is no doubt that the investigation and increased federal scrutiny into industry business practices contributed to that decline as threats of prosecution, convictions, and financial penalties resonated throughout the healthcare provider industry.

At hospitals and healthcare facilities nationwide, the most positive change has been the implementation of compliance programs. Such programs were virtually unknown in the healthcare industry before the Columbia/HCA investigation, with fewer than 15 percent of hospitals boasting such programs. By 2007, more than 90 percent of all U.S. hospitals had such programs, according to the Health Care Compliance Association, a professional and educational organization of healthcare compliance officers.

Hospitals and other large healthcare organizations seemingly embraced compliance, spending hundreds of millions of dollars annually to support internal programs intended to prevent, detect, and report fraud and other violations. Creative consultants and law firms carved specialized practices in the healthcare industry, while large corporations established compliance departments. This trend led to the hiring of thousands of professionals—attorneys, nurses, and accountants—to act as compliance officers. While some may simply be compliance officers in name only, many work in programs that have truly given employees viable means to report fraud within their companies. How effectively those compliance programs deter fraud remains open to debate. The government continues to sign huge settlements, suggesting that many compliance programs are not always accomplishing their intended purposes. But the question remains: Who really oversees compliance? The answer varies.

Many healthcare corporations staff very proactive departments, fielding questions and disseminating appropriate advice to concerned employees as well as suppliers and contractors. Others, however, have adopted the scenario of the fox guarding the henhouse. The corporate CEO or CFO—executives whose compensation and continued employment depends upon the bottom line—often oversees compliance. In some cases, the organization's board of directors monitors compliance, but the board is often far removed from daily operations, which affords it plausible deniability. I believe the real answer is that in many cases, no one is truly responsible for overseeing compliance.

Compliance issues aside, improperly used reserves (the impetus for our lawsuits) have not completely disappeared. Interestingly enough, though, reserve cost reports have vanished almost entirely from the healthcare financial landscape. Those reports, if requested and provided, at least had flagged and identified problematic reserves. Today, it is common practice to not only hold reserves but to camouflage inappropriate ones. Because there is no longer a paper trail in the form of reserve cost reports, problematic reserves are even harder to identify. So who can audit those reserves? The answer is no one.

The Columbia/HCA investigation did heighten awareness within the industry, but I believe that was short-lived. Medicare's regulations are so antiquated, complex, and vague that I fear Medicare fraud has reemerged in a new set of invisible clothes even harder to detect. Calls for my healthcare consulting services to ferret out fraud have increased. My firsthand experiences indicate that healthcare fraud is still rampant, spilling over into the pharmaceutical industry. *Qui tam* settlements have not decreased. In fact, they have increased. According to Taxpayers Against Fraud, settlements in fiscal 2006 reached $3.16 billion, with the majority coming from healthcare.

For a short time, the Columbia/HCA investigation exerted a chilling effect on the provider industry, but the effect fell short of many expert expectations. The investigation and subsequent settlement took seven years to resolve, and along the way prosecutors lost sight of the long-term objective: to prevent and curtail future fraud. Having a defunct division of HCA plead guilty to criminal misconduct wasn't enough to deter future fraud or appropriately punish HCA. The division involved was little more than a corporate shell that was quickly sold off, allowing the corporation to remain a Medicare provider.

And since the 1999 convictions of the Columbia/HCA executives were later reversed by a federal appeals court, healthcare industry executives no longer felt threatened by potential imprisonment. The fact remains that nobody went to jail in this case, and the company as a whole remained guilt-free. When HCA resisted the depositions of its key executives in 2002, I was alarmed. I wondered if the investigators recognized the implications. To me, the implications were obvious. The deposition of high-ranking executives would cause embarrassment, but more important, would ultimately prove a higher level of responsibility and potentially cost the company even more. If this was so glaringly obvious, why did the government retreat from its criminal investigations to concentrate exclusively on a civil settlement?

I believe that the political aspirations of the Frist family played a crucial role in the Justice Department's timing. While the government eventually won a settlement, it conceded by accepting single damages, settling the case for far less than the treble damages and penalties the *qui tam* law allows. The settlement amount, while record-breaking, barely covered the Medicare overpayments Columbia/HCA retained by submitting thousands of fraudulent Medicare cost reports. The government's lack of resolve and inaction reinforced a healthcare industry belief in government incompetence. So while it's true that the Columbia/HCA investigation certainly cautioned the industry, it fell short on delivering a stern and long-lasting warning. Instead of sending the message that Medicare fraud would be prosecuted with vigor, federal regulators conceded that fraud is only a crime if the government can prove it. And it told providers that it's possible to grind out a more favorable legal outcome by stalling and delaying government regulators.

The Columbia/HCA scandal can teach us other lessons. In the last decade, the inspector general of the DHHS, which has the authority to exclude providers from billing government programs and bans around 3,000 individuals and providers annually, has been careful not to restrict access to health services. Only three hospitals have been excluded from the program. Exclusion is called the "kiss of death" in the hospital industry, and providers should fear violating healthcare laws to avoid exclusion. But the inspector general should apply those exclusion authorities more aggressively. Daniel Levinson, who became inspector general in 2004, has been more willing to consider exclusion than most of his predecessors.

Medicare fraud has not been extinguished in the hospital industry, as evidenced by the 2006 whistleblower settlements by Dallas-based Tenet Healthcare Corp. and St. Barnabas Healthcare System in West Orange, New Jersey. For-profit Tenet and not-for-profit St. Barnabas (New Jersey's largest hospital system) together paid more than $1 billion to settle allegations that they gamed the Medicare outlier payment system, which is designed to compensate hospitals for cases incurring extremely high costs.

The healthcare industry, one of the nation's biggest employers, has a nearly $2 trillion effect on our economy. Even with its flaws, it is one of the best healthcare systems in the world. The quality, compassion, and commitment of healthcare providers deserve our respect and admiration. But fraud in federal health programs not only robs taxpayers but depletes valuable resources dedicated to serving seniors, the disabled, and most economically disadvantaged. It would be a national tragedy to allow inaction and apathy to foster the growth of parasitic healthcare fraud and siphon resources from the nation's neediest. While strong leaders such as Senator Charles Grassley and Representative Pete Stark have taken a stand, it is time for younger leadership within the government's ranks to step forward.

After reading my story, you probably realize that becoming a whistleblower is a life-changing process. And if you find yourself in the same position, you must be prepared for those changes. It made me a multimillionaire and allowed me to retire before turning forty. My wealth afforded my family a spacious home, private education for our children, vacations we could only fantasize about before, and luxuries previously impossible to consider.

Most important, it enabled Kirsten and me to spend time with our children. We are active in their lives and support their activities at school. We are trying to offer our children a childhood that they will remember fondly. Unlike our upbringing, they are privileged. That is not something we'd change. But we strive to instill our values and sense of responsibility in our children.

We've learned that wealth demands responsibility. It takes time to manage and preserve assets. Even though we've contributed sizeable donations to several charitable organizations and do have a few toys, we are relatively sensible in our spending. We've taken care that our new wealth has not altered the conservative Midwestern morals and values imbued in us by our parents.

Given the many sacrifices our family made over the years, many people ask if I would do it again. While I am quick to answer, the decision to blow the whistle is difficult to make. Yes, my family and I paid a stiff price when I decided to take on a healthcare giant. My career in the healthcare industry ended abruptly, and we endured many years of emotional and financial turmoil. But in the end, I knew I did the right thing by telling the truth. It is a lesson that I am proud to pass on to my children. I applaud and support others who have already spoken out and attempted to stop corruption in business and government, and I encourage others to come forward.

And when asked if I would do it again, I respond, "Absolutely!"

Ten Years Later

MARK TAYLOR

Healthcare industry insiders said the civil and criminal Columbia/HCA investigations ignited by my whistleblower lawsuit changed the hospital industry and its relationship with government regulators. It also transformed the hospital industry giant now known as HCA, which took itself private when it agreed to a July 2006 purchase by three private equity firms and the family of its founder, Dr. Thomas Frist, Sr., for more than $30 billion in the **largest leveraged buyout in the hospital industry.**

Current and former government officials, healthcare attorneys, healthcare fraud experts, and consumer advocates describe the investigation, trial, and record $1.7 billion settlement as historic. But ten years after the 1997 raids on Columbia/HCA facilities in six states, then the largest search warrant execution in FBI history, what lessons have the hospital industry and healthcare financial professionals learned? How did the country's largest healthcare fraud investigation impact the HCA executives who were indicted, convicted, and later exonerated by a federal appeals court? How did it affect the government investigators and regulators who participated in the seven-year marathon and the attorneys sifting through the aftermath?

To answer those and other questions, I turned to veteran healthcare reporter Mark Taylor, who covered the trial, investigation, and settlement for the hospital industry trade publication Modern Healthcare. Taylor, the magazine's former legal affairs reporter, was familiar with many of the players and knew the issues.

History will judge our actions. It may take years before we know the total *effects of the investigation on the healthcare industry. Here is what industry insiders and experts said in the summer of 2007.*

John Schilling

In 1996, when **John Schilling** filed his lawsuit, Columbia/HCA was the biggest and most feared healthcare provider in the country. The investor-owned company terrified not-for-profit hospitals, then and now the dominant business model in the hospital industry, but also won the admiration of Wall Street for its rising stock value and trend-setting business practices. The company was flying high under the leadership of Rick Scott when the raids of Columbia/HCA offices and hospitals occurred in July 1997, under search warrants partly generated by Schilling's lawsuit and undercover work as an FBI informant. Schilling's name and identity were not known at the time, but his role in the subsequent investigation, criminal trial, and record settlement has spurred lasting changes in the hospital industry—a fact conceded by supporters and critics alike.

Schilling has been both praised and reviled for his actions and the effects they generated. Some executives who have worked for investor-owned hospitals denounced him as greedy, self-interested, and disgruntled, called his lawsuit destructive, and said his case marked the beginning of a deteriorating and adversarial relationship between hospitals and the government. And not-for-profit hospitals and their leaders weren't much kinder, either denigrating Schilling for the damage his actions allegedly caused or refusing comment altogether.

Former Columbia/HCA reimbursement director **Bob Whiteside,** a defendant in the 1999 criminal trial in Tampa, Florida, said he holds no hard feelings against the man whose testimony almost sent him to prison. Whiteside said he remains perplexed by the entire episode and Schilling's role in it.

"Either John was or is stupid or vindictive," Whiteside said. "I hate to think either one of them. I hired him at a low-level position almost as a gopher for me. He was upset when I left that he didn't get my job. But I'd worked for twenty years and he didn't have a lot of experience. He might have been disgruntled. He felt left out and didn't fit in. My big point is I can't understand how the whistleblower act [the False Claims Act] can reward people for their own bad action. John left HCA and came back as a consultant and furthered the act itself."

Whiteside said he doesn't think about Schilling often. "The only time I think of him is when [baseball pitcher] Curt Schilling is pitching," he added.

From the start, Whiteside proclaimed his innocence in the cost reporting fraud, conspiracy, and home health allegations brought by Schilling's civil whistleblower lawsuit and the subsequent criminal investigation. He continues to assert he never did anything wrong. "We really thought we were in the right and were entitled to claim the interest" from the Fawcett Memorial Hospital cost report, said Whiteside. "I think it was the environment at the time. In our situation, the people at the top didn't know what was going on at hospital level."

Whiteside said the judge and jury treated him very fairly, but he reserved harsher judgment for the FBI investigators, Justice Department attorneys, and whistleblower attorneys. "I thought they were kind of ridiculous. The lead FBI agent [Joe Ford] was later dating and then married the Assistant U.S. Attorney [Kathleen Haley] who was prosecuting me. And the FBI agent was friends with the attorney [Stephen Meagher] representing Schilling," Whiteside chuckled. "And they had the gall to say we were conspiring."

Whiteside proclaimed his innocence throughout the process. "I never did anything at all," he said. "I think they got me because I moved up to the corporate offices and they thought I knew more than I did. One, I didn't know anything, and two, I wouldn't have told them anyway. I just stepped in the middle of this."

Whiteside said HCA treated him fairly throughout the investigation, trial, and overturning of his conviction. "I never felt like an outcast," he said. "If this case was in Nashville, it never would have gone to trial. In Nashville, this company is well respected. In Florida, they thought we were a bunch of crooks. I felt I never did anything wrong. But I had faith in the judicial system that everything would work out, and that's what happened."

Whiteside conceded that the HCA investigation did enhance public awareness. "I think everyone is a little more careful now to dot their Is and cross their Ts," he said. But he said the government's crackdown on healthcare fraud was "misdirected."

"The government used blackmail to force companies to pay settlements," he said. "I think it just increased the cost of healthcare. The company had to pay hundreds of millions of dollars to attorneys. At one time HCA was paying for attorneys for more than 200 of its employees being questioned by the government. It was ridiculous, but a great thing for Nashville lawyers. All the good attorneys were busy because no one attorney could represent more than one person. I think it was kind of a waste."

He said the investigation also changed HCA. "They went private again so they don't have to deal with all that publicly traded stuff for Wall Street again," Whiteside observed. "That's one big thing: They're trying to stay out of the spotlight."

Whiteside retired shortly after returning to HCA following the overturning of his conviction in 2002. "When I came back to HCA, all the Columbia people had gone and I felt like a stray cat there. They offered me a severance package and I took it."

Other former Columbia/HCA executives attributed changes in company and industry business practices to the investigation. **Clayton McWhorter,** the former HCA chairman, president, and chief operating officer—who previously served as chairman, president, and CEO for HCA spinoff HealthTrust—said there's no question the company he once led has evolved.

"Unfortunately, coding under the DRG system isn't black and white, but gray," he pointed out, referring to Medicare's prospective payment system for reimbursing healthcare providers for treating patients by diagnosis related groups. "The whole problem is people were upcoding [billing for services at a higher rate than they were entitled to receive]. But after the investigation, they were far more cautious and you probably saw more undercoding going on."

McWhorter, the founder and chairman of the private equity firm Clayton Associates, said many of Columbia/HCA's problems were attributable to the leadership style of Rick Scott. "That started the whole ball rolling," he recalled. "Rick had a strategy for growth that was in our competitors' faces. It aggravated a lot of people. I think that has softened since the investigations. There's more harmony in the marketplace between not-for-profit and for-profit hospitals, more cooperation between them."

McWhorter also agreed that compliance has grown, not just within HCA but throughout the industry. "I think as a result of the investigations people are spending a lot of money to try to do the right and legal and appropriate thing. Back then there were no clear-cut rules. There was upcoding. I don't really believe the people who were charged in Florida were knowingly trying to do something illegal, though it may have been so in the government's eyes. Practices have modified since I was in the business. Hospitals have become much more cautious. I've been out of HCA daily operations for eleven years [he remained a board member until 2000] and I truly believe, knowing the players, that they're committed to doing the right thing."

Sam Greco, former senior vice president for financial operations for Columbia/HCA, worked for Columbia/HCA and its predecessor company, Columbia, from 1989 to 1997. "Without question those suits brought a sense of urgency to compliance and what compliance meant across the board," said Greco, who now operates hospitals. "Before those suits, most of us thought of compliance as a billing department issue. I didn't get the sense that there was the appreciation or understanding how company-wide compliance should have been. If any good came out of it, it was that it made everyone far more aware."

Greco said that before Columbia/HCA CEO Rick Scott was pushed out after the 1997 raids, Scott tried hard to set standards for compliance within the company. "I sat in those meetings and he [Scott] would say we have to figure out how to lead the pack in doing things the right way and be able to measure compliance. He was probably ahead of us on all that," Greco said. "But moving from that statement to implementation was hard. The learning curve was probably bigger than anyone thought."

He said beginning in the mid-1990s, relations with government regulators grew increasingly adversarial. "What hit hard was the government's presumption of guilt. We [Columbia] inherited a lot of the problems we faced. To suggest what happened then was a Columbia thing is wrong. Much of it preceded us. I think Rick was a Boy Scout. I was around him for ten years and he never asked me to do anything except take the high road and do the right thing. I think a number of us took it on the chin for others."

Former Columbia/HCA insider **Jerre Frazier,** now an attorney and consultant in Houston, Texas, witnessed the company's legally suspect business practices when he was an outside attorney asked to conduct an evaluation. "The first obvious thing was they had no compliance program, no one labeled as compliance officer, and their compliance handbook was a ten-page mimeographed effort nobody took seriously. It was easy to see they had some very significant [legal] exposure."

Frazier said that many of the problems preceded Rick Scott's arrival. "There was a lot of pressure placed on managers and that came from the front office, from the top. When the focus is solely on the bottom line you do whatever it takes to make that bottom line."

Eventually, Frazier was hired as compliance director in 1997 and remained there until 1999. "Without the raids being launched, I seriously doubt whether they would have done anything," Frazier said. "Once the raids occurred, it became a high priority."

Frazier said the Columbia/HCA game plan from the beginning was to stall and delay, or assume a "slow play" strategy that would compel the Democrats to settle the case before Bill Clinton left the White House. Frazier said that the policies of Alan Yuspeh, HCA's senior vice president for ethics and compliance, did spur some fundamental changes within Columbia/HCA, including the company's bonus and incentive practices that some contended almost encouraged executives to break Medicare rules and violate healthcare laws. However, he believes that HCA was not chastened by the final outcome of the case but instead emboldened, and believes the rest of the healthcare industry was encouraged by the results.

"Publicly it was viewed as massive because $1.7 billion is a lot of money," he said. "But the public wasn't aware that HCA got off light. Company board members were aware it could easily have been [with triple damages and penalties] $10 billion instead of $1.7 billion. The government spun it well as a big amount of money that should have taught a valuable lesson to the healthcare industry. The truth is that HCA made an informed decision that crime pays. Their calculated business judgment was that there were very slim odds that they'd get caught and very slim odds that even if they were caught that they'd have to pay back all the money. And it was unlikely that anybody would go to prison. It looks like their strategy worked."

Frazier himself became a whistleblower when he sued Franklin, Tennessee–based Iasis Healthcare in 2005. In that suit Frazier, who served as the for-profit hospital chain's vice president of ethics and compliance and chief compliance officer, alleged that the company paid kickbacks to doctors who performed medically unnecessary procedures. His lawsuit, which was filed in U.S. District Court in Phoenix under the False Claims Act, was unsealed in July 2007. The same law firm that represented Alderson and Schilling filed the suit for Frazier. Frazier alleged that Iasis paid doctors for phony medical directorships, offered office and lab space leases for less than market value, and other improper incentives.

Frazier said that John Schilling and Jim Alderson made valuable contributions through their lawsuits. "The hospital industry is indebted to John and Jim. It's encouraging to see somebody stand up to the system. They're among a handful who chose not to go along to get along."

Thomas Scully, the former administrator of the Centers for Medicare and Medicaid Services (formerly known as the HCFA), attributed some of HCA's legal troubles to its dynamic and controversial leader and his aggressive style. "Rick Scott is a good guy, but not a sensitive healthcare guy. He came in as a Southern capitalist dynamo who thought he was going to change the world. He thought he'd kick butts and change the way healthcare operated. But I think he was a little naive about politics."

Scully said Scott scared not-for-profit hospitals into becoming more efficient. "There was this perception that the Columbia Mongol horde would come in and wreak havoc. But he was doing a lot of good stuff. The Premier Hospital Quality Incentive Demonstration project [a later CMS initiative intended to improve quality in hospitals] was a pure copycat of what Columbia was doing," Scully said. "Columbia was way ahead of everyone else on measuring performance and quality. His problem was he approached running hospitals the way you run other big businesses."

But Scully conceded that Scott created a culture "where people who weren't ethical could upcode and do things they shouldn't have done, a culture that made people think they could or should push the envelope."

Scully said he warned Scott not to move into the Northeast, where longstanding not-for-profit traditions and the heavy presence of unions opposed him. "It was different in the South and West, where people looked at healthcare like any other service and were more receptive to for-profit healthcare companies," he recalled. "But once he went into Massachusetts and Rhode Island, he was villainized as a huge corporate monster and a menace. Was Rick Scott a great defrauder? No. Was there bad stuff going on within his company? Probably, and maybe Rick Scott should have understood it better. He made an easy target. I tried to warn Rick. Before HCA blew up he went too far too fast and was too radical in a field where most people were very traditional. Rick drove a lot of the changes in healthcare and pushed not-for-profit hospitals to do things they couldn't have done, dealing with managed care and low-cost services that they wouldn't have done without competitive pressures."

Scully denied that politics influenced the outcomes of the Columbia/HCA criminal investigation and eventual civil and criminal settlements. "That's complete nonsense," he said.

He attributed some of the company's legal troubles to a bitter union organizing battle between a Las Vegas HCA hospital and the Service Employees International Union and cited congressional pressure from U.S. Representative Pete Stark (Democrat of California) on the Justice Department to investigate what some legislators considered a destructive influence in healthcare. "That didn't come from the White House, but from Congress. There was more pressure, yes. At the close of the Clinton administration, they wanted to settle because Republicans were coming in, and why leave it for the next crowd to get all the credit for your hard work."

Scully said it was ludicrous to imagine he intervened to help HCA, a company that formerly helped pay his salary as president of the Federation of American Hospitals and whose leaders—Rick Scott, Tom Frist, and Jack Bovender—he counted among his friends. "I never got involved in the HCA case," he said. "I stayed 100 miles away. I said then that I wasn't required to recuse myself, but I did anyway and left the room when the topic arose."

He disputed assertions by some that George W. Bush's appointments of him and Homeland Security Secretary Michael Chertoff benefited HCA in its final settlement. Chertoff, whom Bush first named to head the Justice Department's Criminal Division, served as HCA's lead lawyer when he was with Latham & Watkins before his appointment. "That's an outrageous idea. I didn't even know Chertoff. This was a huge, pressworthy settlement. It's absolutely ridiculous to think we had anything to do with that. I personally think they [HCA] could have settled many years earlier and I don't know why they didn't. I think that once lawyers get involved in the case, it was not in their interest to settle. Lawyers change in the Justice Department, they come and go. I was surprised it took so long."

Joe Ford, the FBI special agent who is now the associate deputy director of the FBI and its chief operating officer, said he always viewed the HCA investigation as a landmark case on several levels. "It was the first time the government took on probably the most complex aspect of investigating healthcare fraud, Medicare Part A medical costs," Ford said. "If you look at the stats at the time, 90 percent of Medicare dollars were spent on Medicare Part A and only 10 percent on Part B, but 90 percent or more of investigations were directed at Part B. When John Schilling's complaint came in, I saw this as a good opportunity to have a high impact on a major part of healthcare expenditures in this country."

Ford said in most investigations, the defense team paints the government as a powerful Goliath picking on the little guy David. "This is one case when the defendant had greater resources than we did," Ford remembered. "HCA spent more than $300 million on its defense. The government spent $20 million to $30 million in the HCA case, about $30 million in the Enron case. We were outmatched and outgunned."

He credited HCA with fielding a great defense strategy. "They looked after their employees," he said, characterizing the company's strategy as delay, divide, and conquer. The company's two leading defense attorneys for the case, with the firm Latham & Watkins, went on to enjoy high-profile government careers. Michael Chertoff became the secretary for Homeland Security. Alice Fisher, who now heads the Criminal Division of the Justice Department, took the job Chertoff left when he was appointed secretary.

Though outspent, the FBI could muster up a crowd of agents. Ford said the day that the search warrants were delivered, about 500 agents participated, more than 330 in Florida alone. "Today if an HCA-type case presented itself, we could marshal the resources we needed," he said.

Ford said the case offered great challenges to government prosecutors. "The issue of healthcare fraud was so arcane only a handful understood it," he said. "And cost reporting fraud is the most complex fraud I've seen next to the structured financial transactions in the Enron case. But once we understood the schemes and what motivated the fraud, it became a lot easier for us to conduct interviews and put the evidence together."

He said that Schilling played a large role in the criminal investigation, particularly in the early stages. Ford said that the government amassed more than 13,000 boxes of documents providing evidence for the criminal and civil investigations. "He would teach the subject matter and identify targets," Ford explained. "I came to respect John for the actions he took. He had a young family. His wife had medical problems. That had to play on his mind and add a lot of stress to his life. But he was available any time I needed him. John saw something wrong and also realized it was a way to make money. John stuck his neck out further than anybody I ever saw. He was quietly meticulous and self-deprecating throughout."

He said Schilling also brought evidence. "John had the KPMG audit reports. It was pretty blatant. It was the nail in the coffin for HCA. And he had copies of the reserve cost reports."

Ford said he asked Schilling to wear a wire to obtain evidence. "He handled it very well, very professionally. He didn't have to do it. It became difficult for him. I know John was motivated by the success of his *qui tam* and the payoff it could bring. But I believe he was first motivated to do the right thing, to right a real wrong. As an accountant, John saw keeping a double set of books and some of the other HCA practices as blatantly wrong."

Ford, who was also involved in Jim Alderson's whistleblower lawsuit investigation, said hospital cost reporting fraud was rampant at the time. "If you were going to rip off the government, this was the way to do it. There was nobody looking," he said. "The way hospitals were defrauding Medicare Part A, there were multiple schemes in multiple locations. . . . I 'got it' from Alderson's case, but I didn't know how big or prevalent it was. I thought it might have been just a few hospitals or maybe it was confined to Quorum alone. I knew when I first saw it [Schilling's lawsuit] that this was a good case."

He recounted how a later witness in the Tampa criminal trial, former Florida HCA reimbursement official Steve Dudley, said everyone was doing 100 miles per hour. "Dudley said everyone was breaking the law to some degree," Ford remembered. "He said if you didn't, you wouldn't succeed in the hospital industry."

Ford knew the indictment would command HCA's attention. "We would not have unsealed the indictments right away if we'd been able to get a plea from Whiteside, if he'd cooperated. That was our strategy. When he didn't, we unsealed them."

He said by August 2000, government investigators and prosecutors had reached a point of critical mass in the case. "We knew we had to make an affirmative case against the corporation. It was a big turning point. We sat down with all the evidence and analyzed it for them by subject area and showed them the incidents weren't isolated, that it wasn't just one hospital, but many. We tied the witnesses to the testimony and to the documents, and that was the straw that broke the camel's back.

We showed them the depth and width of the fraud. We had e-mails and documents and correspondence and witnesses. We showed them it was corporate-driven, not the actions of a few rogue employees."

Ford said the publicity surrounding the case hurt HCA's image nationally. The company pleaded guilty to criminal charges and paid a $1.7 billion settlement. "That's not chump change," he observed. He noted that while HCA "may have gone private equity" and no longer has to follow Securities and Exchange Commission rules for publicly traded companies and may not be required by the Sarbanes-Oxley law to provider greater public accountability, "They still have to follow Medicare rules."

Ford said the HCA investigation also changed how government views, investigates, and prosecutes healthcare fraud. "It made us realize that companies operate locally, nationally, and globally. The HCA case helped us see that companies operate in global markets. Prior to HCA, we investigated some companies locally and a few nationally as well, but never really looked at the global implications."

He said the lawsuits filed by Schilling and Alderson and the investigations they sparked dramatically impacted the hospital industry, both in the short term and over time. "When the indictments were unsealed, it put the brakes on that [cost reporting fraud] for a while. Other hospitals thought, if HCA could get caught, anyone could," he observed. "The deterrent effect was remarkable. It showed the ineptness of HHS. Shortly after we indicted [Mike] Neeb, [Jay] Jarrell, [Bob] Whiteside, and [Carl Lynn] Dick, it was amazing how many hospitals began sending amended Medicare cost reports to Medicare carriers because of 'errors they'd just discovered.' They said they just noticed the mistakes on the very same issues we were investigating or had indicted upon. The fiscal intermediaries were getting checks every week, a lot of them for $300,000 to $400,000. These hospitals figured if HCA could fall, so could they."

There were other effects as well. "It really changed the healthcare industry. Hospitals were gobbling home health agencies at the time as a way to spread their costs," he said. Home health agencies were reimbursed by Medicare on a cost basis, meaning they were paid what they told the government that it cost them to provide the care. Hospitals were reimbursed on a Prospective Payment System, which meant they received a fixed amount per diagnosis related group. Ford said that after the word spread about the lawsuits and criminal investigation into HCA's purchases of Olsten's home health agencies, those agencies became "almost worthless." And the Health Care Financing Administration later changed the rules. "The HCA case opened their eyes."

Ford applauded HCA's public embrace of compliance, but said that in his current position he hasn't followed its program closely and couldn't vouch for its effectiveness. But he cautioned that if the company's compliance program is only a paper exercise, "Then we will see them again." He pointed out that another for-profit hospital chain, Dallas-based Tenet Healthcare Corp., which paid a $900 million fraud settlement in 2006, also settled fraud allegations a decade earlier when it changed its name from National Medical Enterprises and agreed to pay $378 million. "History repeated itself because that company did not change its culture. For compliance to succeed, the culture has to change," he said, while admitting, "I don't know whether HCA is complying fully or not."

Ford called the HCA investigation historic for several reasons. It was the largest healthcare fraud investigation ever and the largest coordinated search and execution of search warrants, he said. "We're still doing that today. We look at the way we coordinated those investigations with the civil side of the house," he said, noting that lessons were learned there as well. "Unless you stay focused on the criminal case all the way, something gets lost. Civil cases often don't always lend themselves well to criminal investigations."

Ford said he learned his toughest lesson from the HCA investigation. "After Columbia/HCA, I realized people, individual corporate officers, had to be held accountable for the actions of their companies. And after HCA the government did a better job of focusing on individuals. . . . Instead of just giving us [the government] money, people need to go to jail. I learn from my mistakes and this was my first big one," said Ford, who later headed the Enron investigation and the FBI's White Collar Crime section. "After HCA, we went after Enron, Qwest, WorldCom, and HealthSouth. In those cases people went to prison for their corporate crimes."

James Sheehan, the former Associate U.S. Attorney in Philadelphia and perhaps the best known healthcare fraud prosecutor in the United States, said that after the failure of President Clinton's health plan, both Congress and the administration sought to reduce healthcare costs. "And everyone could get behind antifraud efforts. The perception was there was a lot of fraud going on. The FBI and OIG [Office of the Inspector General] started putting resources behind it and the results supported it."

Sheehan said the HCA investigation greatly pushed the corporate compliance movement in two ways. He said appointing respected defense industry compliance specialist Alan Yuspeh as its chief compliance officer marked a significant change for HCA. "He came in with a mandate to create a compliance program. Up to that point, HCA epitomized a tough-it-out approach," said Sheehan, who left the Justice Department early in 2007 to become the inspector general of New York State's Medicaid program. "The HCA investigation demonstrated that was not a successful strategy and showed that the government was serious about pursuing the case against the nation's largest provider. And that gave the compliance industry a huge push. People believed if it could happen there, it could happen anywhere. I don't know if this would have happened without HCA's near-death experience. The Health Care Compliance Association was an industry response to the issues raised by the HCA case."

Sheehan said the case also showed that with so many *qui tam* relators and such big dollars involved, there was a need for a process to handle multirelator cases. "The Justice Department had to figure out a process that worked and develop the expertise to do it. It emphasized the need for nationally coordinated investigations."

He said after the HCA case, the healthcare industry accepted internal processes and controls relating to compliance earlier than some other industries and anticipated requirements similar to the Sarbanes-Oxley law requiring greater accountability in publicly traded companies.

Sheehan declined to speculate whether politics affected the final outcome of the HCA civil and criminal cases. "What do you mean—after George Bush was elected and appointed Tom Scully, the head of the federation, of which HCA was the biggest member, and named HCA lawyer Michael Chertoff to head the Criminal Division of Justice?" He said the 1990s was a different era and Janet Reno a markedly different attorney general. "How often has [former] Attorney General [Alberto] Gonzales talked about healthcare fraud?" he asked.

D. McCarty "Mac" Thornton, the former chief counsel for the DHHS inspector general who is now in private practice with the Washington office of the law firm Sonnenschein, Nath & Rosenthal, said the HCA case continued a trend begun a few years earlier of large *qui tam* cases.

"The notion that the government could take on the leading hospital chain and eventually recover $1.7 billion just heightened tremendously the overall anxiety of the industry and absolutely helped the compliance movement find some priority in the healthcare companies," he said.

Thornton, whose office worked on the HCA investigation and corporate integrity agreement, said there was a sense of being a part of something very big and very successful. "Everybody was having a great time and feeling like they were really accomplishing something. We were pretty confident once we saw the evidence that these companies would have to settle. We were looking at gigantic monetary recoveries. It was heady days to be a part of the prosecutorial efforts."

Gabriel Imperato, a healthcare defense attorney with the Fort Lauderdale, Florida, office of the law firm Broad & Cassel, said Schilling and Alderson "provided information that resulted in the most ambitious fraud enforcement action to that date and ended up having the most pervasive impact on corporate compliance in the healthcare industry."

Imperato said the HCA settlement and corporate integrity agreements resulted in what today is the model for such agreements. "The compliance program was adopted by the largest hospital system in the country. That in itself had a direct effect, as well as a sentinel effect, on the rest of the industry. And the success of these whistleblowers was well publicized and had a direct impact on the volume of future whistleblowers and the kinds of matters they blew the whistle on," he said.

While Imperato pointed out that the government fell short of its ultimate objectives on the criminal side of the investigation, he said the deterrent effect was still very dramatic, "almost indistinguishable from if Jarrell and Whiteside had been convicted. The effect that the indictment, trial, and conviction had on corporate executives was the same, even though they were ultimately exonerated on a legal technicality."

Dr. Sidney Wolfe, the director of the consumer activist organization Public Citizen's Health Research Group, said all the government scrutiny and focus on compliance have not caused healthcare fraud to disappear. "Why isn't anyone going to jail?" Wolfe wondered. "Companies can always write off financial penalties. They still seem to be chuckling on the way to the bank. Companies are making very cold, calculated financial decisions.

They know they might get caught. I think there's more awareness of it [healthcare fraud] going on, but it's still here."

William Mahon, the former executive director of the National Health Care Anti-Fraud Association, said the HCA case may have derailed the presidential aspirations of Senator Bill Frist. "If ever an organization had family connections, it was the Frist family. That combined to make it the landmark case it was that caused such a big impact in the hospital industry," he said. Mahon, now heading his own consulting group in Great Falls, Virginia, said the investigation garnered so much attention because of what Columbia/HCA was at the time. "It had a huge ripple effect on the industry and brought the compliance function into the forefront," Mahon said. "This was not some 100-bed community hospital but the biggest player in the industry. It was like throwing a boulder into a pond. It sent a message to the industry that no one was immune. If they could go after the biggest outfit in the country with the biggest dollar volume, they could go after anyone."

Mahon said he remains surprised that ten years later, a steady stream of False Claims Act cases continues to make headlines, indicating that problems still exist. "What I expected to exert a significant deterrent effect just hasn't. That's been a perennial surprise. Many providers haven't seemed to have gotten the point that the government is serious about this stuff."

A number of healthcare industry leaders and association executives chose not to comment for this book. HCA spokesman **Jeff Prescott** said, "There is no interest here."

Chip Kahn, the president of the Federation of American Hospitals, of which HCA was a founding member, also would not comment. The investigation, criminal trial, and first settlement preceded Kahn's arrival at the federation, which is the industry trade and lobbying organization for the nation's for-profit hospitals. Kahn did say that the suits made some lawyers, consultants, and whistleblowers very rich.

Jay Jarrell could not be located for comment, and his attorney, **Peter George,** did not return phone calls.

Michael Neeb, currently the president of HCA's International Division in London, did not return phone calls or e-mails seeking comment.

The American Hospital Association, the primary trade and lobbying organization for American hospitals and a group that unsuccessfully challenged the False Claims Act, declined comment as well. In an e-mail, AHA Senior Counsel Melinda Hatton said she wouldn't talk about it and advised other AHA staff members similarly to refrain.

Surprisingly, leaders from the Health Care Compliance Association, whose growth was fueled in part by the HCA investigation, also would not comment for the book and refused interviews. However, the organization for compliance officers did release a statement. "The growth of the HCCA can be largely attributed to three factors: the complexity of the healthcare regulatory scheme, coupled with active enforcement; the industry's desire to respond appropriately to the regulatory environment; and the hard work of many dedicated volunteers," the HCCA said.

Officials from several other healthcare professional associations did agree to discuss the investigation and its impact.

Peter Leibold, CEO of the American Health Lawyers Association, said the Schilling/Alderson lawsuits had "a massive impact on the hospital industry." Leibold said that because of the HCA suits and the government scrutiny they drew, healthcare organizations have spent considerable resources on compliance. "Hospitals and healthcare companies grew very nervous about the HCA investigations and wanted to protect themselves and comply with the evolving landscape." He said at least partly because of the lawsuits, there is probably less fraud and wrongdoing in healthcare today. Leibold said the government's successful settlement emboldened prosecutors to pursue other big national healthcare providers. "Government also grew more amicable about *qui tam* relators and conducting large-scale investigations across the healthcare continuum," he explained.

Dick Clarke, president and CEO of the 35,000-member Health Care Financial Management Association, a Westchester, Illinois–based professional organization for healthcare financial executives, said the cost reporting fraud investigation and ensuing trial gripped his membership. "It certainly raised the cost reporting issues onto everyone's radar and got people to pay more attention, as any lawsuit would do," Clarke said.

"These laws were on the books, but like immigration laws, people weren't necessarily focusing on them. Enforcement had not been strong in this area and therefore hospitals had not focused on them. Those lawsuits changed all that and caused much greater focus."

He said the suits spurred tighter reviewing of cost report processes, both by management and external auditors, and spearheaded a whole new industry: compliance. "That is a positive thing that came about as a result of those lawsuits. They got providers to be more attentive to how they do things and it broadened beyond Medicare financial reporting to other areas, causing some broad-based changes within healthcare. And to that extent, I think hospitals have become better corporate citizens and more attuned to complying with laws and regulations, most of which were designed to protect the public. And I would say that's a positive thing."

Fredric Entin, the senior vice president and general counsel for the American Hospital Association from 1990 to 1999, said the HCA investigation fundamentally changed the relationship between healthcare providers and the government. "I thought it significantly altered that dynamic between the government as the payer of Medicare and Medicaid and hospitals as providers and recipients of federal healthcare money," said Entin, now with the Chicago office of the law firm Foley & Lardner. "Prior to that time the relationship was looser, more collegial. If the fiscal intermediary [the companies the government contracts with to administer Medicare in every state] questioned a bill, generally a conversation would occur and the hospital would either concede the error or explain why it occurred. Those first HCA cases ended that relationship. Those conversations didn't occur."

Entin said hospitals started receiving letters from the government explaining that they were liable to pay money under the False Claims Act or civil monetary penalties authorities. "The industry was really shaken by what turned out to be a very aggressive approach by the government," he said. Entin recalled a visit from a Justice Department official who came on behalf of then–U.S. Attorney General Janet Reno. "I thought he was coming to talk about how we can educate our members about these new risks. But he told me that the Justice Department wanted the AHA to turn our members in. It was a 2 × 4 between the eyes." He said the AHA pushed back. "We said, 'You're punishing providers for not complying with rules and regulations so complex that perfect compliance is impossible.' We believed that with the huge volume and complexity the government would always find problems." Entin said relations eventually improved and the AHA worked with the DHHS inspector general to develop the first compliance guidelines for hospitals.

Entin said the lawsuits represented an immense change in direction by the government. The settlement "reflected that something was there and we began to see significant changes within HCA and by extension, with everyone else. Much has gone into compliance since then. I don't think even 10 percent of hospitals had compliance programs then."

Entin admitted some positive impact from the lawsuits: the large recoveries the government has collected from providers. "Last year (2006), it was $3.1 billion. Getting money back to taxpayers is always good. Has it improved the quality of healthcare? The government got the industry to keep its eye on the ball with greater acuity than ever before. Are they doing it because it's the right thing? Yes. Are they doing it because they're afraid? Yes. At the end of the day a massive investment in compliance is the lasting legacy of those lawsuits. It's hard to measure the effects of these lawsuits. They were probably a benefit to taxpayers. And they probably made the *qui tam* bar and a lot of other lawyers, consultants, and whistleblowers rich."

Schilling's attorneys and others from the whistleblower community witnessed a different side of his personality and saw the sacrifices and pressures imposed upon him and his family. Not surprisingly, they viewed the impact of his actions far differently than many in the industry.

Patrick Burns, a spokesman for the whistleblower support organization Taxpayers Against Fraud, said the suits filed by Schilling and Alderson were "transformative. These were very, very big cases. They showed that a hospital company could be nailed hard and forced to sell off assets and change management and business practices."

Burns said Schilling's lawsuit was filed during an era of massive consolidation within the healthcare industry, with clinical laboratory companies, nursing home chains, dialysis centers, and hospitals merging and acquiring competitors to grow bigger, please shareholders, and achieve economies of scale. But he said the catalyst for that consolidation was fraud. "They all discovered how to game the system and used the profits to go out and buy more hospitals and other facilities," he said.

"Schilling and Alderson were the edge of the wedge exposing this con solidation in the hospital industry. And when those cases came forward, they exposed another problem: the incapacity of the Justice Department to actually deal with these really big cases. The department had the desire, but not the manpower or expertise. In the Quorum and HCA cases, they turned to whistleblower law firms to do much of the work."

Finally, he said, the Schilling and Alderson suits demonstrated the power of the False Claims Act. "Schilling understood the mechanics of how this worked. He really was David with five smooth stones to slay Goliath," he said. "These were extremely complicated cases that used to be tougher to sell to government prosecutors. Now they get it and everybody understands how much money is at stake and how much is and has been stolen."

Stephen Meagher, one of Schilling's whistleblower attorneys, said the HCA case remains the "gold standard of cooperation between the government and private individuals when it comes to large litigation. This required more Justice Department personnel and other law firms. It was a multiyear project spanning almost ten years. They went in with an army and a lot of bravado."

He said Schilling and Alderson drew attention to the possibility of being a successful whistleblower. "Before that there weren't many prominent ones in the hospital industry. Hospitals then had not sustained a large hit. Today hospitals have a heightened sensitivity to this," said Meagher, formerly of the *qui tam* law firm Phillips & Cohen but now practicing solo in San Francisco. "That said, I don't think the fraud has stopped."

He said in his small world of False Claims Act law, news of the lawsuits quickly spread and attracted the interest of other whistleblowers. "The word got out that there's a way of being financially rewarded for doing the right thing. More cases came forward. More states are passing their own false claims acts and that will spur even more cases," he said. "The Schilling case and others like it focused attention on healthcare fraud generally and the vast government resources squandered and lost to fraud."

He said hospitals have realized that they could benefit from some internal processes to recognize and respond to complaints. "If both John Schilling and Jim Alderson had a kind ear to go to without fear of firing, they would have used that process themselves. I saw what a struggle it was for John and Jim."

Meagher said he was astounded when Schilling and Alderson told him that they had agreed years earlier to join their lawsuits and divide the whistleblower's recovery fee without benefit of a contract. "We argued and tried to convince them otherwise, but it still sticks in my mind that they agreed to split $100 million on a handshake."

John Phillips, partner in the whistleblower law firm Phillips & Cohen, said the Schilling/Alderson suits sparked the filing of many others against HCA. "Many other lawsuits against HCA were spawned by press coverage of our case," Phillips said. "The government realized that within HCA there were other people who knew things and were coming forward."

He said the government was on the verge of declining Alderson's case when his firm offered help. He said HCA was delaying and delaying in the hope of wearing the government down. "The last thing the government wanted to do was to pass on the case and have us [Phillips & Cohen] bring it on our own and collect a substantial recovery." He said the Alderson and Schilling cases showed that the False Claims Act was working in the private/public collaborations the way Congress intended when it passed a revised version of the law in 1986. "We [Phillips & Cohen and the firms and experts it hired] did much more than half the work, perhaps 75 percent to 80 percent of it on the civil case," he said. "We marshaled resources necessary to bring and prosecute the case. There was no way the government could have done it all on its own. We provided the extra lawyers the government asked for. We spent and risked millions of dollars because we knew we had a strong case and we'd get the money back."

Phillips said Schilling exemplified "the best of whistleblower character. He was a great witness who worked hard and was very knowledgeable. John did all the right things."

One of Schilling's other attorneys, **Peter Chatfield,** a partner in Phillips & Cohen, said that after the lawsuits became public, hospitals took a much less aggressive posture on filing cost reports than they had in the past. "It changed the way the industry went and the way consultants advised hospitals," Chatfield said. "The HCA case also showed a model of how to work big False Claims Act cases in cooperation with the government."

He said Phillips & Cohen, then a small firm with a handful of lawyers, was not intimidated by the size and power of HCA. "The bigger concern was trying to figure out why a case that looked so good to us had the government dragging its feet. We were surprised by resistance to the Alderson case."

He said the biggest challenge in the HCA case was how to create pressure to bring the long ordeal to a settlement. "There was so much money at stake for HCA that it was actually cheaper for them to pay lawyers $30 million per year than to pay up the debt," he said. "So the case just sat there indefinitely. It was to HCA's advantage to drag it out as long as possible." He said his firm applied pressure by moving forward on the depositions of the top HCA executives. "We were concerned that the longer the case dragged on, the easier it would be for HCA to nibble down the damages, and we were looking for ways to show them that the damages would go up," he said.

Chatfield said that Phillips & Cohen's experts continued to dig deeper into each individual hospital's cost report histories with claims mapping, which he said found growing legal liability. "We were able to demonstrate this [claims mapping] would significantly increase claims damages to the company and we were going through the depositions asking about those," he said. "That added some pressure."

He thinks HCA should have paid a higher civil settlement. "The government was being extremely conservative, ridiculously conservative in its approach and steeply discounted the value of the claims. The odds are HCA did pay too little," he said. "But I think the Department of Justice felt like there needed to be a total cap on what's recoverable without the case going on forever. That's part of the complexity of such a large piece of litigation. There really was a fundamental difference in philosophy between us and the government in what was doable and [what] wasn't."

The fact that no HCA executives went to prison for their roles in the fraud scheme constituted "a miscarriage of appellate justice," he said, referring to the Eleventh Circuit's overturning of the convictions of Whiteside and Jarrell. "I was surprised and disappointed. I think it was a wrong decision by the court, something that never would have happened in a street crime."

In retrospect, he said the legacy of the case is the message it sent to the healthcare industry. "This was a major shot across the bow about the ability of government and whistleblowers to bring complex cases. It put the private sector on notice that these kinds of cases can be prosecuted. It also showed the effectiveness of the False Claims Act statute in prosecuting fraud by a major violator."

He called Schilling "an incredibly brave guy" who never lost his cool and withstood aggressive defense attorney questioning.

Fellow HCA whistleblower **Jim Alderson** agreed, describing Schilling as "a true hero of whistleblowers. What really differentiated John from the others was his willingness to wear a wire and work for the FBI. That had to cause a tremendous amount of tension." Alderson said Schilling went to trial "knowing the defense attorneys would come at him with everything they had. The biggest law firms in the country were trying to destroy him," he said. "I thought it was absolutely amazing how well he held up under that situation and move the case forward."

He said what most impressed him about Schilling's ordeal was when he asked both his father and his wife not to attend the trial. "He didn't want them to see it and I thought that has to just tear at him. You want them there, but know you'll be called everything in the book and see yourself destroyed. Who wants your dad or wife to see that? That is the ultimate sacrifice."

Alderson said that HCA was scared by the lawsuits and the government's intervention. "They knew they were guilty of what we were accusing them of doing," he said. "They knew we were different. We were hitting at the nerve center of the whole company's profitability. These reserves were over $1 billion on their books and they knew it and knew we knew it. If the truth ever came out, they knew they were wrong."

He said HCA changed some of its business practices after publicly being pilloried. "They took their hospital administrators off an incentive system designed to make dishonest people out of honest people," Alderson said, explaining that half of a hospital administrator's compensation was awarded in salary and the other half in bonuses, bonuses awarded only if that hospital achieves its ever increasing financial targets. "That put enormous pressure on people who were missing their bottom line," he said. "It was easy to walk down to accounting and ask the accountant to change a journal entry. Journal entry changes make a lot of money for people. They did away with that system and adjusted their salaries appropriately, and in the long term, that was for the good of the company and the industry."

In addition, he said Quorum, the HCA spinoff sued by Alderson, stopped processing the cost reports of the hospitals the company managed. Quorum officials "told each hospital it had to do its own cost report," he remembered. He also believes that fiscal intermediaries began cracking down on fraudulent accounting activity. "After the *60 Minutes* piece on our case was aired, everyone was asking whether these practices were happening in their hospitals. If you're a fiscal intermediary auditor and you hear fraud is going on in one of your client hospitals, it has to scare the hell out of you. FIs began looking deeper in those cost reports."

He said when then DHHS Secretary Donna Shalala said in 1998 that the department would reduce reimbursements to physicians and hospitals, she faced a big backlash. "Shalala came back later and said Medicare payment errors due to fraud, abuse, and mistakes dropped from $22 billion in 1997 to $12 billion in 1998," Alderson said. "I think that some of that decrease was due to the HCA investigations. What we did had a long-term effect. Our efforts saved billions a year for several years at least," he said.

Senator Charles Grassley (Republican of Iowa) said the HCA lawsuits and settlement provoked a deterrent effect that rippled throughout the hospital industry and the government and protected taxpayers from fraud. "We had to wake up the whole hospital industry," said Grassley, a coauthor of the modern version of the False Claims Act and one of its ongoing champions in Congress.

He said the investigation also proved the importance of the False Claims Act. "The whistleblowers' only sin is committing the truth," he said. "They tend to be very patriotic Americans who want things to be right. I think whistleblowers are so important that I've advised the last four presidents they should honor whistleblowers with a Rose Garden ceremony." Grassley said if the president did that, it would send the strongest possible signal that whistleblowers should be honored for their actions, not reviled.

"Sometimes whistleblowers are considered unpatriotic, about as popular as skunks at a picnic," he said. "But I think they're very patriotic. Their sin is telling the truth."

Grassley said he still wonders whether HCA got off lightly. "There's a great deal of reason in the public's mind to question whether the final results were as punitive as they should have been," he said, declining to criticize the Eleventh Circuit for overturning the convictions of Jarrell and

Whiteside. "From my judgment, it doesn't look like justice was done as much as it should have been." He said former CMS Administrator Thomas Scully "probably tried to avoid answering our questions, and there was some evidence that maybe he tried to use his influence in his position to try to get the Justice Department to go lightly on HCA."

Grassley said the HCA investigation sparked two pieces of legislation he introduced and that Congress passed in 2005. The first encourages states to pass their own false claims act laws by awarding states a larger portion of Medicaid fraud settlements if they do. The second law requires healthcare organizations receiving more than $5 million in Medicaid money annually to educate their employees, physicians, contractors, and vendors about state and local false claims laws. "If you look at the $20 billion coming into federal treasury since 1986 from False Claims Act settlements, well, that speaks for itself. It is real money," he said.

Grassley was less certain of the lawsuits' deterrent effects on industry behavior. "That is something that cannot be measured," he concluded.

Ultimately, the impact of Schilling's actions will be measured not only by the savings to the Medicare program, changes in industry practices, and deterrent effect on fraud, but by a change in industry attitude about the integrity of government health programs and the importance of listening to insiders' complaints about wrongful practices. Healthcare industry insiders predict that there will always be fraudulent providers seeking to exploit loopholes and take advantage of vulnerable government programs, the cost of which will be borne by increasingly impatient taxpayers and program beneficiaries in higher program costs and reduced benefits.

With watchdogs like John Schilling, however, both taxpayers and beneficiaries stand a fighting chance of having their interests protected.

Mark Taylor

The Fawcett Interest Issue

The Fawcett interest issue, which was at the core of my whistleblower lawsuit and the criminal indictments against four Columbia/HCA officials, was a debt interest expense question emanating from a mortgage loan from Manufacturers Hanover to an HCA predecessor company, the for-profit hospital chain Basic American Medical, Inc. (BAMI). The original loan of around $15 million was to Fawcett Memorial Hospital, one of five hospitals then owned by Indianapolis-based BAMI.

In 1982, 46 percent of the loan proceeds were targeted for capital expenditures, and 54 percent were allocated to operations. In 1983, the loan was included in a $13.25 million refinancing package with Northwest National Life. The fiscal intermediary (FI, the contractor Medicare hired to review the bills hospitals submitted to the federal health program) ultimately concluded—and Fawcett agreed—that 39 percent of the new debt was used for capital purposes, and 61 percent was spent on operations.

Although it was clear that a substantial portion of the refinanced debt was directed to non-capital purposes, Fawcett filed cost reports for 1984 and 1985 characterizing the interest expenses as entirely capital-related. This was a lie. And it was significant because Medicare reimburses hospitals through their Medicare cost reports at a higher rate for debt interest used for capital expenditures, as opposed to operational expenditures. The change in categorizing the debt interest resulted in Fawcett Memorial Hospital gaining hundreds of thousands of dollars in unwarranted Medicare reimbursement.

In 1986, Fawcett's deceptive scheme began to crumble when a consultant's prepared cost report demonstrated that the debt was not entirely capital-related. After discovering what had been done, Fawcett sought to amend the 1986 cost report to make it conform with those filed in previous years. The effort, however, was rejected by the fiscal intermediary and thus only highlighted the interest issue. The FI did not explain its reasons for the rejection. When providers amend their cost reports, they must explain why. Fawcett would have disclosed that it was changing the interest expense allocation, which would have raised a red flag to the FI that it should examine this area during an audit.

Until 1994, there was generally a delay of two or more years between the date Fawcett's annual cost reports were submitted and the date the FI "settled" the reimbursement claim. In the meantime, Fawcett typically was awarded most of the reimbursement it claimed, recognizing that any overpayment would need to be repaid once the "audit" procedure was completed.

Consistent with the then typical delay in audit processes, the fiscal 1986 Medicare cost report that Fawcett filed with Blue Cross & Blue Shield of Florida in early 1987 was not fully reviewed by an intermediary auditor until 1989. At that time, auditors noted Fawcett's effort to amend the 1986 cost report and the inconsistency with which it treated this interest issue between 1986 and the previous two years. The intermediary then reopened Fawcett's cost reports for 1984 and 1985 to resolve the discrepancy fully. At first, the intermediary planned to recategorize all of the interest expenses as non-capital expenditures for each of the three years. However, after BAMI and the hospital submitted work papers that justified treating 39 percent of the original amount claimed as capital-related, the intermediary disallowed only 61 percent of the interest expenses as capital items.

Significantly, neither BAMI nor the hospital ever submitted documentation supporting Fawcett's original claims that the interest was 100 percent capital-related, apparently because no good faith basis ever existed to support that claim.

By the time the audit of Fawcett's 1986 cost report was completed, the hospital already had filed cost reports for 1987 and 1988. Those reports contained the same misallocation of 100 percent of the interest expense as capital-related that had appeared in the 1984–1986 cost reports. Fawcett first filed a report reflecting the ruling made in the audit of its 1986 cost report when it submitted its cost report for fiscal 1989. Despite the corrections made by auditors in 1989 to Fawcett's fiscal 1984–1986 cost reports, the companies made no effort to correct the as yet unaudited reports Fawcett had filed for fiscal years 1987 and 1988. Despite their duty to disclose overpayments, the companies left it entirely up to the fiscal intermediary's auditors to find and correct the false claims that continued to exist in those reports.

Auditors, however, sometimes make mistakes. So when Fawcett's 1987 cost report was finally audited, the new auditor assigned to the account missed the interest issue and thus incorrectly allowed the 100 percent allocation of such interest to capital-related expenditures to remain as filed. Despite their knowledge that the claim was false as submitted and that the allocation had previously been corrected by the FI on Fawcett's 1984–1986 cost reports, the companies took no further steps to alert the intermediary of its error. Instead, they chose to retain the additional, unwarranted payment to which they were not entitled. Moreover, they seized upon the error as an excuse to resume claiming the improper allocation in subsequently filed cost reports.

Beginning in 1989, the companies reverted to claiming 100 percent of the interest paid on the relevant notes as capital-related expenditures, though they knew there was no basis for that claim. In reserve cost reports and related papers kept secret from the auditors, the companies next calculated what their reimbursement for such costs properly would be if they had filed their cost reports in accordance with the true nature of the interest expense. They then held the reimbursement impact of their false claims "in reserve" in case the overcharge was discovered.

The error made by the new intermediary auditor responsible for the 1987 report was carried forward when the fiscal 1988 cost report was audited in 1990. Again, neither BAMI nor Fawcett corrected the misallocation or informed the auditor of the previous resolution of the issue. The error was then compounded in 1991, when the auditor was faced with the companies' fiscal 1989 cost report—the only one ever filed in accordance with the representations the companies had made to the intermediary during the audit performed on the fiscal 1984–1986 reports.

Apparently relying on the improper treatment of such interest that mistakenly had been permitted to stand in Fawcett's fiscal 1987 and 1988 cost reports, the intermediary's auditor changed the proper interest allocation included in the companies' filed 1989 report to the improper allocation that had escaped correction in the cost reports filed for the two previous years. This meant that the companies gained even more undeserved Medicare and Medicaid reimbursement for those interest expenses, almost as if the borrowed principal had been spent 100 percent on capital-related items. And once again, the companies accepted the windfall without notifying the auditor or the intermediary.

Continuing the pattern of deception, the companies continued to claim reimbursement on their mortgage interest expenses as 100 percent capital-related in cost reports filed for fiscal years 1990–1993. Auditors, time and again relying on the erroneous treatment of the issue in immediately preceding years, likewise continued to accept that portion of the cost reports as filed.

United States v. Whiteside: Granting a License to Steal?©

PETER CHATFIELD, PHILLIPS & COHEN LLP*

On March 22, 2002, a panel of the United States Court of Appeals for the Eleventh Circuit issued an opinion reversing the convictions of Robert W. Whiteside and Jay Jarrell for making false statements in Medicare reimbursement cost reports on the ground that the prosecution failed to prove beyond a reasonable doubt that the defendants' statements were not true under a reasonable interpretation of the law. *See United States v. Whiteside*, 285 F.3d 1345, 1351–52 (11th Cir. 2002). The decision is especially noteworthy because of the stark contrast between the Court's ultimate conclusion that criminal responsibility had not been proven and the damning recitation of the facts that appears at the beginning of the opinion—facts, evidently accepted by the jury, that suggest quite clearly that the defendants directed and participated in misrepresentation and concealment of a claim for Medicare reimbursement that they understood would be disallowed if Medicare were told the relevant facts.

In light of this contrast, what should one make of the *Whiteside* decision? Was the opinion wrong? Has the Eleventh Circuit effectively granted

* Mr. Chatfield and his law firm represent whistleblowers in civil False Claims Act litigation. Their clients included John Schilling and James Alderson, who were engaged in a False Claims Act lawsuit against HCA that included, among other claims, allegations relating to the misconduct alleged in the criminal suit discussed herein. He would like to acknowledge the contribution of Paul Hoeber, Esq. and his colleagues at Phillips & Cohen to the analysis in, and final preparation of, this paper.

providers a license to steal in the area of Medicare reimbursement? Are Medicare regulations so hopelessly complex as to provide no clear guidance as to what constitutes proper treatment of cost-reporting claims? Did the prosecution fail to frame the case properly? Or does the outcome of the *Whiteside* opinion merely reflect differences in the burden of proof between criminal false statement cases and civil False Claims Act actions? The answer, perhaps, is that a little bit of all of these things played into the outcome. Properly construed, however, the *Whiteside* opinion should be read narrowly, even in the criminal context. And it ultimately says very little at all about when civil liability under the False Claims Act is warranted.

The Reimbursement Claim at Issue

The *Whiteside* case centered on the defendants' treatment on Medicare cost reports[1] prepared for Fawcett Memorial Hospital in Florida of interest expense for refinanced loans (the "Citizens Fidelity loans") that were originally used in part to purchase capital equipment and in part for general operating costs of the hospital. The distinction between how different portions of the loans should be deemed to have been used was critical for Medicare reimbursement purposes because, at the time of these events, the Medicare program reimbursed hospitals for a much higher proportion of their capital costs relating to patient care than it did with respect to administrative and general costs.

It appears to have been undisputed at trial that the original use of the relevant borrowed funds was only 39 percent capital-related (and 61 percent administrative and general—or "A&G"—related). Defendants argued, however, that in years following these initial expenditures, they believed that the hospital should be entitled to claim reimbursement for the interest paid on these loans as 100 percent capital-related as long as the hospital chain remained short on cash and its annual capital expenditures were greater than its cash on hand. 285 F.3d at 1348. They thus continued to claim the interest costs as 100 percent capital-related even after being told by the fiscal intermediary (FI) that audited their earlier cost reports that such treatment was not proper. Moreover, they did so notwithstanding their decision not to appeal the FI's rejection of their initial effort to claim the interest expense at issue as entirely capital-related. *Id.*, at 1348–49. This had the effect of increasing the hospitals' reimbursement from Medicare by up to half a million dollars per year.

For years, the provider got away with the overcharge. The evidence at trial was clear, however, that defendants understood that the hospital's good fortune stemmed not from any decision by the fiscal intermediary to reverse its original determination of what Medicare rules of reimbursement required but rather because a new FI auditor assigned to the hospital mistakenly failed to apply the prior-year audit results properly to the hospitals' subsequent cost reports. *Id.*, at 1349. That mistake was perpetuated by the hospital later when, in response to an FI request in 1992 for documentation supporting allocation of the interest being claimed on the relevant debt 100 percent to capital expenditures, defendants' subordinate "falsified the papers sent to the FI" so that they would support the claim despite the fact that "Fawcett's books and records supported only the 39/61 percent split" previously discussed. *Id.* When the FI again asked questions about the issue in 1995, Whiteside told another subordinate, John Schilling, that the hospital had been receiving excess reimbursement on its capital interest claims because the "FI had made a mistake during a previous audit."[2] Thereafter, Whiteside and his codefendant Jay Jarrell discussed with Schilling ways in which they wanted Schilling to try "to divert the FI's attention from the interest issue" should the auditor ever raise the subject again. *Id.*, at 1350.

Despite this clear record of shenanigans, the Eleventh Circuit reversed the jury verdict in favor of conviction. Reasoning that the United States failed to prove any "Medicare regulation, administrative ruling, or judicial decision exists that clearly requires interest expense to be reported in accordance with the original use of the loan," the Eleventh Circuit panel concluded that the prosecution had not proven beyond reasonable doubt that the defendants' proffered interpretation of the law was unreasonable. *Id.*, at 1352.

Is the *Whiteside* Decision Wrong?

A strong argument can be made that the Eleventh Circuit's decision is simply wrong. The stated premise of the opinion—that a criminal false statement cannot occur unless the prosecution proves that the statement could not be true under *any* reasonable interpretation of the law—

accurately characterizes an abstract proposition of criminal law.[3] However, the panel's application of that principle does not meld cleanly with the facts and circumstances of the case, even as the Court itself describes them.

The only potentially "reasonable" interpretation of the law that the Court offers as a possible justification of the defendants' position was the one advanced by the defendants themselves at trial: i.e., their purported belief that, notwithstanding the fact that the original loans were used initially 39 percent for capital expenditures and 61 percent for administrative and general expenditures, the hospital could justify treating 100 percent of the interest paid on those loans in later years as a capital expenditure, provided that the hospital was short on cash and its total capital expenditures for the year exceeded its cash on hand. Such a justification, however, relies on the premise that a change of circumstances in fact occurred that logically could support the conclusion that an exception was warranted to the normal rule that proper treatment of interest expense for Medicare reimbursement purposes is controlled by how the borrowed funds were initially used. See 42 C.F.R. § 413.153(b)(1) (defining "capital-related interest expense" as "the cost incurred for funds borrowed for capital purposes").

While recognizing that this regulatory standard exists, the panel decision notes that "the regulation does not explain how to define the underlying debt; that is, whether the initial use of the loan proceeds provides the *sole* basis for the debt's character." 285 F.3d at 1352 (emphasis added). I emphasize the word "sole" because its inclusion in the Court's analysis is a key qualification that confirms what seems obvious from the plain language of 42 C.F.R. § 413.153(b)(1) cited above: Any effort to define debt as capital by reference to something other than the purposes for which funds were borrowed would have to be an exception to the normal rule. The Court, however, fails to provide any legitimate reason in fact or law to conclude that there was a *reasonable basis* to believe that such an exception existed with respect to the particular loans at issue in the *Whiteside* case.

The most fundamental flaw in the Court's analysis is that it appears to accept the justification Jay Jarrell offered at trial for believing that treating the interest expense as 100 percent capital-related in later years without critically evaluating whether it makes logical sense.[4] Once again, Jarrell's purported basis for concluding that interest on debt whose proceeds were originally used for A&G expenditures can subsequently be transformed to a capital-related expense is his observation that BAMI was short of cash during the period at issue and his purported belief that, in such circumstances, "all interest paid in a year should be treated as capital-related if BAMI's expenditures for capital assets were greater than its cash on hand." There is, however, no logical reason to apply such reasoning to conclude that it is capital treatment of the interest—and not administrative and general treatment—that should be the preferred way for Medicare to reimburse interest on preexisting debt where a provider becomes strapped for cash. Typically, a hospital's A&G expenditures (which includes, for example, all of the hospital's employee salaries and benefits) in any given year substantially exceeds its capital expenditures. Thus, it can be argued with at least equal weight as Jarrell's proffered defense that, in circumstances where a hospital is short on cash, all interest on existing debt should be treated as an A&G expense rather than as capital. The real point, however, is that neither Jarrell nor the Court ever expressed any good reason why the circumstances Jarrell described at BAMI years after the loans had been taken and spent should lead to *any* change in allocation of the debt between capital and A&G at all, much less a change that could properly justify favoring capital treatment of all the interest over A&G treatment (at far greater expense to the Medicare program). Absent some articulated, principled reason to conclude that a bias would exist under Medicare in favor of treating interest expenses as capital expenditures rather than A&G expenditures, there can be no logical foundation at all for the *Whiteside* defendants' proposed interpretation of the law.[5]

A second flaw in the Court's analysis was the panel's improper reliance on the purported concession at trial by the fiscal intermediary auditor who first examined the Fawcett interest issue that "the regulations do not answer the specific question whether the character of interest can change from capital to operating, and in fact 'can be interpreted in different ways.' " 285 F.3d at 1352. In fact, however, the witness was discussing whether, in a hypothetical example posed by defense counsel, the proper treatment of interest on a debt for a CT-scan can be in doubt if the CT-scan is first purchased with cash *because the loan in process to finance the CT-scan could not be completed in time to meet the hospital's need for the equipment* and the cash is then replenished in two or three months when the loan is finally financed. What the FI auditor actually was describing at trial thus was a very specific situation in which a good argument could be made to treat interest in accordance with the original purpose of a loan, even though the actual flow of cash did not fit the normal pattern for such loans. He was not, however, describing a situation even remotely akin to the circumstances at issue in the *Whiteside* case. Moreover, far from stating "that the regulations do not answer the specific question of whether the character of interest can change from capital to operating," as the Court ascribed to him, the witness actually indicated that there *are* clear guiding principles that would govern the decision whether to treat this kind of claim as a capital loan, i.e., the use to which the proceeds of the loan were put.

There is an additional problem with the panel's reliance on the FI auditor's purported "concession." Even if the testimony of the auditor were as the panel stated, it would not establish in any way that the issue of whether the character of interest can change from capital to operating "can be interpreted in different ways." In *Heckler v. Community Health Services of Crawford County*, 467 U.S. at 64–65, the Supreme Court noted that the Medicare rules make it "perfectly clear" that fiscal intermediaries cannot resolve policy questions on behalf of the United States of the kind the panel decision seeks to derive from the witness's testimony. Such questions must instead be resolved by the Secretary of CMS (the Centers for Medicare and Medicaid). The fiscal intermediary is described by the Supreme Court as a "mere conduit," and providers are held to know that fact if they certify familiarity with Medicare rules. *Id.* Indeed, it is generally improper even to turn to "expert" testimony as the basis for reaching a conclusion about what the law requires. *See Montgomery v. Aetna Cas. & Sur. Co.*, 898 F.2d 1537, 1540 (11th Cir. 1990). A jury, moreover, would be free to weigh and reject that testimony, even if it truly were on point and properly admissible. The Court's reliance on such testimony to overturn the jury's verdict is thus unwarranted under any circumstances.

The panel's reference—*see* 285 F.3d at 1352—to HCFA (the Health Care Financing Administration)'s endorsement of Administrative Bulletin 1186 regarding the possibility that borrowing that is deemed "unnecessary" one year may be found to have become necessary in a subsequent year similarly says nothing more than that there can be exceptions to normal rules *when special circumstances warrant*. However, the particular issue addressed in that Bulletin—whether borrowing is "necessary" or not[6]—is an entirely distinct inquiry under Medicare regulations from whether borrowing is related to capital or A&G expenditures. The Bulletin thus provides no insight whatsoever into whether a plausible case exists in the circumstances of the *Whiteside* case to believe reasonably that an exception to the general rules about how to treat interest expense on a cost report might apply.

The panel's reference to the "fungibility of money" also appears misplaced. *Id.* The proceeds of the 1983 loans (used to refinance 1981 debt) certainly were spent long before 1992 and 1993, the years for which the cost reports at issue in the *Whiteside* case were prepared and filed. *See* 285 F.3d at 1347. Cash is no longer "fungible" once it is spent. There is no evidence cited in the panel opinion that suggests any of the costs on which the loan proceeds actually were spent ever changed from A&G to capital. Thus, there is no reason to suppose that an exception might actually have existed in the circumstances of the *Whiteside* case that would warrant changing the normal Medicare reimbursement rule that it is the use of funds for which a loan was taken that determines whether interest expense should be treated as a capital or A&G expenditure.

The Protest Rule: An Important Issue Overlooked

As indicated above, there are a variety of reasons to question the conclusion the *Whiteside* panel reached based on the arguments the panel itself offered in support of its decision. The most compelling argument of all for concluding that a crime actually was committed in the *Whiteside* matter, however, is one that the Court did not address at all.[7] Whether or not there is room for legitimate debate about the reasonableness of Jarrell's and Whiteside's rationale for contending that Fawcett's interest cost could be treated as 100 percent capital-related, once they were on notice that the fiscal intermediary had rejected such treatment of the costs, they were not free to continue to make such claims for Medicare reimbursement without making use of Medicare "protest" procedures.

In observing that "no Medicare regulation, administrative ruling, or judicial decision exists that clearly requires interest expense to be reported in accordance with the original use of the loan," 285 F.3d at 1352, the *Whiteside* panel overlooked the significance of prior audit determinations made by fiscal intermediaries in resolving ambiguities that otherwise might exist in determining how particular reimbursement claims must be filed. In *United States v. Calhoon*, 97 F.3d 518 (11th Cir. 1996), a previous Eleventh Circuit panel noted, in another criminal case involving false statements in Medicare cost reports, that fiscal intermediaries' prior audit determinations cannot be ignored by providers with impunity:

> While it is true that a provider may submit claims for costs it knows to be presumptively non-reimbursable, it must do so openly and honestly, describing them accurately while challenging the presumption and seeking reimbursement. Nothing less is required if the Medicare reimbursement system is not to be turned into a cat-and-mouse game in which clever providers could, with impunity, practice fraud on the government. . . . [I]f a provider disagrees *with the intermediary's past decisions*, with the instructions or guidelines in the Provider Reimbursement Manual, or with the regulations, *the provider must file the cost report "under protest."*

Id., at 529 (emphasis added) (sustaining criminal conviction where a cost report preparer failed to use protest procedures to flag and challenge claims he filed that he knew were presumptively non-reimbursable). *See also* Medicare Provider Reimbursement Manual, Pt. II, §§ 115–115.3.

Similarly, the Eighth Circuit, which the *Whiteside* panel cites in support of the general rule that the United States must negate reasonable alternative interpretations of ambiguous rules to prove beyond a reasonable doubt that a defendant's statement is false, has recognized that issues of ambiguity become moot once the Medicare program's expectations about how a particular kind of claim should be treated on cost reports has been made clear. "If [plaintiff] shows the defendants certified compliance with the regulation [as is required whenever Medicare cost reports are filed] knowing that the HCFA interpreted the regulation a certain way and that their actions did not satisfy the requirements of the regulation as the HCFA interpreted it, any possible ambiguity of the regulations is water under the bridge." *Minnesota Association of Nurse Anesthetists v. Allina Health System Corp.*, 276 F.3d 1032, 1053 (8th Cir. 2002).

By limiting its consideration of relevant, clarifying authority only to "Medicare regulation[s], administrative ruling[s], or judicial decision[s]," the *Whiteside* panel thus overlooked a critical source of clarification of how the particular costs at issue in that case were expected to be treated by the Medicare program.

The issue, moreover, is one with respect to which substantial evidence was entered at trial in support of the government's charges against Jarrell and Whiteside. Indeed, all the facts needed to demonstrate conclusively that Jarrell and Whiteside violated the principles discussed in *Calhoon* appear in the statement of facts presented by the Eleventh circuit *Whiteside* panel. The following is a summary of the central facts and time line set forth at pages 1347–50 of the panel decision:

1. The refinancing loan that was in place during the critical period (1992 and 1993, when the cost reports charged upon were filed) was established in 1983.

2. Fawcett Memorial Hospital's cost report preparing consultant, Providers Reimbursement Consultants (PRC), thought that the proper treatment of interest relating to this loan was that it related 39 percent to capital expenditures and 61 percent to administrative and general expenditures, and that it had made a mistake by claiming the interest expense as 100 percent capital-related in Fawcett's 1985 cost report. Jarrell nonetheless asked PRC to try to amend the 1986 cost report—which PRC had originally filed in the manner it believed to be correct—to claim the interest as 100 percent capital-related.

3. PRC did as Jarrell asked while the 1986 cost report was being audited by the fiscal intermediary. The fiscal intermediary, however, rejected the proposed 100 percent capital treatment and applied instead the 39–61 percent split that was supported by the hospital's books.

4. By the time Fawcett's 1988 cost report was filed, the fiscal intermediary had issued a Notice of Provider Reimbursement for Fawcett's 1985 cost report. In the audit that preceded that notification, the fiscal intermediary treated only a portion of the interest expense at issue in this case as being capital-related, not the 100 percent Jarrell sought to claim. Nonetheless, in preparing the hospital's 1988 cost report, Jarrell asked PRC again to claim 100 percent of the Citizens Fidelity interest expense as a capital expenditure. PRC's vice president, Jerry Lenon, advised Jarrell

that—if they went that route—they should do so using the protest
line of the cost report in order to flag it for the fiscal intermediary's auditor and preserve the hospital's appeal rights. Jarrell disagreed with that plan. Lenon told Jarrell that not using the protest
procedures in light of the fiscal intermediary's prior determination might constitute fraud, and therefore demanded that BAMI
(Fawcett's corporate owner at that time) send him a letter directing him to file the 1988 cost report claiming the interest as 100
percent capital-related, so that the provider accepted responsibility for the decision.

5. In 1989, Steve Dudley was hired by BAMI and asked to study the
interest issues relevant to this case. Dudley concluded that, as of
late 1984, the proper interest split was 39 percent capital and 61
percent A&G. He also told Jarrell that, while the fiscal intermediary's calculations *for 1986* were wrong (because the intermediary
applied the 39 percent/61 percent split to *all* of the hospital's interest and not just to the interest relating to the Citizens Fidelity
loan), Fawcett's records *would not support* treatment of the Citizens Fidelity interest as 100 percent capital-related. Jarrell claims
to have disagreed with Dudley and to have believed that, since
BAMI was short on cash, all interest paid in a year should be
permitted to be treated as capital-related if BAMI's expenditures
for capital assets were greater than its cash on hand.

6. *In October 1989,* Dudley contacted the fiscal intermediary auditor
and told her BAMI disagreed with the intermediary's treatment
of Fawcett's claimed interest expenses for its 1984 through *1986*
cost reports. The fiscal intermediary agreed to revisit the issue,
and after doing so, limited the 39 percent/61 percent split to just
the Citizens Fidelity loan interest at issue in this criminal case
(precisely the result that Dudley had told Jarrell was appropriate).
As the panel decision notes, "*BAMI did not object,* and as a result
of these adjustments, Fawcett received over $135,000 in addi-
tional Medicare reimbursement for 1985 and 1986." (The increase in overall reimbursement resulted from the fact that the
fiscal intermediary stopped applying to all other hospital debt the

39 percent capital/61 percent A&G split that was appropriate only with respect to the Citizens Fidelity debt.)

7. Thereafter, when the fiscal intermediary mistakenly allowed 100 percent of the interest as capital as was claimed in the hospital's 1987 cost report, BAMI *knew* that the treatment was the result of a fiscal intermediary mistake and even made inquiries to outside counsel whether it was obligated to notify the FI of that "mistake." In making the inquires, however, Fawcett did not tell its outside counsel all the relevant facts, and outside counsel testified that he would have told them to tell the fiscal intermediary of the mistake if he had been told the true facts about what the provider's books showed about the use of the proceeds of the debt at issue.

8. Jarrell then asked Dudley to send a letter asking the fiscal intermediary to allow an amendment to Fawcett's 1989 cost report to claim 100 percent of the Citizens Fidelity interest as capital-related. At first, the fiscal intermediary declined the request. Dudley admitted that he then sent the fiscal intermediary *falsified* work papers to support the request. Based on those falsified work papers, the fiscal intermediary permitted the amendment.

9. Thereafter, defendants continued to file cost reports claiming the interest at 100 percent capital-related, including the 1992 and 1993 cost reports with respect to which their convictions apply. When later asked about the issue by John Schilling, a new employee, Whiteside informed Schilling that the FI had *made a "mistake"* in allowing this to get by in the past. He and Jarrell thereafter directed Schilling to distract a fiscal intermediary auditor who was then asking about the past reopenings on this issue so that she would not pursue the matter further.

Most significant among the matters set forth above are the facts that (a) Jarrell advanced (within BAMI only) his supposed theory regarding changed financial circumstances of the hospital to justify treating the Citizens Fidelity debt interest as 100 percent capital-related *before* the fiscal intermediary *rejected* Fawcett's request for approval to claim the interest as 100 percent capital-related in Fawcett's 1984 through 1986 cost reports, and (b) "*BAMI did not object*" to the fiscal intermediary's decision. These events all occurred well before the 1992 and 1993 cost reports were filed. Moreover, the evidence shows that the defendants understood that the fiscal intermediary's allowance of 100 percent capital-treatment of this interest on subsequent cost reports was a "mistake"—one perpetuated at least in part by the hospital's admitted submission of *falsified* work papers in support of that claim.

In light of the above facts, any ambiguity about what was required to file a proper Medicare claim for the Citizen Fidelity interest expense that reasonably could have been said to exist before 1989 clearly *ended in 1989*. That is when the FI addressed—with respect to Fawcett's 1984 through 1986 cost reports—*precisely the same situation* regarding supposed changes in Fawcett's financial situation that Jarrell contended at trial was the justification for his treatment of the interest as 100 percent capital-related in the 1992 and 1993 cost reports upon which his conviction was based. Jarrell's effort to claim the interest as 100 percent capital-related on the 1984–1986 cost reports was rejected in that 1989 audit, and BAMI chose not to object or appeal. As the Eleventh Circuit's decision in *United States v. Calhoon* makes clear, at that point it was no longer an option for the *Whiteside* defendants simply to reject the FI's decision and silently to continue to file for Fawcett's interest expense in the manner that they preferred. Where an FI has previously disallowed the *very same* treatment of the *very same* expense at the *very same* hospital under the *very same* circumstances that defendants contend justify their later treatment of that expense on other cost reports, it must be said that the claim in 1992 and 1993 treating interest on the Citizen loan as 100 percent capital-related is at least "presumptively non-reimbursable."

Calhoon states unequivocally: "[I]f a provider disagrees *with the intermediary's past decisions*, with the instructions or guidelines in the Provider Reimbursement Manual, or with the regulations, *the provider must* file the cost report "under protest." *Id.*, at 529 (emphasis added). Despite being informed by Mr. Lenon of PRC that the use of the protest line of the cost report was the proper way to proceed if BAMI wished to contend that the Citizens Fidelity interest expense should be treated as 100 percent capital-related despite previous audit determinations, Jarrell and Whiteside refused to take the honest approach of disclosure and open discourse. If we apply the evidence cited by the panel in *Whiteside* to the Court's previous opinion in *Calhoon*, we see—quoting from *Calhoon*—that Jarrell's and Whiteside's argument:

> misses the crux of [their] offense: the filing of reports intended and designed to mislead the auditors for the purpose of obtaining reimbursement of costs [they] knew to be at least presumptively, if not clearly, non-reimbursable. Available time and resources do not permit audit of more than a fraction of the cost reports filed. [Jarrell's and Whiteside's] filing of reports claiming costs that were at least presumptively non-reimbursable while concealing or disguising their true nature [as was done when the hospital falsified work papers sent to the FI in support of the 1989 treatment of the claim and when Jarrell and Whiteside directed Schilling in 1994 to distract the fiscal intermediary auditor from following up on her questions about prior reopenings of Fawcett's cost reports] was a deliberate gamble on the odds that they would not be questioned.
>
> *The evidence amply sustains the findings of falsity* . . . . *Id.* (emphasis added).

Thus said the Court in *Calhoon*, as it also should have stated in *Whiteside*.

The *Whiteside* Decision Does Not Displace *Calhoon*

Although the *Whiteside* panel makes brief reference to the *Calhoon* case, *see* 285 F.3d at 1352, it does not address the prior decision's discussion of the protest rule or purport in any way to overrule or limit *Calhoon*'s holding. Nor could one panel of the Eleventh Circuit make such changes to Circuit precedent even were it inclined to do so. *See Bonner v. City of Prichard*, 661 F.2d 1206, 1209 (11th Cir. 1981) (*en banc*) (only the court sitting *en banc* may overrule the prior decision on a prior circuit panel). This rule extends both to explicit and implicit holdings; issues determined previously by one panel may not be "examin[ed] . . . anew" by another. *Johnson v. DeSoto County Board of Commissioners*, 72 F.3d 1556, 1561 (11th Cir. 1996). Thus, panel overrulings *sub silentio*, whether by design or oversight, are banned. *Grabowski v. Jackson County Public Defenders Office*, 47 F.3d 1386, 1402 (5th Cir. 1995) (Smith, J., concurring in part and dissenting in part). It is thus clear that, whatever the proper precedential scope of the *Whiteside* decision might be, it cannot be read to create immunity from criminal prosecution where a provider silently ignores prior FI adjustments because it does not agree with them. Indeed, to be reconciled with the earlier *Calhoon* decision, it is clear that precisely the opposite must be true: The *Whiteside* decision *must be viewed as one based on a simple failure of the prosecution to anticipate and meet the standard of proof it ultimately would be required to allege and prove at this criminal trial. The* Whiteside *Court was never presented a theory of prosecution that relied squarely on Jarrell's and Whiteside's failure to follow Medicare protest rules.* Perhaps, as noted previously, such a theory should not have been necessary to sustain the defendants' convictions. If it had been added to the theories presented clearly in the indictment and trial, however, the result of defendants' appeal likely would have been very different.

The *Whiteside* Decision Does Not Materially Affect False Claims Act Cases

A final point to address is the impact of *Whiteside* on cases brought under the False Claims Act. Ironically, the fact that the Eleventh Circuit's decision does not materially affect False Claims Act cases is uniquely clear with respect to the False Claims Act lawsuit John Schilling initiated against Columbia/HCA for precisely the same misconduct that was at issue in the *Whiteside* case. This is because *a criminal guilty plea has already been entered with respect to the Fawcett Memorial Hospital interest overcharges on behalf of corporate defendants to the False Claims Act action,* and that plea is supported by a stipulation of fact conceding that, from 1990 through 1994, "Fawcett was entitled to claim only 39 percent of the interest on [its Citizen Fidelity] debt as capital-related" and that, despite this fact, "Defendant and certain executives with management responsibilities for Fawcett knowingly and willfully caused the Fawcett cost reports for 1990, 1991, 1992, and 1993 to be prepared and to fraudulently reflect 100 percent of the interest expense attributable to that debt was capital-related." December 14, 2002 Stipulated Facts Relating to Columbia Management Companies, Inc. Information, at 12–13.

More broadly, it is also clear that the *Whiteside* decision does not significantly change the legal landscape with respect to proof of False Claims

Act violations in cost-reporting cases, or in any other matter involving regulations that must apply broadly to circumstances in which it is impossible for regulators to draft rules that will clearly cover every possible factual scenario. First, with respect to cost-reporting matters, the relevance of *Whiteside* to False Claims Act cases is constrained by the principles of *Calhoon* and the Medicare "protest" procedures in the same fashion that broad application of the ruling is constrained in criminal cases.

Second, the standards of proof invoked in *Whiteside* do not apply to civil cases. A premise of the *Whiteside* decision is that, in criminal cases, a court can only apply the law as it clearly existed at the time of the alleged crime, either in written code, regulation, or rule or through established precedent. This is because, in a criminal case—unlike a civil case—the court cannot decide after the fact what an ambiguous regulation means, but is instead limited to deciding whether the regulation was really ambiguous and, if so, whether the government proved that the defendant's statement was false under all reasonable interpretations of the regulation.

In a civil False Claims Act case, the court would have to resolve this disagreement between the parties by determining whether the defendants' interpretation of the law was correct or not, not just whether it was reasonable at the time the interpretation was made. If the interpretation was incorrect, it is "false" within the meaning of the civil False Claims Act. To impose liability, however, the court would need to find both that the claim was false (i.e., incorrect) and that the defendant acted with the required knowledge of that falsity (i.e., actual knowledge, willful blindness to the truth, or reckless disregard of the truth or falsity of the claim). *See* 31 U.S.C. §§ 3729(a) and (b). The Ninth Circuit explained this clearly in *United States ex rel. Olive v. Parsons Co.*, 195 F.3d 457, 462–64 (9th Cir. 1999):

> *Hagwood [v. Somona County Water Agency*, 81 F.3d 1465 (9th Cir. 1996)] does not stand for the proposition that a "reasonable interpretation" of a regulation precludes falsity [within the meaning of the False Claims Act]. . . . [W]hile the reasonableness of Parsons' interpretation of the applicable accounting standards may be relevant to whether it knowingly submitted a false claim, the question of "falsity" itself is determined by whether Parsons' representations were accurate in light of applicable law. . . . In short, Par-

sons' petition arguing that the sky will fall upon government
contractors if they are precluding from relying on a "reasonable
interpretation" is not only unsupported by the case law, it is also
ungrounded in reality. It ignores the fact that the FCA requires
more than just a false statement—it requires that the defendant
knew the claim was false. 31 U.S.C. § 3729(a)(1). A contractor relying on a good faith interpretation of a regulation is not subject
to liability, not because his or her interpretation was correct or
"reasonable" but because the good faith of his or her action fore-
closes the possibility that the scienter requirement is met. (Emphasis in original.)

Thus, if we imagine *Whiteside* as a civil False Claims Act case, a court
would determine the meaning of the regulations and (putting aside evidence issues) decide either that the defendants were entitled to reimbursement for this interest expense or that they were not. If the latter,
then the claim would be "false" (leaving questions of defendants' beliefs
for the scienter determination). "Scienter" refers to the level of awareness
of wrongdoing that a defendant must have in order to be found legally
responsible for misconduct. To be found liable under the False Claims
Act it is not enough to prove that an overcharge was made as a result of
an honest mistake or mere negligence. At the very least, the plaintiff must
prove that the defendant acted in reckless disregard of the truth or falsity
of the claim for payment made. Recklessness might exist, for instance,
when someone knows that there is a substantial chance that they are
charging too much but decides not to make a reasonable effort to verify
the proper amount to claim.

It is well understood that the very same conduct may be immune from
criminal conviction yet subject to civil liability. This is so with regard
to the rule applied in *Whiteside*, as we can divine from that case itself.
Immediately before its holding, the *Whiteside* Court quoted *United States
v. Mallas*, 762 F.2d 361, 363 (4th Cir. 1985): "Here, 'competing interpretations of the applicable law [are] far too reasonable to justify these convictions.' " That is the rule for criminal cases, and, in *Mallas*, the Court
reversed criminal-tax convictions because "the prosecution and the defense can in this situation both offer plausible support for their positions." But the Court then carefully explained that the government *could
pursue the matter by seeking civil liability and penalties*:

Nothing here is meant to imply that one of these solutions is not a better construction of tax law, or that civil liability—with appropriate civil penalties—may not be imposed on these defendants for deductions claimed without a foundation in sufficient coal reserves. Compare *United States v. Dahlstrom*, 713 F.2d 1423 (9th Cir. 1983) with *Zmuda v. Commissioner of Internal Revenue*, 731 F.2d 1417 (9th Cir. 1984) (criminal conviction vacated but civil liability imposed in connection with same tax shelter). We merely find that there has been no "fair warning . . . given to the world in language that the common world will understand, of what the law intends to do if a certain line is passed." *McBoyle v. United States*, 283 U.S. 25, 27 (1931) (Holmes, J.). The government may face a difficult task in translating the deductibility of annual advance minimum royalty payments into language that the common world will understand. But without that fair warning, the government may not institute criminal proceedings. As this court noted in *United States v. Critzer*, "the appropriate vehicle to decide this pioneering interpretation of tax liability is the *civil* procedure of administrative assessment," not a criminal prosecution. 498 F.2d [1160,] 1164 [(4th Cir. 1974)]. 762 F.2d at 364–65. [Emphasis in original.]

Conclusion

The conclusion I reach upon close examination of the *Whiteside* opinion is that the defendants in that action escaped criminal sanctions for conduct that should have been punished as a crime. The decision itself, however, rests so heavily on facts and legal theories peculiar to the case that, even if the matter was decided incorrectly and prosecuted on inadequate grounds, the precedential implications of the decision are quite limited. While the opinion does not represent a triumph of justice or judicial insight, neither does it constitute a license to steal. And the prosecution itself, although ultimately reversed, no doubt has had a salutary effect on an industry that had let its obligations to report costs accurately to Medicare for taxpayer reimbursement digress into a cat-and-mouse game where Medicare was always the loser.

Notes

1. Cost reports are complex accounting documents submitted annually by hospitals and other healthcare institutions (such as skilled nursing facilities and comprehensive rehabilitation facilities) in order to receive reimbursement from Medicare, Medicaid, and CHAMPUS/Tricare (the military healthcare benefits system) for the fair share of capital and overhead costs associated with treating patients insured by those federal programs. Cost reports are then audited by fiscal intermediaries, or FIs (generally, insurance companies) hired by the United States to administer its healthcare programs. Fiscal intermediaries' interpretation of reimbursement rules and how they apply to particular cost claims can be appealed by providers to the Provider Reimbursement Review Board, to the Secretary of the Department of Health and Human Services, and ultimately to the federal courts. However, that does not mean that hospitals are free to ignore interpretations of the rules by FIs with which they disagree. Medicare regulations permit providers who disagree with FIs' interpretations about how certain costs should be treated for federal reimbursement purposes to claim the costs as the provider believes fit on filed cost reports, but only if they do so through use of "protest" procedures set forth in the Medicare Provider Reimbursement Manual (PRM), Pt. II, §§ 115–115.3. Indeed, the Supreme Court held years ago that fiscal intermediaries lack the authority unilaterally to bend or waive Medicare regulations and rules. *See Heckler v. Community Health Services of Crawford County, Inc.,* 467 U.S. 51 (1984).

2. Schilling eventually retained Phillips & Cohen to represent him as a *qui tam* plaintiff in the False Claims Act cost report litigation against Columbia/HCA.

3. *See, e.g., United States v. Migliaccio,* 34 F.3d 1517, 1525 (10th Cir. 1994) ("In cases arising under 18 U.S.C. § 1001 . . . the government bears the burden to negate any reasonable interpretations that would make a defendant's statement factually correct when reporting requirements are ambiguous"); *United States v. Johnson,* 937 F.2d 392, 399 (8th Cir. 1991) ("This court has previously held in a section 1001 case, 'the government must negate any reasonable interpretation that would make the defendant's statement factually correct' . . . . Title 18, section 1001's language prohibiting false and fraudulent statement sweeps broadly. However, . . . '[c]riminal sanctions should not be imposed for conduct which is not clearly illegal' "); *United States v. Anderson,* 579 F.2d 455, 459–60 (8th Cir. 1978) ("In light of these ambiguities . . . it was incumbent upon the government to introduce proof sufficient to establish the falsity of the statements . . . . In carrying out that burden the government must negate any reasonable interpretation that would make the defendant's statement factually correct").

4. Another problem with the Court's treatment of this issue is its apparent acceptance of Jarrell's representations of his actual belief in this theory as established fact. *See* 285 F.3d at 1348 ("[Jarrell and Dick] firmly believed that the interest was

100 percent capital-related"); *Id.* ("Jarrell was displeased with Dudley's report [concluding that Fawcett's records could support only the 31/69 percent split between capital and noncapital treatment of the interest] because he believed that, since BAMI [the hospital chain that owned Fawcett prior to its purchase in 1992 by Columbia Hospital Corporation] was short on cash, all the interest paid in a year should be treated as capital-related if BAMI's expenditures for capital assets were greater than its cash on hand"). The jury, of course, was not obligated to accept Jarrell's assertion as reflecting his true beliefs at the time, and the appeals panel should have been evaluating the evidence in the light most favorable to the prosecution's case. *See, e.g., Schlup v. Delo,* 513 U.S. 298, 340 (1995). Thus, if the panel's decision actually was premised in whole or part on an acceptance of Jarrell's proffered beliefs, such reliance was improper.

5. Although the Court did not focus on *mens rea* issues in deciding first whether an improper *actus reus* had been proven, that Jarrell never was willing actually to advance to the FI his purported justification for believing that treating the interest as 100 percent capital-related in later years is a telling fact, and one that should at least have given the Court pause to conclude that Jarrell's stated interpretation of the rules was even arguably reasonable under the circumstances in which the claims were actually made.

6. The basis of this rule is that Medicare will not pay for interest on loans if the provider has cash funds available to it that make it unnecessary for a loan to be taken at all. Where, however, a loan that is deemed to have been unnecessary at the time it was taken would have become necessary in later years, Medicare has decided to permit interest to be claimed as a reimbursable expense as of the date on which borrowing actually became necessary (i.e., as of the date that cash the provider had available to it would no longer have sufficed to meet the provider's needs in providing patient care). The reasonableness of this concession to hospitals is self-evident. How that exception could logically be expanded to cover a situation anything like that described by Jarrell to defend Fawcett's treatment of its interest expense as 100 percent capital-related is a mystery neither Jarrell nor the Eleventh Circuit endeavored to make clear.

7. Review of the briefs in the *Whiteside* case shows that, while the protest rule is mentioned, it is not a focus of the government's discussion. Perhaps this is because the prosecution failed to foresee that the defendants' clear failure to follow the protest rule would prove so important to the success of its case.

Index